ORDER OUT OF CHAOS

A volume in the series

Religion and Conflict

Edited by Ron E. Hassner

For a list of books in the series, visit our website at cornellpress.cornell.edu.

ORDER OUT OF CHAOS

Islam, Information, and the Rise and Fall of Social Orders in Iraq

David Siddhartha Patel

CORNELL UNIVERSITY PRESS   ITHACA AND LONDON

Copyright © 2022 by Cornell University

All rights reserved. Except for brief quotations in a review, this book, or parts thereof, must not be reproduced in any form without permission in writing from the publisher. For information, address Cornell University Press, Sage House, 512 East State Street, Ithaca, New York 14850. Visit our website at cornellpress.cornell.edu.

First published 2022 by Cornell University Press

Library of Congress Cataloging-in-Publication Data

Names: Patel, David Siddhartha, 1977– author.
Title: Order out of chaos : Islam, information, and the rise and fall of social orders in Iraq / David Siddhartha Patel.
Description: Ithaca, New York : Cornell University Press, 2022. | Series: Religion and conflict | Includes bibliographical references and index.
Identifiers: LCCN 2022013884 (print) | LCCN 2022013885 (ebook) | ISBN 9781501715419 (hardcover) | ISBN 9781501767944 (paperback) | ISBN 9781501715426 (epub) | ISBN 9781501715433 (pdf)
Subjects: LCSH: Islam and politics—Iraq—History—21st century. | Iraq War, 2003–2011—Peace. | Iraq—Politics and government—2003– | Iraq—Social conditions—21st century.
Classification: LCC DS79.769 .P38 2022 (print) | LCC DS79.769 (ebook) | DDC 956.7044/31—dc23/eng/20220429
LC record available at https://lccn.loc.gov/2022013884
LC ebook record available at https://lccn.loc.gov/2022013885

Contents

Preface	vii
Note on Transliteration	xiii
1. Order, Authority, and Identity	1
2. The Sanctions-Era Roots of Postinvasion Developments	20
3. Collapse	40
4. The Emergence of Local Orders	52
5. The Geography of Order	89
6. Ayatollahs' Networks and National Authority	119
7. The Limits of Sunni Religious Authority	162
8. Beyond Basra and Beyond Sermons	173
Notes	179
References	203
Index	215

Preface

At one level, this book is a story about what happens when an authoritarian and controlling state suddenly disappears. How do individuals establish some sort of order until the state reestablishes itself under new leadership? Many Iraqis in April 2003 looked to the mosque and found cues in Friday sermons, which I argue was neither "natural" nor expected. And because clerical institutions in Shi'i Islam and Sunni Islam are organized differently, Iraq's Shi'i clergy were a lot more effective in binding people in a functioning national-level community, inadvertently contributing to the salience of sectarian identities. At another level, this book uses postinvasion Iraq to speak to big and enduring questions—the origins of social order, the source and limits of political authority, and the salience of collective identity—that cross borders of academic disciplines and popular interest.

As is often the case with fieldwork, my field site chose me. In September 2003, a friend working in Iraq with a humanitarian nonprofit organization offered me an unexpected opportunity to visit Basra. At the time, the US-led invasion of Iraq seemed like it might be one of the most important events to occur in the region in my lifetime (today, that still seems true). That thought led me to change my plans, fly to Kuwait, and cross into southern Iraq. At the time, there was no checkpoint or immigration on the Iraqi side of the border; after passing the Kuwaiti authorities, one could drive unhindered into the border town of Safwan, Iraq.

Once in Basra, where I lived with a local Iraqi in their home throughout my time there, I began to talk with various people to try to make sense of what was happening after the fall of Saddam and in the absence of a functioning state. As I did, I realized that Basrawis were doing essentially the same thing that I was doing, and they seemed almost as confused about what was happening in their neighborhood, city, and country as I was. Everyone was in the same boat, trying to make sense out of anarchy.

I collected ethnographic data during seven months of field research in Basra, where I was immersed in Iraqi society from September 2003 to April 2004. I had plans to remain in Iraq for at least another six to nine months, but escalating violence forced me to suddenly suspend my fieldwork much earlier than anticipated, and I was never able to pick up where I left off. When I left, I was field-testing a survey and a field experiment and had begun to collect systematic data on indicators of social order. I had conducted dozens of interviews and had many more planned.

But in the first week of April 2004, the situation in Iraq for foreigners changed dramatically, virtually overnight. Militiamen affiliated with Moqtada al-Sadr clashed with coalition forces throughout southern Iraq and in Baghdad after the Coalition Provisional Authority (CPA) closed a newspaper associated with his movement and arrested one of his top aides. At the same time, US Marines began an offensive in Fallujah in response to the killing of four armed Blackwater contractors in the city. I happened to be in Baghdad when this all occurred and could not return to Basra because Sadrist militias controlled points along both of the roads I could have taken from Baghdad south to Basra. This was the moment when insurgents and opportunists began to kidnap foreigners in large numbers. At least a dozen foreigners were abducted that week in Iraq, and over seventy were taken hostage by the end of 2004. Rumors passed among journalists and foreigners in Iraq that gangs were trying to sell hostages to violent jihadists instead of or in addition to collecting ransoms from families and employers.[1] After the kidnapping spree began, and unable to safely travel west or south from Baghdad, I went north to Iraqi Kurdistan, crossed into Turkey, and made my way to Amman, Jordan, to wait for things to settle so that I could return to Basra and continue my fieldwork. I did not see Basra again for more than seven years.

I remained in Jordan from April to September 2004, interviewing Iraqis and aid workers there and anticipating resuming my fieldwork in southern Iraq. A second round of fighting between Sadr's militiamen and the US military, as well as the kidnapping of a British freelance reporter from his hotel in Basra in August 2004, convinced my contacts in Basra that it would be unsafe for me in their city.[2] By this point, my presence in Basra also would have significantly increased risks to those Iraqi contacts: militias and criminal gangs knew that people with access to money could and would pay sizable ransoms for relatives, friends, and coworkers. The anthropologist Hayder al-Mohammad conducted fieldwork in Basra after 2005 and later wrote, "Many of my friends and acquaintances have been kidnapped. Most did not survive."[3]

When Iraq held elections in January 2005, it seemed that things might be improving to the point where I could resume fieldwork. I flew to Jordan in April 2005 and was emboldened in May when I heard that an American freelance journalist, Steven Vincent, had moved into a hotel in Basra and was collecting material for a book on the history of the city. If Vincent was in Basra, I could be too! It took two months of cajoling and waiting in Amman before the Iraqi embassy there gave me a visa. On 2 August, two weeks before I was to return to Basra, Vincent was abducted off of a main street in the city by men wearing police uniforms and driving a police vehicle.[4] He was tortured and executed, less than three months after arriving in the city. Two days earlier, Vincent had published an op-ed in the *New York Times* stating that "Basran politics (and everyday life) is increasingly coming under the control of Shiite religious groups" and that "a few police officers are perpetrating many of the hundreds of assassinations—mostly of former Baath Party members—that take place in Basra each month."[5] The following month, an Iraqi journalist and stringer in Basra, Fakher Haider, whom I knew and respected, was abducted from his home by masked men claiming to be police officers. His body was found hours later, "with his hands bound and a bag over his head in a deserted area on the outskirts of Basra."[6] I had interviewed people in, and planned to return to, the neighborhood where Haider had been abducted. The murders of Vincent and Haider, in rapid succession, erased any hope I had that I could safely restart my fieldwork in Basra.[7]

Vincent's reporting had accurately described the influence of Islamist militias and the spread of conservative mores in Basra. For reasons I describe in this book, local social orders based on mosques could not scale up to provide district-level or citywide order. And the spread of religious discourses and symbols helped Shi'i Islamist militias operate with impunity, including from within police ranks. Kidnappings for ransom and assassinations increased dramatically in Basra from 2003 to 2005. The police chief of Basra Governate, General Hassan al-Sade, admitted to the *Guardian* in May 2005 that half of his force of 13,740 officers was working for political parties and militias and was involved in assassinations.[8] Gangs and militias made Basra ungovernable for weak central authorities and far too dangerous for me to conduct fieldwork. Several preachers and officials whom I had interviewed were assassinated. More than a dozen of my contacts fled the city; several others were murdered. The situation in Basra deteriorated further in early 2007 when the US military increased operations in Baghdad's Sadr City in an effort to degrade the militias' capabilities. The Mahdi Army and other militias relocated their seasoned fighters and bomb makers to Basra to prevent them from being killed or captured.[9] The central government did not reestablish control over the city until early 2008, when the Iraqi Army launched its first major operation since the collapse of the state in 2003, Operation Charge of the Knights. I finally returned to Basra in June 2011, seven years after I had left and four years after I had filed my dissertation.

During my time in Basra, I was fortunate to land and remain on good terms with several key individuals connected to militias in the city, including Moqtada al-Sadr's local representative, Sheikh Abdul Satar al-Bahadali. On several occasions I had run-ins with Sadr militiamen, and being able to mention Bahadali's name and phone number, as well as the names of other clerics in the Office of the Martyred Sadr II, prevented tense situations from escalating and saved me from being detained or possibly harmed. I learned ways to quickly figure out which militia controlled any particular checkpoint or building; this made it easier to know which names to mention and which to avoid mentioning. This would have been more difficult in Baghdad, a larger city with more actors. There were two particularly dangerous Shiʻi Islamist militias operating in Basra while I was there—TharAllah (God's Revenge) and Fifteenth Shaʻban.[10] Both were rumored to be linked to the Quds Force of Iran's Islamic Revolutionary Guard Corps or the Sadrists, or both. These two militias were widely thought to be responsible for a series of assassinations of alleged Baʻthists, sympathizers of the nascent insurgency, and alcohol sellers. Members of these militias knew who I was: I was introduced at a meeting to a TharAllah official whom I believe was their leader, Yusuf al-Mosawi, and an Iraqi contact later told me members of TharAllah had asked employees at a restaurant I frequented, Qasr al-Sultan, for the names of Iraqis with whom I met.[11] I always had the sense that someone, perhaps in the Sadr Office or with the Badr Organization, had vouched for me and instructed those and other groups to leave me alone. Elsewhere, things might not have been as fortuitous for me.

I have always been aware that I was able to enter Iraq, to remain there, and to leave when I did because of who I was and the passport I held. Although it was the British Armed Forces and the British-led CPA South that were present in Basra, the fact that it was my country, the United States, that had led the invasion and occupation of Iraq influenced my fieldwork. I hope this book makes at least a miniscule contribution to our understanding of the impact of those actions on Iraqi society.

Along the tortuous route I took to complete this book, I incurred more debts than I can acknowledge here. I am privileged to have the support networks that allowed me to conduct field research in Iraq, safely leave when I had to, and then make sense of what I saw unfold.

This research began while I was a graduate student at Stanford University. I thank David Laitin for encouraging and supporting my foray into Middle Eastern and Islamic studies, despite the university offering few avenues at the time to do so. Avner Greif's teaching, writing, and feedback deeply influenced how I view institutions and strategic beliefs. I thank Jim Fearon for repeatedly pushing me to be precise in my arguments and reminding me not to allow my claims to go further than what the data allow. Jeremy Weinstein provided pointed feedback that, to my regret, I brushed aside until a manuscript reviewer echoed similar concerns. Although they were not part of my committee, Russell Hardin and Barry Weingast each had a greater influence on my thinking than I realized until years later.

Among my graduate school colleagues from Stanford, I received particularly constructive comments and criticisms—often over beers—from Kimuli Kasara, Peter Lorentzen, Ebru Erdem, Leo Arriola, Catherine Duggan, Desha Girod, Todd Sechser, Nahomi Ichino, Moonhawk Kim, Nikolay Marinov, Kay Shimizu, Jake Shapiro, Heather Stoll, Martin Dimitrov, and Matt Carnes. I owe them all another round.

Cornell University is a wonderful academic institution and intellectual environment, and I failed to take full advantage of it while I was an assistant professor there. In particular, I thank Val Bunce, Ron Herring, Ken Roberts, Chris Way, Chris Anderson, and Nic van de Walle for their feedback, support, and sound advice.

I never would have completed this book if not for the scholars and staff of the Crown Center for Middle East Studies at Brandeis University. I thank all my colleagues there for their feedback and intellectual support. At our annual retreat, Eva Bellin gave me invaluable insights into how I might frame and link various topics in the manuscript. Most critically, I will be forever grateful to Shai Feldman for his confidence in me, encouragement, patience, and seemingly endless supplies of carrots and sticks. My trajectory would be dramatically different if not for him and the center he built.

Over the years, I presented parts of this book at seminars or panels at Duke, Yale, Princeton, Cornell, Michigan, MIT, the Central European University, the National Defense University, the Royal Institute for Inter-faith Studies in Amman, and several academic conferences and workshops. I am appreciative of all the discussants' and participants' insights and questions in those forums. For particularly insightful and useful feedback, I thank Juan Cole, Timur Kuran, Ron Hassner, Lisa Blaydes, Melani Cammett, Nathan Brown, Stathis Kalyvas, Abbas Kadhim, Vali Nasr, Larry Diamond, Adria Lawrence, Quinn Mecham, Dan Corstange, Pascal Menoret, Lisa Wedeen, Charlie Brown, Peter Sluglett, Toby Dodge, Reidar Visser, Harith Hasan al-Qarawee, and Gabriel Young. I thank the Middle East Studies Association for awarding me its Graduate Student Paper Prize for a paper that became a section in this book.

I owe a special thanks to Jake Shapiro, Val Bunce, Richard Nielsen, and Marsin Alshamary, who each read full versions of the manuscript at various stages and offered extensive comments.

Roger Haydon at Cornell University Press was an extremely patient, helpful, and supportive editor for this project. I am deeply grateful for his input and that of the three excellent reviewers he found. The book is better for their feedback. I thank Jeff Blossom for helping improve the figures for publication and Enid Zafran for creating the index.

Numerous Iraqis invited me into their homes or took the time to speak with me during my fieldwork. I can never repay their generosity and hospitality.

I regret having to turn down uncountable meals and requests to return. In particular, I thank Suad, Farook, Aladdin, Rihab, Abu and Umm Farook, Sufian, Kaysar, Hasan, and Hussein. From all of you, I think I have begun to understand what it means to be Iraqi and Arab. I especially thank Suad for her hospitality, Farook for his friendship, and Aladdin for his advice and insights.

To Yasser, Safa, Majid, Ali and Abbas, Abeer, Hasanayn, Abu Ridha, Raed, and Taha: I thank you for your insights and hope some of what appears in this book is familiar. I am grateful for Laura Ingalls's peripatetic companionship during that time in our lives. I thank Dumeethra Luthra and the late Anthony Shadid for conversations in Iraq about what was occurring as it occurred.

My parents, Aneel and Jean Patel, and my family, Padma and Akhil, all suffered far too long as I "finished" this book. I thank Padma for shouldering responsibilities and for her patience as I spent long hours revising and editing. I apologize to Akhil for failing to include any pictures of dinosaurs, and I will try to do better next time.

Note on Transliteration

This book employs a simplified transliteration style, based on the one used by the *International Journal of Middle East Studies*, that leaves out diacritics except for ' for 'ayn and ' for hamza. When possible, it uses widely accepted transliterated spellings of words or names, even if they leave out some letters, including an 'ayn (e.g., ulama instead of 'ulama; Iraq instead of al-'Iraq). Anglicized plurals are used (e.g., fatwas instead of fatawa; mujtahids instead of mujtahidoon; hussainiyas instead of hussainiyat), although the Arabic plural is used when an Anglicized plural might be confusing, such as with words that end in an 'ayn or hamza (e.g., maraji' as the plural of marja' instead of marja's, which could be mistaken for a singular possessive).

ORDER OUT OF CHAOS

1
ORDER, AUTHORITY, AND IDENTITY

Abbas Hayder lives in Basra, a city in southern Iraq. On the morning of 7 April 2003, he saw three men walking down the street carrying chairs and light fixtures—goods that they had looted, he correctly surmised, from a nearby municipal office. He immediately knew that the Ba'th regime's grip on Basra must have disintegrated and that the British Army, after two weeks of waiting outside the city, finally had entered it. What he did not yet realize, however, was that the Iraqi state was collapsing and, looted to its foundations, would not be quickly reconstituted. Abbas now was living in a newly stateless society.

The sudden absence of a functioning state quickly impacted his family's quality of life and safety: uncollected trash rotted and raw sewage congealed in the street, a staccato rhythm of gunfire routinely echoed, and criminals roamed unchecked. In the following weeks and months, Abbas came to understand a way through which he could work with neighbors to achieve common goals and substitute for some, but not all, missing state services. By doing relatively simple things in a coordinated way, Abbas and his neighbors managed to keep their street tolerably clean and provide a modicum of security. This book is about how Iraqis were able to produce social order in the absence of a state, the limits of that order, and the unintended consequences of their reliance on particular ways to achieve order.

The central claim of this book is that Abbas and many of his fellow Iraqis turned to the mosque after state collapse because it had an unparalleled ability to communicate in ways that helped them coordinate their activities with others. The influence of religious authorities is due not only to the message of Islam but also to the ability of Islam to deliver messages in ways that render them common knowledge. But in postinvasion Iraq, the power of the mosque and clerics was limited by the number of persons the message reached and by the types of endeavors to which it could induce individuals to contribute. Mosque sermons could facilitate coordination, but only rarely could they get people to comply with costly edicts, such as situations in which individuals had incentives to free ride by letting others do most or all of the work. Clerics could foster contributions only when the actions required of followers imposed relatively small costs; as costs rose, the effectiveness of clerics diminished. This distinction demonstrates that preachers derived their influence not solely from followers' piety but also from an institutional capacity to solve informational problems. It helps demarcate the limits of religious authority: whom religious leaders can lead, when can they lead, and the set of issues over which they have authority.

Order from Clerics' Orders

A week after the Baʻth regime fell, the imam at the mosque near Abbas's house, for the first time in anyone's memory, modified the ritual form of the afternoon prayer on Friday and included a pair of brief sermons. In his first sermon, the imam recited a sura from the Quran and stated that from then on, on Fridays they would hold the special congregational prayer (*salat al-jumʻa*) instead of the midday group prayer (*salat al-dhuhr*) that is held on other days. He described ritual differences between the two prayers (e.g., two prostration cycles instead of four) and matter-of-factly stated that this form of prayer was now permitted and preferable. He sat for a moment and then rose and began his second sermon, which focused on the breakdown of law and order after the collapse of central authority. The preacher condemned the looting of public buildings, told listeners to shun looters, and said looted goods should be turned in at a designated mosque.

This ritual of Friday congregational prayers and associated sermons was new for most of Iraq's Shiʻi Muslims. Except in a few mosques, most notably for a few years in the late 1990s, such sermons had not been heard in Shiʻi mosques in Iraq since the 1950s, and even before then they were relatively rare. Although they are an essential worship rite in Islam, Shiʻi scholars have disagreed for centuries about the legitimacy of holding Friday sermons in the absence of the Mahdi, the prophesized redeemer. Abbas and his neighbors began to attend these Friday congregational prayers when it suddenly became an acceptable ritual in most Shiʻi mosques. Like many Iraqis, they were pious and had lived amid a general increase in religiosity in Iraqi society over the previous decade or two. But the local imam, as well as the more senior scholars with whom he was affiliated, were widely known to be proponents of a clerical tradition that disdained politics and mundane affairs. They were respected as guides on religious and spiritual matters, but Abbas and other Shiʿa did not expect—and many did not want—clerics to try to mobilize Iraqis.

Silently sitting together, Abbas and his male neighbors heard the preacher's messages about looting, rubbish, and security (the few women who attended sat in a separate section). The preacher proposed group actions that, if done by enough residents, would improve their shared situation, and—critically—attendees knew that others in attendance also heard these messages. When the solution to a problem was one in which everyone wanted to do what everyone else did, such as where everyone should dump their trash, this ability of the sermon to generate common knowledge provided preachers the social weight to determine which solution from among the plausible ones would be selected by the community. Coordination ensued. The preacher's authority—his ability to induce compliance with edicts—began to ratchet up week after week as neighbors came to expect each other to look to messages from the mosque to solve other collective dilemmas. In this sense, sermons and the mosque loudspeaker amplified, literally and figuratively, preachers' preexisting authority, and the guidance and advice they offered touched on a gradually wider set of issues, moving from the traditionally religious to the more temporal and mundane. But this augmentation of clerical authority had limits. When the proposed solution to a dilemma entailed sufficiently high costs for individuals, it was in listeners' self-interest not to contribute to the group action and instead to free ride on others' contributions, if there were any. Knowledge that others had the same knowledge was insufficient for compliance. In such cases, preachers—unable to punish noncompliance—could foster contributions only when the actions required of followers imposed relatively low costs on them.

Like ink drops on a page, enclaves of social order—centered on Friday mosques—emerged out of anarchy. But the power of "Islam" to generate social order via mosque sermons was limited in two ways: how far the message reached and the types of collective behaviors it could produce. And Iraqis would soon see, although they may not have realized why, that achieving order via this mechanism had important and unintended consequences: religious discourses flourished, and those discourses included some Iraqis but excluded others; emergent norms varied across congregations; less order emerged in areas where Sunnis and Shiʿa lived as neighbors; and, perhaps, it contributed to the stunting of civil society.

Identity from Orders

As 2003 wore on and US-led transition efforts stumbled, debates raged inside Iraq about how to reconstitute the Iraqi state and select a government to lead it. A cacophony of voices tried to influence Abbas and secure his support: Basrawi regionalists, secular nationalists, monarchists, new and old Islamist movements, and elders of his clan. But beginning in late June, Abbas and millions of other Iraqi Shiʿa increasingly came to rely for guidance on a single voice that rose above the din. An esteemed septuagenarian cleric, cloistered in the holy city of Najaf and long considered apolitical, began issuing statements regarding the transition process. Although he almost never appeared or spoke publicly himself, his pronouncements spread widely because he sat atop a hierarchical network that included the majority of the mosque preachers who had been independently promoting local coordination in their communities since the collapse of the state in April. Abbas and his neighbors heard their local preacher—to whom, over the preceding months, they had already begun to look for shared understandings of what they ought to do in many situations—convey Grand Ayatollah Ali Sistani's opinions on aspects of the transition process, including perhaps most importantly his call for direct elections and rejection of the Coalition Provisional Authority's (CPA) plan to select a group of Iraqis to draft a constitution. These were new and complex issues for Abbas and other listeners, and their opinions on many of them converged on Sistani's viewpoint partly because they shared in the collective hearing of it. When Sistani's preachers later called on followers to engage in low-cost collective actions in support of these positions, many obeyed. A few months later, in January 2004, Abbas participated in his first political rally, traveling with a group from his mosque to join tens of thousands of other Basrawis in a northern neighborhood to listen to Sistani's foremost representative in the city repeat these positions. A year later, when Abbas voted for the first time in his life, he did what he knew others would do: he supported the electoral list that Sistani's preachers endorsed. This list—the United Iraqi Alliance—was dominated by Shiʿi Islamist parties, none of which Abbas particularly liked.

Yet, despite this seemingly immense power, Sistani's influence remained limited. The grand ayatollah's authority vis-à-vis many political issues—that is, his ability to get Iraqis to follow his messages—depended on Iraqis' expectations that other Iraqis also would obey his messages. Sistani's edicts would be unsuccessful if the cost of compliance demanded of individuals was too high. This gave him an incentive to avoid issuing rulings he knew would be ignored or disobeyed by large numbers of his followers. Sistani could induce Shiʿa to coordinate, but he largely avoided asking Iraqis to participate in activities that entailed significant costs and for which many had an incentive to free ride on others' obedience. Like all grand ayatollahs, Sistani must consider competition from other clerics for followers; if enough of his edicts were ignored, Iraqis would be less likely to expect other Iraqis to act on his future messages and might look elsewhere for guidance. Sistani's statements and fatwas reflected these constraints. Sistani was unable to stop many Shi'a from retaliating against Sunnis after the bombing of a Shi'i shrine in February 2006. As his messages demanding restraint went unheeded, he dramatically scaled back his political involvement as Iraq descended into sectarian conflict.

Abbas had never thought of himself first and foremost as a Shi'i Muslim; he still does not, but in many ways, he acts as if he does. Until mosques affiliated with Sistani began delivering similar messages in Friday sermons, Abbas did not know what other Shi'a thought about the myriad of issues facing Iraq or what they would do in new circumstances. Although his life, like many other Iraqis', had been steeped in Shi'i narratives and symbolisms, that background did not automatically lead to a "we-ness" with other Shi'a or a shared understanding of new issues, such as how an interim constitution should be written. In this sense, the mosque as a technology of communication made it possible for listeners to be part of a much larger community concurring on (or acquiescing to) shared positions. It increased the social and political relevance of "being Shi'i," albeit without calling it such. But that technology did not reach all Iraqis; the boundaries of the imagined community did not include Sunni Muslims or non-Muslims. Over time, a cohesive imagined community of Iraqi Shi'a came to dominate Iraq's political order. This was unintentional sectarianism: Sistani's messages were overwhelmingly "Iraq-centric," not "sect-centric."[1] While they may have been directed at all Iraqis, the means by which they were delivered limited them to the Shi'a.

Many Sunni Arabs in Iraq also had come to rely on messages from their local mosques to produce social order. Both Sunni and Shi'i preachers gained influence in their local communities because they derived their power from a similar source: their ability to solve problems of coordination and low-cost contribution. But Sunni clerics in Arab Iraq are less hierarchical than their Shi'i counterparts; they lack the organizational equivalent of a grand ayatollah who can consistently induce preachers to deliver the same message in different localities. Sunni Arabs did not act cohesively on the national level. It is often claimed that one of the central issues in postinvasion Iraq is "Sunni inclusion," which, in effect, often implies national-level leaders who can represent Sunni Arabs as a group. This assumes that Sunni Arabs exist as a coherent group and share a sense of "we-ness." But sharing a culture did not automatically translate into community or a shared set of beliefs about what should be done when confronted with new issues. During the US-led occupation, Sunni Arabs did not adopt unified bargaining positions or electoral strategies. Most did not think of themselves as a group, and they did not have a set of institutions—like Shi'a did—that could bring them to collectively think of themselves and act as a group. Their mosques advocated different strategies, leaving them split regarding how and under what conditions they should participate in the political process. No unifying national-level Sunni Arab leaders emerged.

Iraqis' reliance on mosque sermons and religious networks for information and the production of social order contributed to an increase in public expressions of piety, including assertive expressions of sectarian identity.[2] Mosque messages were couched in religious terms, and the ways that Iraqis coordinated reflected clerics' preferences. In some locales, residents came to tolerate or even condone the enforcement of conservative norms by militias, including attacks on alcohol sellers and insufficiently covered women. The sounds and images of Shi'i Islam permeated public discourses and spaces, including those associated with the Iraqi state. Pictures of martyred Shi'i clerics replaced those of Saddam Hussein at intersections and even on many government buildings. The pervasiveness and public acceptance of "sectarian" iconography was partly an unintended by-product of the mechanisms by which Iraqis had come to collectively understand a new Iraq. But Sunni Arabs felt increasingly alienated from this order; to them, their country and its government felt occupied by something foreign, even after coalition authorities and troops withdrew. Sunni Arabs remained fractured and, over the years, some turned to violence, others engaged in elections, and some did both. No strategy led to a sense of "groupness" or "we-ness" that was sufficient for Sunni Arabs to act as a cohesive group, which created fertile ground for extremist groups, including al-Qaeda and its descendant Islamic State (ISIS).

Three Central Puzzles

Although this book seeks to help explain specific phenomena in post-Saddam Iraq, a larger goal is to speak to three problems of enduring significance for social scientists and political theorists. These are the problem of how societies create social order in a stateless environment, the origins and limits of political authority and leadership, and the social and political salience of collective identity. Often discussed in separate literatures, this book shows the interconnectedness of these topics and treats them as sequential problems.

After the collapse of the state and in a postauthoritarian environment where people did not have strong preexisting trust or ties to spread information, why were individuals in some localities but not others able to work together to produce a modicum of order? Under what conditions were people able to coordinate their activities, and what were the limits of their cooperation? Tribal and religious ties predated the state collapse, but when did sharing a tribal or religious "culture" translate into a set of beliefs about what other members of that group would do in new and unforeseen circumstances?

Amidst a vacuum of political authority, a wide variety of political entrepreneurs with different messages and resources tried to influence others and offer up a vision of how to understand the world. Why were some actors (and ideas) more successful than others? In the context of Iraq, why did the most senior Shi'i clerics—who followed a tradition that disdained involvement in politics—surprisingly become the most influential opinion leaders among Shi'a, instead of established and richly endowed parties and movements, both Islamist and secular? How did Sunni Arab clerics outmaneuver their secular rivals and become prominent leaders for many Sunni Arabs? From what did their power derive, and why did some clerics, but not others, possess such influence? What were the limits, if any, of that influence? And why did people follow messages from actors whom they knew had their own agendas?

Why did religious and sectarian identities become increasingly salient for Iraqi Arabs, rather than class or other identities? Why did so many Iraqis quickly come to accept religious symbols and discourse in the public sphere? And why did Shi'a come to express a relatively cohesive notion of political community, while Sunni Arabs remained fractured? To what extent does history alone explain such trajectories?

Existing Explanations

The literature on social order is vast, yet much of it ignores the question of how individuals come to coordinate. Much more attention has been paid to examining how individuals can solve collective action dilemmas plagued by free riding. Coordination is often seen as basic, simple, and uninteresting. Prior experiences help people solve coordination problems, but what happens when there is little history of coordinating—when people do not share cognitive presuppositions, or when they share too many? We know far too little about how new institutions emerge out of anarchy or the conditions under which existing ones take on new roles. Coordination problems are ubiquitous in social life; how does the way one outcome is "selected" affect the solving of other problems among the same population?

Most explanations for the increased authority of religious leaders or sectarianism in Iraq fall into two broad categories that can be labeled "primordial attachments" and "historical path dependencies." The first, favored by journalists and policymakers, holds that there is something special about Islam and its sects, or religion more generally, that garners inherently deeper and more emotional attachments than other identities. Maybe religious discourse is easy for people to understand, or when times are difficult or uncertain, individuals are inclined to seek refuge in faith. From this perspective, when the Iraqi state collapsed in 2003, traditional or ancestral loyalties—tribal, religious, sectarian—became even more important than they had been before. The influence of clerics and other traditional authorities is assumed to increase when people face such uncertainty. Regarding sectarianism, Iraq is often described as consisting of three distinct communities that have been stuck in an artificial state for more than eight decades.[3] Arguments in this category tend to focus on the failure of the Iraqi state to create a durable national identity to unify groups and pry allegiances from the latent capacity of sectarianism.

Answers in the second category, favored by academic specialists on Iraq, are diverse but share the idea that particular historical events shaped or constrained the development of the Iraqi state and society. Scholars have analyzed sectarianism as a legacy of Ottoman governance, the privileging of Sunni Arabs and marginalization of Shi'a when Iraq was fashioned under the British mandate, the Ba'th Party's atomization of society, pan-Arabism, the 1991 uprisings in Iraq and their aftermath, and deprivations of the 1990–2003 sanctions period. Other scholars blame US officials and exile parties for disenfranchising Sunni Arabs through de-Ba'thification and imposing ethnosectarian quota systems that institutionalized sectarian representation in ways that made it difficult to change. In contrast to answers based on primordialism, these explanations claim that the prominence of sectarianism is a legacy, a contingent product of history.

These explanations for the prominence of clerical authority, political Islam, or sectarianism in post-Saddam Iraq tend to describe outcomes in broad brushstrokes and provide, at best, partial answers to specific puzzles. For example, saying that Iraqis "turned toward religion" could mean many things: local religious networks (e.g., based in hussainiyas or prayer groups), geographically dispersed religious networks (e.g., Sufi), rituals and narratives associated with people or events (e.g., Muharram observances of Imam Husayn's death), or a huge variety of political entrepreneurs speaking in the name of religion (e.g., local clerics, senior clerics, sayyids, pious lay notables, millenarian preachers, leaders of religious parties). Leaders of identity groups need not be exemplars of those groups; sectarians can be secular.

Iraq was not a blank slate in 2003; history (particularly social changes in the 1990s) is important for understanding what came after. But the preceding decades did not foreshadow the immense role that would be played by clerics who had long been distant from politics. Before 2003, Iraqis held these clerics—Shiʻi "quietists" like Sistani but also many Sunni imams—in esteem as authorities on religious issues, but they did not traditionally look to them for political guidance. After 2003, however, clerics quickly expanded their writ. What are the limits of authority and leadership; what is the set of things that someone will do in the name of identity, "for the tribe" or because of religion? This book is built on a claim that focusing on the distribution and control over information at the local level contributes to explaining the above puzzles.

An Informational Approach

In contrast to other accounts, this book argues that the breakdown of order did not lead Iraqis to simply reveal "where their true loyalties and identities lay."[4] The influence of preexisting solidarities and the ability of extant authorities to expand their writ are not assumed. Instead, I treat individuals' motivations to follow "rules" or messages from claimants to authority as something that must be explained as part of the proposed mechanism. Similarly, the salience of particular identities is not taken as exogenous and assumed to affect individuals' behavior.

My approach begins by focusing on the situation in which Abbas and other ordinary Iraqis found themselves when the state collapsed and it became clear that occupation authorities were ill-prepared to replace it. Raw sewage and trash had accumulated in the streets for a month, and convicts, newly released from jail, roamed freely. Looting had stripped government buildings to their foundations. British troop strength in Basra peaked on the day they entered the city, at five thousand.[5] By the end of 2003, there were nine thousand total coalition troops combined across Iraq's four southern governates.[6] For the approximately 1.2 million residents of Basra and 4.6 million residents of those governates, there was no Leviathan.

The approach of this book, developed more thoroughly in chapter 4, is to attempt to simplify a complex world by focusing on the core interactions that, I claim, helped produce and define the limits of social order, political authority, and collective identity. I focus on a city dweller in a suddenly stateless environment who, to address matters that affect them and their neighbors—such as sewerage, trash removal, and safety—must find ways to act in concert with those neighbors. I build on insights from rational choice theory—particularly work on culture and coordination by Thomas Schelling, Russell Hardin, Michael Chwe, Avner Greif, David Laitin, and Michael Hechter—to explain the conditions under which many Iraqis were able to coordinate their activities and cooperate under anarchy.

Following state collapse, Iraqis suddenly had to work together to achieve common goals and create social order. Basic, local social order—in neighborhoods, among several dozen households—was more immediate and causally prior to broader social orders, such as establishing political, legal, and constitutional orders.[7] Ameliorating many of the negative effects of living without a state required Iraqis to work with their neighbors because many conditions affected, and could only be solved in, geographically concentrated areas. But situations in which people can work together can be divided into two types: (1) coordination dilemmas and (2) contribution problems.[8]

Coordination dilemmas are those situations where each person wants to participate in a group action but only if a sufficient number of others also participate. They are dilemmas because solving them requires individuals to have shared information about how to solve them, know that others also know this information, and believe that others will act on this information. Forming such shared expectations and solving coordination problems requires something game theorists call common knowledge: knowledge of other people's knowledge.[9] This was difficult in Iraq because of the way the Ba'th regime had atomized society. In this context, I argue that particular Muslim religious leaders—mosque preachers—controlled the most effective way Iraqis could acquire common knowledge, first at the most local level and later at the national level. This provision of common knowledge—accompanied by the belief that others will act on this knowledge—helped rational, self-interested actors to coordinate their behavior under conditions of anarchy. What distinguished preachers from other claimants to authority—tribal elders, leaders of political parties, the CPA, other religious figures—is that their voices echoed from mosque megaphones on a regular schedule and in a way that a geographically co-located audience heard the message and knew that others had also heard it. Friday sermons create common knowledge among attendees, facilitating *intra*-congregational coordination. Once Iraqis saw their neighbors act on mosque messages, they came to expect them to act on future ones. This occurred even though Friday sermons were a new institution for the majority of Iraq's Shi'a. Week by week, clerical authority ratcheted up to encompass more, and more complex, ways to coordinate together.

Contribution problems differ from coordination dilemmas. Solving these situations requires individuals to bear costs—perhaps time, money, or risk—and it is in an individual's self-interest to not contribute to the solution, even if others are doing so, and instead to free ride on others' efforts. Inducing compliance usually requires either externally provided rewards or sanctions. Mosque sermons were less effective at solving these sorts of situations; preachers' edicts were less likely to be obeyed as the costs they imposed on the individual rose. Clerical authority could not be ratcheted up further to solve costly contribution problems because clerics (at least those without enforcers or a militia at their disposal) could not sanction or otherwise impose external incentives for people to alter their behavior. Alternative explanations for the "turn to Islam"—including those rooted in Weberian understandings of authority—imply that preachers should have been able to induce more of these sorts of behavioral changes than what was observed. Instead, my admittedly functionalist approach helps account for how a particular group of religious *figures*—preachers—became religious *leaders* because they had an ability to solve problems of coordination.[10] It also helps explain the limits on how far this authority could expand.

A few weeks after the invasion, Grand Ayatollah Sistani, who had religious (and financial) authority over a vast network of Friday mosque preachers, began to coordinate messages across geographically dispersed localities, generating *inter*-congregational common knowledge and coordination. Most other grand ayatollahs lacked such networks, although clerical supporters of the late Grand Ayatollah Mohammad Mohammad Sadiq al-Sadr rekindled his Friday mosque network and combined sermons with coercion from militias, allowing the Sadrists to sometimes spur followers to engage in costly forms of collective action.[11] A new organization of Sunni clerics, the Association of Muslim Scholars, attempted to mimic Sistani's and the Sadrists' coordination of sermons across locales. They had limited success, although they surprisingly did become arguably Iraq's most influential Sunni Arab political grouping in the immediate postinvasion years.

Sistani's commands were rarely disobeyed. Why? Because except in extraordinary situations or when he had miscalculated, he only issued commands that he knew his followers would obey. He refrained from issuing guidance on many issues, including those we might have expected him to address if he thought that his followers would do anything he commanded. His early warning against clerics holding political office or running in elections was insufficient to deter some from doing so, and his public opposition to several features of the draft constitution did not prevent them from being adopted. Sistani was unable to enforce obedience; his power was limited to coordinating his followers and inducing their compliance only on relatively low-cost edicts. When Sistani's messages were most directly and publicly disobeyed by large numbers of Shiʻa in February 2006, he largely disengaged from politics for several years as sectarian violence escalated, a move that makes sense from the informational perspective developed here. The final part of the argument explores the implications of these processes not only for the rising salience of identity politics in postinvasion Iraq, but also for the internal cohesion of Shiʻa and the relative disunity of Sunni Arabs.

Although religion rose in importance in Iraq in the 1990s, mosque sermons had not previously played a mobilizing role: with a few important exceptions,

Shiʿa did not hold sermons, and Sunni Arabs heard only Baʿth-approved messages meant to indoctrinate. But those years that preceded state collapse might help explain why clerics' messages resonated in the first place. Sistani and the institution of the *marjaʿiyya* (here meaning the system of senior religious scholars issuing edicts for followers, see chapter 2 for more detail) had long been held in esteem by Shiʿa, who looked to senior clerics for guidance and advice on religious issues. But, until late 2003, the most senior grand ayatollahs in Najaf followed a long-established tradition of remaining avowedly detached from political affairs. Some Shiʿa would have turned to the marjaʿiyya for political guidance, but the fact that an overwhelming majority acquiesced to Sistani's political pronouncements demands further explanation.

Methods, Fieldwork, and Limitations

This book's approach identifies a pattern of behavior and attempts to explain how it came to be and what sustains it. Such a mechanism-focused approach is similar to an analytic narrative and Avner Greif's approach to historical institutional analysis.[12] The evidence includes many firsthand observations I made during field research of day-to-day activities of Iraqis.

There is an underappreciated natural affinity between rational choice approaches and ethnographic understanding. Game theory is useful for generating intuitions about situations, such as the real-world one in which Iraqis found themselves when the state collapsed. A game theorist typically starts by specifying the relevant actors, the information these actors have and the actions they can take at various points in time, and the payoffs for each actor for each outcome. Getting each of those elements right is what ethnography and participant observation do best, immersing the practitioner in others' worlds to see the choices they face and how they understand those choices. I believe that conducting ethnography makes game theorists better game theorists, and learning game theory might help ethnographers identify the core reasons that the people they study respond to others in the ways that they do.

From September 2003 to April 2004, I lived in an ordinary and unguarded house with Iraqis in Basra, ate the same food they did, and generally participated, as much as possible, in their everyday lives. I was an outsider, but I was living in the same environment as them, outside of the protective bubble of one of the occupying coalition's Green Zones or hotels catering to foreigners. I spent much of my time doing the things that Basrawis did, like sharing rumors with friends and acquaintances, exploring the commercial district of al-ʿAshair to see the countless new products pouring into Iraq after the easing of embargos, and people watching outside the popular Fustika ice cream parlor on al-Jazaʾir Street. Basically, everyone was learning to navigate life in a post-Baʿth and newly stateless Iraq. In this sense, I was an observing participant of social order and disorder. Other times, I was a participating observer, such as when I attended Friday sermons. I never hid what I was doing or my personal background and motivations, but I think I still became known among many of Basra's clerics and Islamist organizations as "the Indian student from America who is studying Islam in Iraq and will inevitably convert." I took an active part in ritual activities with the intention of understanding their meaning and role from an insider's perspective. I memorized the bodily movements—the prostrations—and the expressions of prayer. But I was not a member of the community; I am not a Muslim, not a Shiʿi Muslim, and not Iraqi. It is possible that, as a nonbeliever, I missed something in the power of the religious message of Islam and the experience of its rituals. This thought recurred each time I sat in on a Shiʿi lamentation, when grown men I knew would begin to cry and beat their chests and heads. Lamentation responses during Friday prayers were subdued compared to those I would experience in hussainiyas during Muharram in early 2004. My functionalist approach to religion de-emphasizes factors rooted in emotion and faith, but it is not inconsistent with them. There is some merit to such explanations, but they miss an important aspect of religion's power and do not tell the whole story.

The physical layout of Basra was easier to study than the social layout. I walked around a lot and took notes on buildings, checkpoints, rubbish, and other signs of order and disorder. I had a vehicle and often drove around the city, noting which neighborhoods fashioned speed bumps and barriers to control traffic. Many of my insights came from informally sitting around with Iraqis, sipping steaming *istikans* and eating date cookies (*kleicha*) or sharing a meal of Iraqi-style *quzi* (a lamb and rice dish), and talking about what they thought their neighbors thought about issues facing the neighborhood, city, and country.[13] I struggled to understand Basrawi colloquial Arabic for most of the seven months I lived there; it differs more than I had anticipated from what textbooks teach as the Iraqi dialect.[14] I regret having had to conduct most of my interviews and informal conversations in a mix of other colloquials and Modern Standard Arabic, and I often wondered if obliging Iraqis to speak to me in a more formal Arabic affected their ability or willingness to give me candid answers. I conducted unstructured interviews, in-depth interviews, and group interviews. Group interviews were usually spontaneous: over lunch after Friday prayers, in clerics' or tribal leaders' receiving rooms, or around a counter in a shop. I never recorded interviews, and the context often made it difficult for me to write down more than jottings or scratch notes during conversations. I never took notes during a sermon; I attended ten Friday prayers in Basra and always participated as a member of the congregation. I asked two preachers if I could record their Friday sermons, and both refused. At the time, I assumed I would have plenty of opportunities in future months to record and transcribe sermons. As soon as feasible after prayers ended, I tried to write descriptive field notes and, if possible, discuss the content of the sermon with someone who also had attended. Twice I happened into impromptu postsermon discussions over kofta kebab sandwiches in the Canary Restaurant, and I learned more from those chance encounters about what Iraqis knew others knew from sermons than from any planned interview on the subject.

When I unexpectedly had to quickly leave Iraq in April 2004, I was in Baghdad, while much of the material I had accumulated during fieldwork remained in Basra. Months later, an Iraqi contact managed to send some of that material to me in Jordan, and I had wisely made backup copies of some other material. But most of what I had left—including logbooks, raw field notes, newspaper clippings, undeveloped rolls of film, printouts of maps on which I had recorded observations—was irretrievably lost. The empirical evidence and narratives in this book would be far richer if I had not lost the materials that I did.

The ethnographic evidence suggests that local social orders did emerge around many Friday mosques, and the evidence is consistent with the informational mechanism I describe. I use geographic information system (GIS) techniques to provide further empirical evidence in support of the argument. My ethnographic data and information perspective focus on process, the mechanism of how social order and authority emerged and worked. Field data include conversations with numerous Iraqis, interviews with preachers and coalition and Iraqi officials, participant observations I made in mosques, and insights I gleaned living immersed among Iraqis. The "larger N" GIS analysis complements these ethnographic data by demonstrating, insofar as available data allow, a relationship between Friday mosque location and one indicator of order.

Southern Iraq is a conservative society, and while I was there, norms of gender segregation were strengthening. I had relatively few opportunities to have extended conversations with conservative Shi'i women, and the women I did speak with regularly were not representative of the majority of women in the city. On several occasions when I was talking with a family or a group, husbands intervened and answered my questions for their wives. Even if I could have spoken to more Iraqi women, some might have felt it inappropriate to talk to me about what other Iraqi women thought, which would have made questions about common knowledge—knowledge about other women's knowledge—difficult. I never knew how many women attended the sermons I attended; the women's section was usually hidden behind a wall or screen. And I learned that at least one local preacher also had no idea how many women attended his sermons; he was surprised and stumped when I asked him. Women in Basra might have found other ways to create order amidst anarchy, and that question deserves more attention than I was able to pay to it.

Why Iraq?

Although the Iraqi state collapsed, it was not a typical "failed state." As Robert Rotberg writes, "The terms 'collapsed' and 'failed' designate the consequences of a process of decay at the nation-state level. The capacity of those nation-states to perform positively for their citizens has atrophied."[15] Iraq was different than other failed states in that the state collapsed in 2003 without collapsing; it was not on the verge of state collapse prior to the invasion. The Iraqi state contracted in the early 1990s because of the multilateral UN sanctions, but as described in chapter 2, the power of the state and the Baʻth Party over society strengthened when the UN Oil-for-Food Programme began in 1996 and increased considerably in 1998 and again by the end of 1999, when the ceiling was lifted on the amount of oil Iraq was allowed to sell. The Iraqi state was bankrupt, but it had access to materials, imported consumer goods, and foreign technical assistance for reconstruction and for use in a steady stream of patronage to supporters. The country's physical infrastructure was dilapidated, but from 2000 to 2003, the state expanded housing construction, water distribution networks, and access to subsidized goods. One influential study of the sanctions regime notes, "In all sectors there were indicators that the government of Iraq put Oil-for-Food [Programme] imports to good use."[16] A construction boom was occurring before the invasion; from 2001 to February 2003, cement production in Iraq increased by 30 percent.[17]

Corruption in Iraq was endemic, but Baʻth rule remained despotic and in control of society via fear, coercion, and an elaborate system of rewards.[18] There was no extended time period of state decay when warlords could take over territory and establish fiefdoms, like what occurred in Somalia before and after the fall of the Siad Barre government in 1991. The Baʻth Party maintained an extensive system of informants and dominated political violence. There was little opportunity for citizens to develop ways of providing goods that were truly independent of the state; although it could not pay adequate salaries, the Iraqi state remained strong enough to suppress or co-opt any such ventures into state patronage networks. There was never sufficient breathing room and freedom from repression for civil society groups to emerge and flourish.[19] What vibrancy existed was intertwined with the state apparatus and the Baʻth Party. As discussed in chapter 2, in the 1990s, social control devolved or was delegated to tribes and other groups, but they were heavily co-opted into networks of state patronage.

Some nonstate actors had influence before 2003 largely because they could access state goods and services. When the Iraqi state collapsed in April 2003, the source of much of their influence vanished. In this sense, post-Qaddafi Libya is a closer, albeit problematic, parallel to Iraq than either contemporary Afghanistan or Yemen. The Libyan state collapsed quickly. In Afghanistan and parts of Yemen, the state had limited authority and capacity to begin with, so Afghans and Yemenis had long relied on other ways, and other authorities, to produce and maintain social order. The Iraqi state did not undergo a downward spiral that provided opportunities for nonstate institutions to develop and incentives for individuals to find alternative ways of providing public goods, especially security, as the state withdraws or weakens. Therefore, Iraq in 2003–2004 is a good place and time to explore these three particular puzzles.

Why Basra?

It was happenstance that I ended up conducting field research in Basra. Yet, Basra offers several advantages for investigating order, authority, and identity in postinvasion Iraq. First, despite being founded in the 630s, the modern city of Basra is relatively new. Basra's location changed over time; the original city of Basra lies approximately twelve miles to the southwest of today's city. That original city declined and was largely abandoned by about 1397; today the associated site is a rocky field alongside a highway. The new city of Basra, which some claim was founded in 1407, grew slowly until the late nineteenth century, when it became more important as a hub for the Gulf economy. And rapid expansion occurred only after the arrival in 1914 of the British, who built a new port and a European-style quarter several kilometers to its north. People settled along the roads the British constructed between settled areas, and the population expanded rapidly only after 1938 and even more so after 1958. All this is to say that the "old" parts of today's Basra are not that old. Most of Basra's mosques date from the late twentieth century, and they were built according to central planning guidelines and do not reflect underlying social or religious divisions.[20] The majority of the city's families moved there sometime in the past seventy years. If I had examined the relationship between mosques and social order in another city, such as Baghdad, I would be concerned that some other factor affected both mosque location and social order. Maybe mosques are a public good, built by cooperative communities! Shi'a in Iraq often rely on buildings called *hussainiyas* for daily prayers, as well as for special rituals commemorating the deaths of the Imams. After the fall of Saddam, hussainiyas sprouted up throughout Basra, and they may reflect such social divisions, but Friday mosques do not.

A second advantage for my field research was that the British, not the Americans, administered Basra during my time there. If I had been in the American zone, many Iraqis likely would have thought that I was working for the US military or the Central Intelligence Agency. They might have responded to me and my questions differently, particularly when I asked about what they thought their neighbors knew. In contrast, the British military maintained a minimal presence in Basra, leaving day-to-day order to neighborhood groups and sanctioned militias. CPA South, headquartered in Basra Palace after 15 October 2003, and responsible for the four most southern governates of Iraq, was a modest but professional operation compared to CPA Baghdad. I interviewed officials from CPA South, including the astute members of its political office. In contrast, Baghdad's Green Zone seemed impenetrable, and, I assume, individuals there would have had much less insight into life outside their walls than the staff in Basra had about their region of responsibility. I once tried to enter Baghdad's Green Zone, but my US passport was insufficient to get me past the guards at the infamous Assassins' Gate.

This book proceeds as follows. Chapter 2 addresses the extent to which recent Iraqi history can explain the rise of religious actors and sectarian politics after the invasion. It begins by describing the effects of sanctions from 1990 to 2003 on the Iraqi state and its relationship to society, including the regime's Faith Campaign. The chapter also examines the history and nature of Shiʻi and Sunni clerics' authority and network structures. These factors contributed to the initial resonance of clerical messages postinvasion, but alone they do not explain how clerical authority expanded, the limits of that expansion, and why other religious actors were not as influential. Chapter 3 describes the looting of Basra and the collapse of the Iraqi state following the US-led invasion. It then sets the stage for the rest of the book by describing the situation in which Iraqi Arabs found themselves the day after.

Chapter 4 presents the core argument of the book, linking an ability to generate common knowledge to coordination. It then explores why some institutions (Friday mosques and sermons) motivated Iraqis to coordinate, while others (e.g., tribes, occupation authorities, political parties, other religious organizations) could not. It provides a framework to understand the types of issues on which mosque messages could and could not induce neighbors to work together to address. Chapter 5 provides ethnographic evidence showing how Friday mosque sermons helped some communities coordinate to solve local problems. It then explores how prevalent this phenomenon may have been by using GIS to spatially link Friday mosques to a sample of murders in Basra. I collected the information on mosques, and the data on murders come from a collection of US Army field reports from 2004 to 2009. The weekly Friday sermon rendered messages common knowledge within the geographic catchment area of individual mosques. I use spatial analysis techniques to try to assess the extent to which the social orders that emerged reflected these catchment areas. Using murders as a measure of social order, I find that fewer murders occurred in areas that fall within the catchment area of a single Friday mosque than in places where two or more mosques' areas overlap.

The next two chapters turn to the national-level expansion of Shi'i and Sunni clerical authority and its limits. Chapter 6 explains why Grand Ayatollah Ali Sistani and Moqtada al-Sadr, instead of religious party leaders or other elites, surprisingly became Iraq's most important political entrepreneurs. I use insights from social network analysis to trace how Shi'i ayatollahs, who control hierarchical networks of clerical deputies, could reliably and consistently disseminate similar messages in different mosques and generate common knowledge, coordination, and low-cost cooperation across dispersed Shi'i congregations on national-level issues like federalism and voting strategies. In the first year after the invasion, other political organizations, such as tribes, parties, occupation figures, and media outlets, lacked a sufficient ability to routinely generate the wide common knowledge necessary to coordinate Iraqi Arabs across localities. Electoral data from the time are analyzed and shown to be consistent with the argument. The chapter also examines the limits of authority. It argues that the postinvasion augmentation of Sistani's authority was constrained by the individual-level cost of commands he could issue. Sistani's edicts fostered large-scale participation when they asked Shi'a to coordinate or to engage in low-cost endeavors. When the costs of complying with a command rose, however, followers were less likely to follow. Knowing this, and to maintain followers' expectations that others will follow future commands, Sistani limited what he asked his followers to do. I examine postinvasion issues about which he chose to issue a statement or fatwa and those that he chose not to address. In other words, it was not only Sistani's worldview and socialpolitical philosophy that determined when and how he intervened in postinvasion developments; his widely noted pragmatism was also partly a strategy to protect his future influence.

Chapter 7 turns to Sunni Arabs and compares their clerical structure to that of the Shi'a. Following state collapse, Sunni clerics also facilitated intracongregational coordination, but the preexisting network structure of Sunni clerics did not provide a comparable institutional capacity to disseminate similar messages in geographically dispersed mosques. But the two most prominent Sunni Arab political organizations after the invasion both reflected clerics' newfound authority. Yet, Sunnis remained relatively fractured and leaderless at the national level. They failed to adopt coordinated positions on many issues during the transition process. Finally, the often lamented problem of Sunni inclusion in post-Saddam Iraqi governments is reexamined in light of this argument. The challenge was not so much finding suitable Sunni leaders; the dilemma of post-invasion Iraqi politics was bargaining between groups when one side—the Shi'a—is highly coordinated and another other side is not.

Chapter 8 extends the argument about order making to other places and other cognate forms of producing order via information. I go beyond Basra in looking at the coordination of Friday sermons in other places and times, including attempts to unify sermons across Egypt. I go beyond sermons in explaining how the argument speaks to broader issues of culture and social order; we can think of other rituals and technologies—unrelated to Islam or religion—that can produce a similar unifying effect. The information mechanism is generalizable: how people come to know what others know and then collectively act, especially when order or political authority is highly fluid and contested.

2

THE SANCTIONS-ERA ROOTS OF POSTINVASION DEVELOPMENTS

There is a growing consensus among analysts of Iraq that the roots of the post-2003 rise of religious actors and sectarian politics must be attributed in part to social and political changes during the sanctions period, from 1990 to 2003. Some see continuities before and after regime change, arguing that a weakening of the Iraqi state and the destitution caused by sanctions led to the growth of groups that maintained an uninterrupted trajectory, more or less, from the sanctions era to the postinvasion period. Peter Harling, for example, writes, "The invasion revealed, enabled, and exacerbated pre-existing phenomena more often than it generated them in and of itself."[1] The influence of tribal sheikhs is often explained in such terms. Other scholars focus on the attitudinal effects of specific Ba'th policies, such as discrimination against Shi'a and the suppression of their religious institutions and rituals. Fanar Haddad links a variety of historical factors to the post-2003 advent of identity politics, placing particular emphasis on the 1991 uprising and competing interpretations around it. He says that the 1990s was "a decade that altered Iraqi society for generations to come."[2]

This chapter examines these roots, focusing on the alleged weakness of the Iraqi state under sanctions, Saddam's Faith Campaign, and the nature of the authority that Shi'i and Sunni clerics held before the invasion. This consensus on the importance of historical context is not wrong; the past matters. There is merit to these explanations, but they all miss an important issue or do not tell the whole story. After 2003, both Shi'i and Sunni clerics were able to extend their preexisting religious authority to temporal and mundane issues, but how this augmentation occurred and its limits are not well explained by preinvasion factors. While the seeds of many postinvasion developments were planted in 1991 and during the sanctions period, later chapters will show that the direction and length of the postinvasion sprouts that grew from those seeds can be understood only by also looking at the informational capacity of different actors when the state collapsed in April 2003. Some roots withered, while others flourished in unanticipated directions.

Iraqi State and Society under Sanctions

Iraq was neither a failed nor a failing state on the eve of invasion in 2003. Although over twenty-two years of war and twelve years of international sanctions had decimated the country's economy, infrastructure, and population, the Ba'th Party and the Iraqi state proved to be remarkably resilient and adaptable. Scholars of Iraq, building on Kanan Makiya's foundational work, traditionally have emphasized the role of surveillance, fear, and coercion in explaining the Ba'th's control over Iraqi society.[3] Although the authoritarian welfare system built after the nationalization of the oil industry in 1972 had atrophied amid war and sanctions, recent scholarship based largely on the captured archives of the Ba'th Party highlights the extent to which Iraqis remained reliant on and entangled in the regime's elaborate system of patronage and rewards.[4] The party did not weaken or lose its control over the population, and party membership expanded in the late 1990s. As the state contracted fiscally, the party delegated some tasks to tribes, religious actors, and local specialists in violence, but this devolution of authority can be understood as a deliberate state strategy and should not be conflated with a loss of control over society. The regime continued to oversee a stable and functioning dictatorship characterized by multiple overlapping power centers at the local level. Writing in 2005, Sultan Barakat described Iraq under the late Ba'th as a "functioning, modern state," rich in liquid assets and human resources, whose grip "over the population in the central and southern regions was to remain total up to the moment of intervention by external forces."[5]

Sanctions

Changes in international sanctions strengthened the state and regime after 1996, particularly after 1998. Under international sanctions from August 1990 until 1996, the Iraqi state was allowed to import almost nothing other than medicines and food, and it could receive no external funds. The economic situation began to change in 1996, when the Iraqi government reached an understanding with the United Nations over the implementation of the Oil-for-Food Programme.[6]

Under this program, Iraq was allowed to sell up to $1 billion worth of oil every ninety days, and 53 percent of the proceeds went into a UN-controlled escrow account that was used to pay for imports that Iraq requested and a UN committee approved.[7] The amount of oil Iraq was allowed to sell increased in early 1998 to $5.26 billion every six months, and in December 1999 the ceiling on oil sales was lifted.[8] The Iraqi state could not access cash, but it could sell as much oil as it could extract and use approximately 70 percent of the revenue to import a wide variety of nonmilitary products for (re)construction and to distribute as patronage. Oil trading and smuggling outside of the UN-administered program also increased and provided additional revenue.

Although the figures remain controversial, the horrific humanitarian toll of sanctions on the lives and health of everyday Iraqis has been documented in malnutrition and child mortality rates, and much of the population became dependent on a state-provided food basket for survival.[9] Throughout this sanctions period, the regime effectively used this food rationing system (the Public Distribution System, or PDS) to control society and expand the state's reach further into the daily lives of the population.[10] The PDS allocated mainly domestically produced basic food supplies from its establishment in 1990 until 1996 and then Oil-for-Food imports from 1997 to 2003. The government stripped ration cards from political opponents, public sector employees who did not show up for work, and, occasionally, entire families as a form of collective punishment.[11] The sanctions-era food allocation system created another lever of control for the regime and increased the strength of the state vis-à-vis society.[12]

The Iraqi economy grew in the years leading up to the invasion; between 1996 and 2000, Iraq's GDP tripled from $10.6 billion to $33 billion, and the currency stabilized, although inflation remained high.[13] With the assistance of a constellation of UN-affiliated agencies, home construction and agricultural production increased, and the water distribution network expanded after 2000. From 2001 to February 2003, cement production increased by 30 percent.[14] In a comprehensive study of the sanctions on Iraq, Joy Gordon writes, "In all sectors there were indicators that the government of Iraq put Oil-for-Food imports to good use."[15] Joseph Sassoon estimates that by late 2000, Iraq's "infrastructure was more or less back to its pre–First Gulf War strength."[16]

New Tribal Authorities

In the 1990s, the Ba'th's support for loyal tribal leaders increased, and many sheikhs saw their status elevated as they were brought into state patronage networks through personal relations with Saddam, security agencies, or party offices.[17] This can be understood as part of a regime strategy to delegate some state functions to substate actors, to reduce expenses, and, perhaps, to deliberately further fragment power structures to reduce the risk of a coup.[18] It also served as a way to reward tribes—Sunni, Shi'i, and mixed ones—that had remained loyal during the 1991 uprising. Saddam rewarded these loyal "Arab" tribes. In some cases, the party gave tribes weapons and tolerated (or cooperated with) their smuggling. In exchange, tribes policed rural and border areas and may have helped monitor and control their tribesmen who had moved to towns and cities.

Those new sheikhs of the 1990s, however, were not autonomous from the state. The Ba'th Party's control over them remained high because they relied on the state for goods and services needed to maintain their influence. What looks like the hollowing out of the state and fracturing of authority in the 1990s was really a deliberate regime strategy of delegation and control. The "new tribalism" of the sanctions period does not explain the influence of tribal leaders after the invasion. When the state collapsed in 2003, many sheikhs who were influential under the Ba'th lost their access to state resources, and their authority over their tribesmen declined precipitously. Sheikhs who could provide protection or predatory opportunities to their tribesmen, however, rose in influence.

This is all to say that the Iraqi state collapsed in April 2003 without first going through a pronounced period of decline in state control. As mentioned in chapter 1, Robert Rotberg notes that the terms *collapsed* and *failed* usually designate consequences of a process of decay.[19] States fail, and a few collapse, because the capacity of the state to provide goods and maintain order declines over time, often in a downward spiral. This decline provides opportunities and incentives for substate groups—mafia organizations, militias, grassroots organizations, kinship groups, religious charities—to provide services alongside or in lieu of the state. A weakening state might create, in Daniel Posner's words, "breathing room and freedom from repression for civil society groups to emerge and flourish."[20]

But in Iraq, the collapse of the state in 2003 was so sudden that there was no chance for nonstate actors to gradually fill in the vacuum left by the disappearance of the state. The next chapter will examine what transpired when the state provision of goods and order in Iraq ended suddenly. Before the invasion, there was no extended period of time when substate actors could take over the provision of services. There was no parceling out of territory into fiefdoms.

Rising Religiosity and the Faith Campaign

It is widely claimed that religiosity increased in Iraqi society in the 1990s. After acknowledging the difficulty in empirically assessing this perception, Fanar Haddad agrees with it, saying, "After the war and under the shadow of sanctions, Iraqi society underwent a marked turn towards religious identity and practice."[21] Scholars point to both regional and Iraq-specific factors for this turn: the decline of leftist and Arab nationalist ideologies after 1967; the 1979 Iranian Revolution; the Baʻth regime's Faith Campaign after 1993; years of war and domestic violence; and impoverishment caused by international sanctions. On these latter factors, Faleh Jabar summarizes the conventional wisdom, "Fear, dislocation, destitution, uncertainty and social ills drove masses to the warmth of religious charities and fraternities."[22]

Some writers conflate religiosity in society with state-sponsored efforts to promote a Baʻthist interpretation of Islam, and the relationship between "bottom-up" and "top-down" expressions of piety—particularly during the sanctions period—is complex and a source of debate. For Amatzia Baram, state followed society. He sees the Baʻth regime, and Saddam personally, as undergoing a dramatic U-turn in identity and belief system from "staunch secularism ... with a whiff of atheism" to Islamism, beginning in 1986 and culminating with the initiation of the Faith Campaign in 1993.[23] For Baram, this "Islamic about-face" was done to align with Iraqi society. The party "jumped, in a calculating and even cynical way, on the bandwagon of the public's growing religiosity" after "the president learned that the Iraqi people were returning to the mosque."[24] In contrast, Samuel Helfont, working with documents in the Baʻth Party archives, argues that Baʻthism was neither "secular" nor "anti-religious," and he sees a continuity over time in how the Baʻth understood and sought to employ proper Islam.[25] The regime's Faith Campaign was a culmination of earlier plans; it simply took time for the regime to train cadres of loyal yet credible religious figures who would transmit the Baʻth's views on religion to the public. More will be said in later chapters on these clerics, many of whom surprisingly became influential local actors after the invasion.

Baram's and Helfont's research elucidates the regime's use of religion in the 1990s, and the unprecedented rate of (Sunni) mosque building is well documented. We know much less, however, about how religiosity changed in Iraqi society: many claims are based on anecdotes and assumptions, and it is unclear how often Iraqis conformed to regime discourses. It is often said that Iraqis went more often to mosques to pray in the 1990s than in previous decades, although the vast majority of Shiʻi mosques did not hold Friday congregational prayers or sermons. The most notable exception were mosques affiliated with Grand Ayatollah Mohammad Mohammad Sadiq al-Sadr, who restarted Friday prayers in a handful of mosques from 1995 to 1999. We do know that there was an increase in Shiʻa's undertaking Ashura pilgrimages to Karbala; one estimate says that 2 million went in 1999 and 2.4 million in 2001 (out of a total Iraqi population of around 23 million), although these figures include a large number of Iranian pilgrims.[26]

In general, it is safe to assume that this conventional wisdom is correct: large parts of Iraqi society, like many other Arab societies, did become more pious during this period. This is an important factor in why religious actors would be influential in postinvasion Iraq, but it does not help us explain *which* religious actors. As we will see, Sunni clerics became influential both local and nationally, which is in sharp contrast to many other Arab societies where laymen dominate Islamist movements. Three Sufi orders—the Qadiriyya, Rifaʿiyya, and Naqshbandiyya—flourished under the Baʿth, which promoted them as a counterweight to Salafism.[27] They had national-level political leaders and a network of mosques and practitioners that survived the invasion. But, as chapter 7 describes, their ability to coordinate members was limited.

Sectarianism before 2003

To what extent did Iraqi sectarianism increase in the 1990s? What Haddad calls a "sect-centric political culture" certainly became dominant among the organized Iraqi opposition in exile, particularly the Shiʿa, who came to see themselves as victimized by the regime *as Shiʿa*.[28] This is reflected in documents such as the 2002 "Declaration of the Shiʿa of Iraq," articles and books by members of the opposition, and the adoption of ethnosectarianism as an organizing principle in opposition endeavors.[29]

We know much less about, and there is more disagreement about, the extent to which sectarianism increased among Iraqis in Iraq from 1991 to 2003. In his seminal work on sectarianism in Iraq, Haddad says "it became more salient than ever" because of the events of 1991, how those events were remembered, and the effects of sanctions.[30] Najib al-Salihi, an ex–Republican Guard officer who defected in 1995, claims that the regime actively encouraged sectarian sentiments during the 1991 uprising to deter Sunnis in central and western Iraq from joining the uprising.[31] Baram shares this conventional wisdom, pointing out that the regime killed tens of thousands of Shiʿa while putting down the 1991 uprisings but deliberately limited its violence when putting down Sunni tribal revolts in the mid-1990s.[32]

Documents in the Baʿth Party archives, however, suggest that the extent of the Sunni-Shiʿi divide in Iraq during this time might be overstated. The regime's discourse, at least, was not driving an increase in sectarian sentiment.[33] One scholar notes, "Overtly anti-Shiʿi language is conspicuously absent in the Baʿth

Party's archive during this period—as it was in the 1970s and 1980s."[34] Internal Baʿth documents never characterized any Iraqi as Sunni or Shiʿi.[35] The regime's meticulous registers of high school students recorded a variety of data about students and their families, but they never ask sectarian affiliation (only religion: Muslim or Christian), and that detail is not always evident from place of residence or family name.[36] The Faith Campaign included support for Shiʿi shrines and rituals, and the regime suppressed Salafism because of its anti-Shiʿi tendencies.[37] The regime tolerated Sadr's resumption of Friday prayers and clerical outreach to underserved Shiʿi communities (a toleration that led many outside observers to assume that the regime favored his marjaʿiyya). Internal documents show a fixation by the upper echelons of the regime on Persians in the clerical ranks.[38] Even members of the banned Islamic Daʿwa movement were referred to as "Iranian agents," "criminals," or other similar nonsectarian terms by the regime. Regarding Shiʿi rituals, the regime was concerned, first and foremost, with the Ashura commemoration and gatherings, which had a history of being exploited by opposition groups to mobilize protests and conduct sabotage and assassinations.

More research—and unbiased research—is needed on the extent to which sectarian sentiment increased among ordinary Iraqis during the sanctions period; existing work has focused too much on the exiled opposition and regime. Haddad mentions the difficulty of studying this issue: it was unacceptable to talk about sects and sectarian relations in Iraq before 2003.[39] Throughout my fieldwork in 2003 and 2004, Iraqis I spoke with generally considered open discussions of sectarianism uncouth or even inflammatory.[40] Basrawis focused on who had supported the Baʿth and who did not, and it was widely understood that the regime relied heavily on Shiʿi Party members in areas where Shiʿa lived. There were dozens of assassinations and tit-for-tat killings in Basra during my time there, and I never once heard that someone was targeted because of their sect. In the vast majority of cases someone was said to have been targeted either because they were "a Baʿthi" or because of a personal grudge, some of which were years or decades old. This powerful reluctance to appear sectarian fades as the civil war escalates in 2006–2007, but the sectarian animosity witnessed during that period was more a product of the violence than a precursor to it.

Many claims about the rise of identity politics in post-2003 Iraq assume a latent sectarianism that exiles, lacking a social base, were able to exploit. Freed from Iraq's political correctness, exiles could develop a more assertive form of Shiʿi identity that, allegedly, "resonated with a significant body of Shia opinion" after 2003.[41] The dynamics explored in chapters 4 to 6 offer a complementary way that sectarian divides, to the extent that they preexisted, widened and became more pronounced as an inadvertent result of the ways in which Iraqis created order after the invasion. The argument I develop does not assume a high degree of preexisting latent sectarian sentiment within Iraqi society; my narrative is not one of aggrieved Shi'a deliberately searching for more assertive forms of Shi'i identity or being manipulated by exiles or occupation officials. I analyze the postinvasion increase in the saliency of sectarianism as an inadvertent and unintended by-product of other processes.

The Clerical Structure of Shi'i Islam in Iraq

Iraqi Shi'ism, as practiced today as the Usuli jurisprudential school of Shi'ism, developed relatively free from financial and bureaucratic influence from the Sunni-dominated Ottoman state. Its modern institutional structure, therefore, reflects the need of the religious class to garner financial and political support from the Shi'i laity.[42] Iraq's Shi'i clergy has traditionally relied on followers' donations, especially *khums* alms and monies collected from pilgrims and burials around the Shi'i shrines in Najaf and Karbala.[43] Throughout Iraqi history, and particularly under the Ba'th, the highest echelons of the Shi'i clergy have done and sacrificed what was necessary to maintain their independence from an authoritarian state that repeatedly sought to co-opt and control it.

Usuli Twelver Shi'ism divides Muslims into two categories: individuals formally trained and qualified to extract the rules and commandments of Islam from original sources, and the untrained or unqualified laity. The former—a trained scholar—is called a *mujtahid* (literally, one who exerts himself) in applying limited deductive judgement to answer a legal or theological question. The latter—lay individuals—must choose a living mujtahid and follow his religious rules.[44] Such a Shi'i follower is a *muqallid* (literally, an imitator). A mujtahid who has such followers is known as a *marja' taqlid* (plural *maraji'*)—literally, "a source or reference of imitation." Several maraji' usually live in each Shi'i shrine city. A muqallid is free to change his marja' if he believes another is more knowledgeable. In general, upper-level mujtahids without emulators are called *ayatollahs* and those with emulators are *grand ayatollahs*, although the use of these honorifics varies over time and place. Usually, fewer than a hundred grand ayatollahs with followers exist around the world at any given time; there were at least seven in Iraq in 2003.

Lay Shi'a in Iraq frequently told me that this doctrine of emulation dates back to the first Imam and the year 632. Twelver Shi'i scholars typically date the practice to the Major Occultation, which began in 941 when the twelfth

Imam, Muhammad al-Mahdi, who had disappeared from the earth sixty-eight years earlier, issued a statement via his dying fourth deputy that he would appoint no further deputies to serve as a bridge between him and the community of Muslims.[45] In the absence of a deputy, the Mahdi supposedly instructed believers to emulate expert scholars until he returns to establish justice on earth. In reality, this institution of emulation emerged much more recently: the concepts supporting it developed in the early 1800s, and the first jurist who used the term *marjaʿ taqlid* to refer to himself, Sheikh Muhammad Hasan al-Najafi, died in 1849 or 1850.[46] The concept of one mujtahid having superiority over others dates from the fourteen-year period from 1850 to 1864 when Sheikh Murtadha Ansari, Najafi's successor, was the sole marjaʿ for the entire Shiʿi world.[47] These doctrines of emulation and the nonecclesiastical clerical hierarchies that go along with them are an outcome of the spread of Usuli Shiʿism and the decline of Akhbari Shiʿism in the late eighteenth and nineteenth centuries.[48]

In Usuli Shiʿism, traditional religious authority derives from religious knowledge (*ʿilm*) and reflects a consensus given by other scholars that the individual has the requisite expertise and personal characteristics to interpret God's message. A mujtahid who then aspires to be followed, or emulated, publicly signals so by writing a *risala*, a legal manual summarizing his legal opinions on rituals (e.g., prayer, ablutions) and transactions (business and personal, including marriage). This custom dates only to the 1920s, and in practice, these manuals are usually annotations or commentaries on the manual of a previous marjaʿ (now, often Mohsin al-Hakim's), all of which are essentially footnotes on an influential manual of jurisprudence that is taught in the seminaries.[49] There is little variation between them. Mujtahids who take this step have typically spent decades studying in one or more Shiʿi seminaries under the supervision of famous and learned senior scholars. As a general rule, an aspiring marjaʿ refrains from declaring himself worthy of emulation (i.e., issuing a risala) until his mentor dies or the most senior grand ayatollah in the city dies. There is usually, but not always, deference across generations: ambitious clerics of one age cohort wait for the eldest marajiʿ of the previous one to pass before competition enters into the open to be a wide-ranging marjaʿ. All that said, it is not unheard of for ambitious young clerics in Iraq to ignore this traditional procedure for becoming a marjaʿ. Muhammad al-Shirazi, as well as other members of his extended family, have repeatedly challenged conventional clerical hierarchies, such as in the 1960s and 1970s when he tried to become a wide-ranging marjaʿ despite the prominence of Mohsin al-Hakim and then Abu al-Qasim Khoei.[50] Similar challenges to the established grand ayatollahs of Najaf occurred after 2003.

Grand ayatollahs financially support and train students before dispatching them to serve as their agents in various Shi'i communities to collect religious dues in their name, answer followers' questions, and disseminate their legal and religious rulings.[51] Students and junior clerics need support and certification from a grand ayatollah to conclude seminary studies and find a position in a mosque or other religious institution. Mosque preachers collect religious dues in the name of a grand ayatollah. Grand ayatollahs, in turn, need a stream of loyal students to maintain and increase their influence by disseminating their rulings and sending some collected alms back to the central office. In some Shi'i communities, a cleric might be authorized by two or more grand ayatollahs to be their agent.

Islam—including Shi'i Islam—lacks an ecclesiastical hierarchy. Instead, each grand ayatollah sits atop a pyramid-shaped network and, in effect, competes with his peers for students and followers. Such a network is typically referred to as a *marja'iyya*, although the term has different meanings. It sometimes refers to a single grand ayatollah and the organizations, mosques, charitable institutions, and the preachers, staff, and students he supports. It is this network that binds the marja' with lay followers who emulate him and often provide the financial means that sustains the network. Other times, however, the term *marja'iyya* refers to the leadership of a shrine city's seminaries and religious institutions (*hawza* or *hawza 'ilmiya*, a territory of learning); that leader might be a single individual or a group of senior scholars as a collective. So the marja'iyya of Sistani and the marja'iyya of Najaf are overlapping but different things. There is no centralized mechanism for determining relative influence among ayatollahs.[52] The relative influence of a particular grand ayatollah is a function of his ability to attract followers and maintain a network of agents.

Ayatollahs' networks are typically highly centralized. Describing such networks as they developed in the nineteenth century, Meir Litvak states, "Patronage networks linking the teacher and his former disciples who resided as 'ulama' in various Shi'i localities came close to the ideal type of radially connected network. In this model each member is directly linked to the central figure, i.e. the teacher, and members communicate with one another only through him."[53] When a grand ayatollah dies, his network might disintegrate as disciples independently and sometimes competitively attach themselves to the networks of other senior scholars, including new claimants to such religious authority.[54] Other times, much of the network remains intact and effectively transfers its loyalty to another grand ayatollah or a de facto successor. The former happened after the death of Grand Ayatollah Mohammad Mohammad Sadiq al-Sadr in 1999: his network fractured as his agents and followers attached themselves to clerical contemporaries or several of his students who tried to elevate themselves. A process akin to the latter occurred when Khoei died in 1992. As discussed later in this chapter, there was disagreement within Khoei's network about which member of the next generation of senior scholars they should coordinate around. But there was a consensus among them that they should stay united and consolidate around one; eventually, Sistani ended up being the pick.

This brings us to a key point: the traditional religious authority of a grand ayatollah, therefore, is to offer guidance and direction (*irshad wa tawjih*) to those who have chosen to emulate or follow him. This is nominally done through instructions in his risala but also by answering questions asked of him by his followers. These questions are usually posed to his representatives (*wakils*), who are sufficiently trained in Islamic studies and knowledgeable enough about the grand ayatollah's rulings that they can be trusted to answer on his behalf.

Sources of Authority

Max Weber's tripartite classification of authority is a useful starting point to explore Shi'i clerical authority.[55] It does not fit the rational-legal ideal authority. The hawza is not a bureaucratic institution, and a marja' is neither appointed nor selected to hold a position and apply a set of legally enacted rules. Any obedience given to a marja' is to the person as an individual, not an impersonal order. Weber's traditional model of authority is potentially more applicable. As mentioned, many Shi'a believe that emulating senior scholars has been done for over a thousand years, even though the practice in its current form really developed only over the past two centuries. In this sense, the religious authority of a marja' rests on "an established belief in the sanctity of immemorial traditions and the legitimacy of those exercising authority under them."[56] Most grand ayatollahs behave like a traditional religious authority, leading austere lifestyles, remaining steeped in scholarly study, and rarely venturing out in public. We would expect traditional authority to be bound by precedents handed down from the past.

Years of Quietism

From 1923 to 2003, the dominant characteristic of Shi'i religious authorities in Iraq was quietism, which broadly meant serving as an authority on traditional religious issues (e.g., rituals and transactions—the sorts of things covered in a risala) and avoiding involvement in political affairs. This was justified on philosophical and doctrinal grounds (after all, each of the twelve Imams is understood to have adjusted his involvement based on the circumstances at the time, and most were apolitical), but it was also widely interpreted, both inside and outside clerical circles, as a practical survival strategy. Prior to 1920, senior Shiʻi scholars in Iraq had occasionally involved themselves in politics, particularly in safeguarding the Muslim community from foreign interference, such as in opposing the Iranian shah's granting of a tobacco monopoly to a British firm in 1890–1891 and during the 1905 Constitutional Revolution in Iran and the 1920 revolt in Iraq against the British. In 1922, a group of prominent *marajiʻ* led by Muhammad Mahdi al-Khalisi opposed the Anglo-Iraqi Treaty and forbade Iraqis from participating in elections for a constituent assembly that would ratify the treaty. They failed to prevent the election, and, the following year, Khalisi and several other senior clerics were either expelled or voluntarily went into exile. In 1925, after Khalisi's death, five grand ayatollahs negotiated their return to Iraq on the condition that they pledge not to involve themselves in Iraqi political affairs.[57] This ended a period that Yitzhak Nakash labeled the "years of upheaval."[58] For at least the next three decades—until the early 1950s—the vast majority of clerics in Najaf disdained politics and restrained their rulings and statements to religious and spiritual concerns. This tradition, often labeled "quietism," started as a deal with the British but over time became a (arguably, *the*) defining characteristic of Najaf's hawza.

This tradition of political quietism can be dated to this moment in 1925, and the most senior scholars of Iraq by and large adhered to that tradition until at least the early 1950s. There are, of course, exceptions: Sheikh Muhammad Hussain Kashif al-Ghita supported tribal rebellions in the 1930s and issued a fatwa in 1948 prohibiting communist activities and calling on believers to stand against communism.[59] But, as Fouad Kadhem says, Kashif al-Ghita (died 1954) was "an exceptional and glaring contrast to the dominant conservative current in both Iraq and Iran."[60] Kadhem writes, "'Ulama who were involved in politics [between 1923–1950] were seen as swimming against the stream, deserving no respect, and sometimes even disgrace."[61] This was a period when at least ten senior scholars in Najaf claimed to be *marajiʻ*, leading to fierce competition between them. Not coincidentally, despite the Kashif al-Ghitas' status as an esteemed clerical family, they are known for being relatively poor and, in later decades, in need of state patronage.

There are dozens of key moments in Iraqi history over the past eighty years when Shiʻi clerics *could* have become overtly involved in politics, such as times when governments were overthrown or the Iraqi constitution changed.[62] In general, the senior mujtahids kept their distance and remained uninvolved, even when many Shiʻa called for their intervention. There was tremendous unrest in

Iraq in the late 1940s and 1950s, and Kadhem considers the period 1952–1958 to be a transitional phase in which clerics' political activism became more obvious.[63] But even then, their involvement in politics was limited. Some scholars consider Mohsin al-Hakim a relatively "political" marjaʿ, but, as Elvire Corboz documents, his political involvements (e.g., lobbying against the Personal Status Law in 1959; opposing attempts to nationalize banks and companies in the mid-1960s) were limited and focused on protecting the independence of the Shiʿi religious establishment, which included its wealthy social base.

Hakim's February 1960 anticommunist fatwa is often cited as evidence of his political activism, but the timing and context suggest it was not as bold a move as many suggest. Kashif al-Ghita had issued a ban on communist activities in 1948, and at least one other mujtahid issued a similar fatwa that year.[64] Hakim resisted efforts in 1948 and again in 1953 to get him to issue an anticommunist fatwa, and only after the 1958 revolution—and in collaboration with the new Qasim-led government—did Hakim's marjaʿiyya form a countercommunist organization. Kadhem sees these efforts as consistent with the traditional quietest view because for Hakim's circle, this was about religion and a secular ideology's threat to belief.[65] Hakim issued his anti-communist fatwa only in 1960, a dozen years after Kashif al-Ghita's similar one and at a moment when the Iraqi Communist Party (ICP) had made enemies of all Iraqi political currents. Kadhem sees Hakim's fatwa as merely "rubbing salt in the ICP's wounds." Perhaps more importantly, it was a thank you from Hakim to Egyptian President Gamal Abdul Nasser, under whom al-Azhar University had recently recognized Shiʿism as a legitimate fifth school of Islamic thought (*madhhab*), and it also bought goodwill with the shah, who was battling the communist Tudeh Party in Iran.[66] Hakim's anti-communist fatwa, therefore, was less of a domestic political intervention than it is often thought to have been. Hakim and his marjaʿiyya ceased any activism after the Baʿth, who came to power in July 1968, arrested his son, Mahdi al-Hakim, and broadcast testimony in June 1969 linking Mahdi to a failed coup plot with Israel, Iran, and the CIA.[67] What limited momentum of clerical involvement in politics existed under Hakim ended with his death in May 1970.[68]

Quietism was particularly predominant under Khoei, who was extremely cautious regarding intervention in politics after he succeeded Hakim as Najaf's leading marjaʿ.[69] In 1974, he issued a fatwa forbidding clerics and religious studies students from joining political parties.[70] Corboz describes his doctrine of absolute noninvolvement in politics as "a calculated strategy of survival in the face of a regime attempting to neutralize the religious establishment through mixed policies of repression and co-optation."[71] Khoei repeatedly refrained from involving himself in politics, including when the regime pressed him for fatwas during the Iran-Iraq War. He famously issued two fatwas during the 1991 uprising, both of which were "devoid of political connotations."[72] The first, issued on 5 March, called on people to respect public and private property, bury corpses found in the streets, and refrain from torturing captives. It does not even mention that a rebellion was underway. The second, issued two days later, created a committee to supervise public services in Najaf. Haddad notes that there is "a noticeable absence of any pretensions to political leadership and of any reference to the central government, the rebels or the rebellion."[73]

What clerical involvement occurred typically came not from the very top of the hierocracy, but from "rivals" (usually Iraqi Arab clerics) in the generation of scholars below the most senior *maraji'*, such as Kashif al-Ghita in the 1940s and early 1950s and Mohammad al-Shirazi in the 1960s and 1970s. In the late 1990s, Mohammad Mohammad Sadiq al-Sadr criticized Najaf's dominant quietest tradition and differentiated between the "silent hawza" of Khoei and Sistani and the "active or eloquent hawza," which he linked to Mohammad Baqir al-Sadr and himself. The silent clerical grouping, Sadrists in Iraq told me, focused on trivial religious issues and tacitly complied with the regime, while the alternative helped the masses apply religion to the world, gradually increasing people's resistance to tyranny.

If Shi'a turn to their clergy in moments of existential crisis, as is sometimes claimed, the history of twentieth-century Iraq suggests that the clergy very rarely respond to that call. That was true in 1927, when a Shi'i separatist movement failed due to lack of support by the higher clergy, and it was true in 1991, when many Shi'a begged Khoei to lead or at least support the uprising against the Ba'th.[74] On the eve of the 2003 invasion, the dominant tradition of the leading *maraji'* of Najaf was captured in the title of a 2002 book by a leading Iraqi academic: *Iraq without Leadership: A Reading in the Crisis of Shi'ite Islamic Leadership in Modern Iraq*.[75]

Sistani's Gradual Consolidation of the Marja'iyya

It is commonly claimed that Sistani was designated by Khoei to be his successor and became the supreme marja' and head of the hawza when Khoei died.[76] As mentioned earlier, no institutionalized system exists for the transfer of religious authority, and the story of Sistani's rise is more complex than the conventional narrative suggests. Sistani's official biography says that professors in Najaf's hawza advised Khoei to "groom someone for the office of the supreme religious authority and the directorship of Najaf Seminary."[77] It is implied that Khoei, in response, effectively designed Sistani as his chosen successor by asking him in 1987 (or as late as October 1988) to begin leading communal prayers at the al-Khadra Mosque, where Khoei himself previously led prayers. A number of authors have written about Sistani's background and rise to the marja'iyya, but with very few exceptions, they tend to be hagiographic, repeating the official biography and describing a smooth transition in 1992 from Khoei to Sistani as the most prominent marja'.[78] In reality, Shi'i religious authority in Iraq was fractured throughout the 1990s and into 2003.

The period from 1992 to 1999, if not until 2003, should be understood as the time in which Sistani's standing as "the first among equals" gradually became consolidated while being contested. As Corboz writes, "Ayatollah al-Khu'i's death put the Shi'ite community in a serious leadership crisis as there was no obvious and unchallenged candidate to the position of marja' a'la after him."[79] As was tradition, clerics nominally turned to the senior maraji' of Khoei's generation before staking real claims to authority. There were two venerable grand ayatollahs to whom Iraqis nominally looked after Khoei died—'Abd al-'Ala Sabzwari in Najaf, who died within a year, and then Mohammad Reza Golpaygani in Iran, who died in December 1993.[80] Adding to the confusion, the official Iranian regime–backed marja', ninety-nine year old Muhammad Ali Araki, died in November 1994. By the end of 1994 the floodgates had opened and a number of Khoei's students and rivals issued risalas or sought to widen their marja'iyya. Approximately thirty-two maraji' can be dated from around this time.[81]

When Khoei and then Sabzwari died, Sistani was one of a number of high-ranking and learned mujtahids from his generation in Iraq. Khoei had many prominent students and former students whose names were mentioned alongside Sistani's, including Mirza Jawad Tabrizi, Wahid Khurasani, Taqi Tabatabaei Qomi, Mirza Ali Falsafi, Ali Beheshti, Mohammad Sadeq Rouhani, and Mohammed Hussein Fadlallah. Some of these clerics were based outside of Iraq, which presented them both advantages and disadvantages relative to those who were based in Najaf. All were pressured to issue a risala and welcome emulation after Khoei died; some did immediately, some waited until 1994, and some never did. There were also potential successors from the prominent Najafi Sayyid clerical families, including Saeed al-Hakim, Husayn Bahr al-Uloom, and, of course, Mohammad Mohammad Sadiq al-Sadr.

Sistani was, in many ways, unexceptional relative to these peers. He slowly rose in prominence after 1994, in large part because he was seen by the traditional Najafi clerical families, the al-Khoei Foundation, and both the Iraqi and Iranian governments as nonthreatening and reliably apolitical.[82] The Ba'th knew he would not threaten their regime in any way. Also, as he was an Iranian opposed to the rule of jurisprudent system that underlies the Iranian regime, it was useful for the Baʿth to keep him alive and prominent. He was arrested after the 1991 uprising, but unlike many other clerics, he was released relatively quickly.[83] Documents in the Baʿth Party archives reveal that on occasion, Sistani (like other grand ayatollahs in Najaf) was willing to issue a fatwa at the regime's request, including in 2002 as the invasion of Iraq loomed.[84] Critics say that Sistani did not protest when the regime closed the al-Khadra Mosque in 1994 for "repairs." In contrast, Burujirdi refused to stop leading congregational prayers in the Imam Ali Shrine when the regime asked him to. Burujirdi published his risala in 1997 and was killed a year later. Sistani also was not threatening to the interests of established Najafi clerical families: the Hakims, Bahr al-Ulooms, Sadrs, and others. Sistani had no notable students and was seen as unlikely to develop an independent base of support. By comparison, Mirza Ali Gharawi, another prominent student of Khoei, issued his risala in 1993, after the death of Sabzwari, and was a well-known teacher in the seminary and led congregational prayers in the Imam Ali compound. Compared to other grand ayatollahs in the 1990s, Sistani was almost never in the public eye.

Perhaps most important for cementing Sistani's rise was the decision of the al-Khoei Foundation to officially request his "patronage" in January 1994.[85] Many people say this "made Sistani's marjaʿiyya."[86] The relationship was mutually beneficial. The al-Khoei Foundation continued its activities and collected and spent religious alms, albeit now in Sistani's name. In exchange, the foundation spread Sistani's name and rulings worldwide and linked him to transnational flows of financial and diplomatic support, including from mercantile Khoja communities.[87] Sistani's offices in Qum and London, led by his sons-in-law Sayyid Jawad al-Shahristani and Sayyid Murtada al-Kashmiri, respectively, also played important roles in promoting his marjaʿiyya among Shiʿa outside of Iraq. Finally, for several reasons, Sistani survived when many other grand ayatollahs in Iraq were assassinated in the late 1990s, including Ali Gharawi (June 1998), Ali Muhammad Burujirdi (April 1998), and Mohammad Mohammad Sadiq al-Sadr (February 1999). Sistani survived, and Sadrist clerics in Basra told me in 2004 that Sistani closed his office in Najaf and refused to meet even his followers after 1998.[88]

Although the majority of Shiʿa, both inside and outside of Iraq, nominally followed (as muqallids) Sistani by 2003, there was nothing to indicate that he would ever engage in politics. Before 2003, Sistani had issued only one fatwa that could be considered political: a criticism of Israeli military operations in the West Bank in 2002.[89] For Sistani's followers, the marjaʿiyya was not particularly central to their religious life during the period from 1992 to 2003. They paid their religious taxes to Sistani or, more precisely, to either local preachers or officials in the shrines who collected them in his name. If they had a question about a religious issue, they might consult his risala or, more commonly, ask their local preacher, who would answer it, nominally for Sistani. But a larger number of Iraqis continued to reference Khoei, even years after his death. In the final years of the sanctions period, from 1999 to 2003, popular rituals unaffiliated with Sistani, such as Ashura commemorations and pilgrimages to Karbala, rose in importance. Prior to the invasion, practically no one—inside or outside of Iraq—expected Sistani or the other senior clerics to play a role in postinvasion politics. Iraqis had every reason to believe that the Najafi tradition of clerical noninvolvement would continue and that the hawza under Sistani's guidance would remain an authority solely on religious rituals and transactions.

Sunni Clerics under the Ba'th

The Ba'th regime tightly regulated the training, licensing, and placement of Sunni clerics through the Ministry of Endowments and Religious Affairs and the Ministry of Higher Education. Joseph Sassoon's work in the Ba'th Party archives reveals the extent to which "the regime was obsessed with all religious movements, be they Wahhabi or Shi'i, and wanted to infiltrate them to ensure its control."[90] Party functionaries and the General Security Directorate monitored the content of Friday sermons, the activities of imams and preachers, and who attended mosques. Imams were required to announce that Wahhabism is an infidel movement or face dismissal. Sassoon says that the regime was "involved in every appointment by the Ministry of Endowments and Religious Affairs in any religious institution, and it tried to impose party loyalists in every position. All imams and mosques were under scrutiny.... Every party branch and section was asked to undertake a survey of all mosques and *husseiniyyat* (Shi'i religious centers) in their areas, and to evaluate all the employees from a security point of view."[91] Party functionaries were asked to report whether a preacher had prayed for Saddam in his sermons. Friday sermons—which were held in Sunni mosques before the invasion, unlike in Shi'i mosques—were largely Ba'thist propaganda. They could be used for mobilization only in support of Ba'th initiatives, such as rallies and other party events. Communities did not use sermons for local coordination before the invasion.

In contrast, Baram argues that local clerics in Iraq had significant authority prior to 2003; they were grassroots religious leaders.[92] This claim seems largely based on briefings Saddam received in the 1980s about the "men of religion" (*rijal al-din*) having more influence than they had before. According to Baram, this spurred Saddam to join the bandwagon of public religiosity. The regime co-opted already influential Sunni clerics by giving them prestige, authority, and financial rewards if they served on regime-funded religious awareness committees.[93]

Helfont argues that the Baʿth regime created its own Sunni clerics who were indoctrinated in Baʿthist interpretations of Islam, including Arab nationalism and nonsectarianism. Some Sunni clerics were military chaplains during the Iran-Iraq War, which provided thousands of trusted preachers for the regime, and many of them were presumably still active in 2003.[94] Other Sunni preachers came out of the College of Sharia and Fiqh at the University of Baghdad, which predated the Baʿth. But the bedrock of the Sunni clerical establishment were the graduates of two institutions created in the 1980s: the Institute for the Preparation of Imams and Sermon-Givers (1985), which became the Saddam Institute for Imams and Sermon-Givers, and the elite and prestigious Saddam University for Islamic Studies (1988).[95]

Helfont sees the Baʿth training and employment of Sunni clerics as part of a long-term and consistent strategy to penetrate and absorb religious institutions into the party and state structure. He says that by the 1990s, the regime had created its own cadres of loyal and trusted Sunni religious leaders. He writes, "They had filled a critical mass of mosques with co-opted—or at minimum, compliant—religious leaders, and almost all religious institutions were now firmly rooted in the regime's authoritarian system."[96]

Baram and Helfont thus give somewhat differing accounts of the Sunni religious landscape in the 1991–2003 period. Baram says that the regime co-opted and further empowered the already influential traditional class of Islamic leaders. Helfont seems to disagree; he analyzes how the regime created a new troop of clerics, recruited from the newly urbanized middle class and educated in modern secular schools, who were already loyal to the regime. The regime had Baʿthized Iraq's Sunni religious landscape not by paying them, but by creating them.

What looks like the independence of religious leaders in the 1990s, Helfont says, is really the regime scaling back costly oversight because of fiscal pressures, but also because it could now trust Sunni clerics to support the regime, avoid sectarianism, and instill Baʿthist values in society. They were not independent from the regime. "These religious leaders were loyal to the regime and deeply enmeshed in its authoritarian structures," including committees that helped the security services and other state agencies supervise the general population. He summarizes, "Contrary to the theory that the regime ceded religious affairs to independent or grass roots Islamic leaders in the 1990s, the Baʿth Party's records demonstrate a pattern of increasing control over both Sunni and Shiʿi religious leaders."[97]

It is unclear what percentage of preachers were actually members of the Baʿth Party. A 1998 party survey of preachers in Salah al-Din Governate reported that twenty-four of the forty-one imams (59 percent) working in the governate's seventy-six mosques were associated with the party hierarchy but only four (10 percent) were full members.[98] We do not know how representative the imams of Salah al-Din Governate are of Sunni imams throughout Iraq (Saddam's home village of al-ʿAwja is in Salah al-Din, just south of Tikrit), and the numbers in the survey appear too low to be a full accounting of all imams in the governate (the governate had a population of over one million in 2003). But other scholars working with the same Baʿth Party archive came to similar conclusions as did Helfont. They also note that the regime closely tracked every Iraqi religious leader and mosque and kept detailed data. In 1995, the regime considered only seventy of 1,501 religious leaders in Iraq to be problematic, although many were considered to be "uncooperative."[99]

In general, and unlike in (Usuli) Shiʿi Islam, there is no institutional or clear clerical hierarchy in Sunni Islam. Baram states that national-level senior Sunni religious figures had been in decline since the monarchical period (ended 1958) and the ʿArif regimes (1963–1968), and under the Baʿth, they "disappeared as a national recognized authority."[100] According to Baram, "What was left was some local religious leadership at the level of local mosque imams, but none on an all-Iraqi level." Even under the Baʿth, Iraq lacked a strict hierarchy among Sunni clerics because the Baʿth Party interfered to such a large extent in religious affairs. Iraq lacked a "head" Sunni cleric; the party dismissed the grand mufti of Iraq "a few years into its rule" (presumably in the early 1970s) and never appointed a successor.[101] But Helfont's work suggests that many Sunni clerics by 2003 had interpersonal links because so many of them had studied together in the Saddam Institute for Imams and Sermon-Givers or the Saddam University for Islamic Studies. We know that the regime used those institutions to continue to track and continuously (re-)educate its graduates, and it is not unreasonable to expect that scholarly links of teachers and students flourished under the Baʿth and survived to be influential after the invasion. But, as mentioned above, there was no clear hierarchy within those networks, either between students or between students and administrators at the institute and the university. This would have important implications after 2003 for the ability of those Sunni preachers to coordinate their messages across mosques.

Haddad correctly notes that a generation of Iraqis came of age in the sanctions era and likely were predisposed to religious messages.[102] The extent to which they were predisposed to sectarian appeals is unclear and debatable. Both Shiʿi and Sunni clerics had standing in their local communities, although neither had played any significant role in local mobilization. Both Shiʿa and Sunnis had among their clerics networks that survived the invasion, but they looked quite different. Shi'i clerical networks were old, hierarchical, independent of the state, and based on interpersonal ties and tradition. Sunni clerical networks were new, relatively flat, deeply connected to the state, and based on interpersonal ties and a shared ideology rooted in a Ba'thist interpretation of Islam and Arab nationalism. There was no precedent from pre-2003 Iraq for mosques to serve as focal locations for social organization for either Shi'a or Sunnis. Friday sermons were a defunct ritual for Shi'a and a flaccid one for Sunnis. How those networks revived and reinvigorated sermons and got people to follow messages from them is partially explained by deference to traditional religious authority, but it also needs the context of postinvasion of Iraq to make sense.

3
COLLAPSE

The Iraqi state collapsed, suddenly and completely, over several days, beginning on 6 April 2003. This chapter unpacks the meaning of "collapsed," "suddenly," and "completely" before turning to the implications of collapse for Iraqis.

The Invasion and Fall of Basra

Leading up to the invasion of Iraq in March 2003, the Iraqi government expected Basra and other southern cities to be key objectives of the attacking coalition.[1] The defensive strategy, therefore, centered on urban "defense-in-depth." Various armed units—the Iraqi Army, intelligence agencies, Feda'yeen Saddam paramilitary formations, Ba'th Party militias—deployed with the intention to draw coalition troops into fights within city limits and then defend reinforced fixed strong points such as concrete pillboxes and fortified buildings. Ammunition and supplies were dispersed, hidden, and protected by Ba'th loyalists in neighborhoods. Local party leaders were responsible for preventing internal uprisings and protecting the homes of officials and party members.[2] According to the *Iraqi Perspectives Report*, "Iraqi army planners never seriously considered the possibility of an American attack that would isolate and bypass the southern cities."[3]

To the Iraqis' surprise, US ground forces entered Iraq from Kuwait on 20 March and quickly moved northwest toward Nasiriyah, bypassing Basra.[4] British ground forces established a loose cordon around the city, about three kilometers from Basra's suburbs, but their mission was to secure the oil fields and protect the flank of US forces advancing toward Baghdad. British commanders admit that "there was never any intention to go into Basra city" and that "plans to enter Basra were not very well developed."[5] Coalition commanders did not want the British to get bogged down fighting in Basra in case British troops were needed farther north for what was expected to be the decisive battle for Baghdad.[6]

After sixteen days of waiting, British tanks and armored vehicles finally rolled into Basra on the afternoon of 6 April, on the same day that the first US military planes landed at Baghdad's Saddam International Airport and only three days before the statue of Saddam Hussein was famously toppled in Baghdad's Firdos Square. The British had little idea what was happening inside Basra, and they were ill-prepared to (once again) take over administration of the city.[7]

Looting and the Dismantlement of the State

The British entry into Basra coincided with a sudden and complete collapse of central political authority, and similar scenes played out throughout Arab-majority parts of Iraq. Police and local bureaucrats went home or, in some cases, looted their own places of work before others could. Although British intelligence agencies had identified a risk that lawlessness would break out, the formal authorization for action in Iraq did not contain instructions on how to respond or rules of engagement for postconflict operations.[8] A British colonel described the resulting scene:

> Mayhem occurred. A bit like a cork coming out of a champagne bottle, they all went berserk and started looting and burning, and an area that had been appallingly undercapitalized for years under the Baʿath regime was completely trashed. There was much subsequent criticism—why didn't we stop it? There were hundreds of thousands of people just going berserk, and short of shooting them in large numbers there was no way of deterring them, none at all. If we'd done that, we would have been involved in some hideous wide-scale urban fight against the populace, which would have been totally counter-productive.[9]

The scale, extent, and impact of the looting that occurred when the regime fell cannot be overemphasized.[10] In Basra, the looting began on 6 April, as British forces entered and fighting was still taking place. It continued intensely for a week and sporadically until the end of April. The British reached and protected a few buildings—a power station, food warehouses, oil infrastructure—before they could be looted, but most other buildings in Basra associated with the state were looted: Ba'th Party offices, police stations, hospitals, military barracks and depots, schools, the courthouse, municipal offices, and state-owned companies.[11] During the Iran-Iraq War, the Ba'th Party's Southern Bureau took over many administrative functions in Basra, effectively replacing the municipal government.[12] This commingling of the party and municipal institutions continued through the 1990s and partly explains why the looting in Basra was particularly thorough, even compared to elsewhere in Iraq. The British watched. Major General Graham Binns, commander of the Seventh Armoured Brigade, told the Iraq Inquiry, "We reached the conclusion that the best way to stop looting was just to get to a point where there was nothing left to loot.... We could either try and stop the looting, in which case we would have to shoot people, or we could try and prevent it but knowing that we weren't going to prevent it and take a pragmatic view ... and then when we are ready we will restock it and guard it. But actually trying to interpose ourselves was difficult."[13]

In October 2002, Saddam had issued a general amnesty covering almost all those incarcerated in Iraq to mark a referendum in which 100 percent of the electorate allegedly voted to extend his rule as president for another seven years. Tens of thousands of prisoners were released, the exceptions being murderers who remained unforgiven by their victims' families, those who owed money to the state, people convicted of spying for the United States or Israel, and some categories of non-Iraqi prisoners.[14] Released criminals participated in the looting, but so did excited youths, the desperate poor, informants and corrupt bureaucrats with an interest in destroying records, and many ordinary Iraqis, disenfranchised from the state and seeing a temporary opportunity to improve their fortunes. Looted goods soon reappeared in homes or for sale in new or extant "Ali Baba" street markets.

Office supplies and furniture were stolen, as were vehicles, equipment, and propane tanks. Electrical wiring and outlets were ripped from walls, window frames were removed, ceiling tiles were collected. Tribes from nearby marshes took heavy weaponry from military and party stockpiles and came to Basra to target the Rafidain and Rasheed Banks and the adjacent commercial district. On the other side of the city, to the west, the Basra University campus at Sa'd Square was looted; its library and archives on the Gulf were pillaged and burnt. Along the Shatt al-Arab waterway eighty statues of Iraqi officers and commanders who had died in the Iran-Iraq War, sculpted from photographs of the dead men and pointing east toward Iran, were toppled and carted off for scrap metal.[15] Manhole covers were sometimes lifted from the streets, leaving gaping holes into which a few people fell in the following days.

The material manifestations of the Iraqi state—its buildings, equipment, and icons—were looted to their foundations. Its administrative records and files were stolen or destroyed by informants and workers fearing implication, aggrieved individuals looking for evidence, or opportunists. Much of the human capital of the state also vanished. Many civil servants fled or remained home, fearing retaliation for having been Ba'th Party members, for having taken bribes, or for how they had exercised discretionary authority. Many key technical and managerial professionals fled, and Iraq did not have a deep bench of permanent civil servants behind the senior generation who had been educated in the 1960s and 1970s and had kept the country's infrastructure running through decades of war.[16]

Analyses of postinvasion Iraq tend to emphasize the CPA's decisions in May 2003 to disband the Iraqi Army and implement an expansive policy of de-Ba'thification. The dismissal of hundreds of individuals in the highest-level management positions of the state, regardless of party membership, and the exclusion of thousands of individuals who were members of the top four ranks of the Ba'th Party, regardless of the level of their civil service position, did make filling government jobs with competent individuals difficult.[17] In comparison, though, the effects of the looting have been underappreciated and understudied.[18] At the time of the looting, US Secretary of Defense Donald Rumsfeld infamously quipped that "stuff happens" and "freedom's untidy, and free people are free to make mistakes and commit crimes and do bad things."[19]

In a very tangible sense, the Iraqi state suddenly vanished. The challenge facing coalition officials from day one of the occupation, therefore, was reconstituting a state from the bottom up. What did this mean on the ground? Jay Garner, director of the Office of Reconstruction and Humanitarian Assistance (ORHA—the predecessor of the CPA), asked Don Eberly immediately after the invasion to organize trash collection in central Baghdad. In his memoirs, Eberly recalls the task:

> This would be my first introduction to the tough realities of occupation. Trash removal seemed like a straightforward task. But the size and scope of the problem were staggering. Here we were, facing the need to organize a city-wide operation to remove 60,000 tons of trash that had piled up across the city and another 2,500 tons accumulating each day, in a city the size of Chicago. But many of the 234 trash collection stations had been burned or looted. And of the 600 garbage trucks, we were told that 90 percent of them had either been destroyed in the war or stolen. Eighteen hundred workers, three per truck, had all disappeared. Furthermore, the city had no leaders and no trash compacters. Even brooms had disappeared. So here we were, charged with "reconstruction," needing equipment and labor, and we had no money.[20]

Eberly struggled to even figure out how the old system worked: the managers who had directed operations had vanished, no records were available, and there was no way to contact Iraqis by telephone. He summarizes, "The die was cast during the first month or two after our arrival. The disorder we faced, along with our lack of capacity to forcefully confront those conditions, set the stage for the reality the United States has endured since that time."[21] The CPA would later estimate that the looting cost Iraq twelve billion dollars.[22]

Social Ties and the Problem of Order

The social ties and preexisting institutions that existed in Iraq in April 2003 were usually insufficient to promote high levels of coordination and cooperation amid state collapse. Social scientists have identified a number of mechanisms that can produce social order, but most of these were not feasible in postinvasion Iraq because of how the Ba'th had governed society. Decades of Ba'th rule left Iraqi society atomized and social trust exceptionally weak. Social groups and institutions that might have encouraged cooperative behavior had been systematically eliminated or co-opted into the party over time.

The existing literature on collective action emphasizes the importance of social ties and preexisting institutions in helping groups to both coordinate and cooperate together. After forty-five years of authoritarian rule, including twenty-five years under Saddam Hussein, Iraq had very low levels of social trust and, with few exceptions—such as the clerical networks analyzed in chapters 6 and 7—lacked robust networks of associational involvement or the kind of solidarity groups that people often rely on to work together. In many ways, Iraqi society was atomized, especially after the ties held together by party or state patronage ceased to exist. Authoritarianism shaped social networks, limiting the ways Iraqis could jointly acquire information and know what other Iraqis know. Iraq in 2003 was not a blank slate—a tabula rasa—on which anything could be written. It had a legacy from the Saddam era, one that shaped the challenges Iraqis faced in the absence of a state.

Civil Society

Throughout the 1970s and 1980s, the Ba'th Party worked diligently to destroy or subsume all civil society structures and nonstate organizations, including unions, professional associations, and the media.[23] There were no independent unions left in Iraq, only the twelve unions and professional organizations that were controlled by and served the needs of the Ba'th Party.[24] Laith Kubba and others argue that the regime deliberately fractured society to ensure that the country had no viable alternative to his rule.[25] The regime felt threatened by local collective action, even the seemingly innocuous, fearing it could eventually morph into a threat.

Lacking voluntary grassroots organizations, postinvasion Iraq was left with communities that had a difficult time working together. There was little noticeable ethic of community action. Before the Baʿth came to power, Iraq did have traditions of cultural pluralism and civic activism, but there is little evidence that much of that tradition survived Baʿth rule. The difficulty of local collaboration was a Baʿth legacy.[26]

The Decimation of Social Trust

Documents in the Baʿth Party archives reveal the extent to which state informants existed throughout various strata of Iraqi society: many Iraqis voluntarily provided information for compensation, to settle personal grudges, or for malicious reasons.[27] Up until 2003, the livelihoods of tens of thousands of families depended on informing on others, including their neighbors, friends, and extended family. The regime used informants to infiltrate nascent groups and public spaces. It tracked rumors; the archives contain official "rumor forms" that list sources, analysis, and effects of particular rumors.[28]

The Baʿth Party's reliance on domestic security and intelligence agencies both influenced the flow of information through social networks and shaped those networks in ways that hindered their ability to channel information postinvasion. The General Security Directorate (*Mudiriyyat al-Amn al-ʿAmm*) and the Baʿth Party's security agencies (generically called *Amn al-Hizb* by Iraqis) each maintained extensive networks of local informants.[29] These organizations were complemented in the 1990s by several paramilitaries whose original and primary purpose was to control the population.[30] The most important of these new paramilitaries was the Fedaʾyeen Saddam, which was formed in October 1994 and became the regime's private standing army.[31] In addition to its duties rooting out (and often replacing) criminal networks involved with smuggling and racketeering, the Fedaʾyeen monitored civilians and ran its own informants throughout society.

Ordinary Iraqis were encouraged and paid to report law breakers and criticisms of state policy, officials, or social conditions. The Baʿth Party archives contain numerous reports that family members made about each other. One Basrawi whom I came to know well during my field research told me how General Security agents had come to their house a few years before the invasion and confiscated their contraband satellite dish after a close friend reported that it was hidden on their roof, allegedly for a reward of about $40.[32] Not surprisingly, surveys conducted soon after the invasion show that trust among Iraqis was extremely low, sometimes with 90 percent of respondents saying "You have to be very careful in dealing with [other] people."³³ During my field research, my closest Iraqi contacts repeatedly warned me, "Trust no one in Iraq"; one of them frequently added, "Trust no one in Iraq, including me!"

Under the Baʿth, it could be personally dangerous for Iraqis to associate too often with people whom they did not know well; internal security institutions sometimes assumed guilt by association, and families could be collectively punished if a member ran afoul of the party. The annual registers of high school students, kept by the party from the mid-1980s to 2003, included questions on the "reputation of the student and his family," his family's position on the 1991 uprising, and whether the student had "close ties to someone sentenced for hostility to the party or the revolution."³⁴ One Basrawi told me that the first time they spoke more than pleasantries (*mujamalaat*) to their neighbors was in March 2003, when residents on their street came outside to watch the initial US military strikes illuminate the sky. Despite living in their lower middle-class neighborhood for years, they knew well only one other person living on their street.

Despite Iraqis' seemingly constant consumption of slowly brewed tea (chai), there were few teahouses and shisha clubs in the country by 2003. These spaces are important social and gossip sites in other Arab societies, where people can socialize and share news while drinking tea or coffee, playing board games, and smoking. But the Baʿth regime prohibited all but a few (usually in hotels, and always tightly regulated and monitored), seeing them as places where dissent and conspiracy easily spread. Those that survived were often understood to be open only to known patrons, the educated and "cultured." Surprisingly, almost no teahouses of note existed in Basra during the time of my field research. Both the Iran-Iraq War and the 1991 uprising led the party to view public space in Basra, in particular, as critical to the nation's security.³⁵ Hundreds of such public places later opened throughout Iraq in the years after the invasion.

By 2003, the average Iraqi Arab city dweller was probably strongly connected with and confided in only a few other Iraqis, often immediate family or first cousins. During my fieldwork, I tried to "map" Basrawis' pre- and postinvasion social networks to see if and how they were changing. The survey questions I pretested on Iraqi confidants, however, made them clearly uncomfortable. One bluntly shouted at me, "For safety, you cannot ask these questions." I quickly realized that for Iraqis in 2003–2004, questions about social networks resembled Baʿth-era intelligence-gathering efforts, which frequently asked Iraqis to report on their extended family, friends, coworkers, and associates. But respondents' sensitivity might also have been related to my status as an American asking such questions in a country that the US military was occupying. For these reasons, I abandoned the effort to systematically map social networks.

Immediately after the invasion, most Basrawis I spoke with seemed to know *of* many others in their immediate local community, but nothing *about* them, such as their opinions on issues or expectations of how they would react in new, previously unforeseen situations. Joseph Sassoon relates the story of an Iraqi who was allegedly arrested after telling friends that he dreamed of visiting a shrine in Iran and meeting a famous Shi'i cleric.[36] Whether or not the story is true, at least some Iraqis thought it plausible that someone could be arrested for merely telling their friends about a mildly subversive dream. Ba'th policies splintered and stunted social networks, "effectively atomizing the population."[37] Post-Saddam Iraq was a society in which the nature and strength of people's social connections made them unlikely to be motivated to act on behalf of others.

How quickly did social trust change after the invasion? At least one researcher suggests that trust in Iraqi society continued to decline after 2003. Hayder al-Mohammad notes that many kidnappings were done by people who knew the victim, which often meant death for the kidnapped because they could identify the perpetrators if released. He writes that after 2003, "The acquaintance one has not seen in a while who pops in for a chat was often met coldly with doubt and uncertainty. One never feared close friends and family members, although everyone else was potentially a threat in the climate of terror that emerged after the invasion. Hence, when kidnappings became an everyday occurrence in Basra from 2004 to 2008, the circle of friends and acquaintanceships a person held reduced noticeably."[38]

Public gatherings in Ba'thist Iraq were rare and closely monitored; few public rituals or social practices that could generate useful common knowledge survived the period. Consequently, Iraqi Arabs lacked either common bases for forming shared understandings of many new issues or a way to select a common strategy from many possible ones. An Iraqi might draw analogies from well-known events and Iraqi history: the colonial period, the revolt of 1920, democratic practices from 1921 to 1958, the 1963 coup that forced the first Ba'th government from power, the Iran-Iraq War, Ba'thist persecution, and the 1991 or 1999 uprisings.[39] In my interviews and informal discussions with Basrawis, however, I found that they did not carry *shared* cogent understandings of these events and did not know whether other Iraqis might draw such analogies or what lessons might be drawn. Some interviewees compared, usually in superficial terms, the growing postinvasion insurgency with the 1920 uprising against British occupation, but they did not know whether or what other Iraqis would think about such a comparison. Iraqis in exile in the 1990s created a shared and cogent historical narrative of the March 1991 uprising and its aftermath, but it is not clear to what extent that narrative was shared by Iraqis in Iraq before 2003.[40]

A shared history does not automatically generate "historical memory" or a collective understanding of lessons of the past for the present; individuals must also know if, when, and how others will employ that history. Since the Ba'th regime politicized historical memory to reinforce its hold on power, Iraqis knew that most of what other Iraqis knew about modern Iraqi history reflected Ba'th Party interests and propaganda.[41] I found that the version of history that was most widely shared among Arab Iraqis in Iraq came from two "national culture" subjects (*thaqafa al-qawmiya* and *al-wataniya*) that they studied in school from age thirteen onward. The books used in schools focused on the establishment of the Ba'th Party, Saddam's speeches and guidelines, and the army and revolutions. Even though this version of history was common knowledge among Iraqis in 2003, most Iraqis would not have expected other Iraqis to condition their behavior on interpretations associated with the former regime.

The Occupation's Failure to Reestablish Order

If social ties or groups cannot produce and maintain order from the bottom up, then why did the occupation authorities fail to provide order as a top-down solution? The US government's inadequate planning for the occupation and civic administration of Iraq has been well documented.[42] What passed for prewar planning at the Office of the Secretary of Defense seems to have been based on unstated assumptions that the existing physical and human infrastructure of the state would largely remain in place. ORHA, established seven weeks before the war, and the rest of the US government prepared for crises that did not occur: oil-field fires, massive refugee flows, and intervention by Iraq's neighbors.[43] The phrase "humanitarian assistance" in ORHA's name points to the kind of crises planners expected. The subsequent strategic missteps and organizational pathologies of the US-led reconstruction effort have been analyzed in a series of books on the "business of occupation," which Peter Sluglett memorably referred to as "blunder books."[44] With regard to Basra, there was little planning related specifically to southern Iraq because until January 2003, war plans called for coalition troops to enter Iraq from Turkey. British plans for postconflict operations in Basra were drawn up in the month before the invasion.[45]

There were never enough coalition troops in Iraq to maintain order, and this was particularly true in Basra. On 7 April, the day after they entered the city, there were just over five thousand British troops from six battlegroups in Basra, and as one journalist later wrote, "This was the high point of British troop strength inside the limits of the city. Never again would a British commander in Basra have so many troops at his disposal. . . . This was the high water mark of British rule in Basra."[46] Within a few days of entering the city, "diarrhea and vomiting sickness would sweep across British units in the city, incapacitating hundreds of soldiers for days at a time."[47] Beginning in May 2003, the British rapidly reduced their troop commitments in Iraq; overall numbers fell from 46,000 to 10,500 three months later.[48] By the end of 2003, there were nine thousand total coalition troops in the area known as Multi-National Division Southeast, which included a population of 4.6 million Iraqis.[49]

The British military's initial attempt to reestablish an Iraqi-led municipal administration failed spectacularly. British intelligence identified a tribal leader, Sheikh Muzahim Mustafa Kanan al-Tamimi, whom they thought could help set up and lead a Basra city council.[50] Tamimi was a well-known member of the Ba'th Party and had been a general in the Iraqi Army.[51] Protests erupted immediately, and it quickly became apparent that half of the first twelve members whom the British had picked for the interim city council had Ba'thist links.[52] Six weeks later, the British abandoned their attempt to hand responsibility for city services over to an Iraqi-led authority and set up a "utilities committee," led by a British brigadier general, to coordinate reconstruction and reestablish city services.

Created in May 2003, the Coalition Provisional Authority South would also face a rocky start. Its early headquarters in the electricity administration offices in the center of the city were cramped and spartan. The initial head of CPA South, Danish ambassador Ole Wøhlers Olsen, left suddenly in late July, two and a half months into an expected six-month stint. His replacement, Sir Hilary Synnott, arrived two days later, and he admitted in his memoirs that the small staff he inherited was overwhelmed with basic day-to-day challenges.[53] At the time, the United Kingdom had approximately thirty officials seconded into CPA South.[54]

A team from Human Rights Watch visited Basra and issued a report six weeks after the invasion.[55] They found an abysmal security situation. Hospitals were reporting sixty-seven violent homicides daily and an equal number of nonfatal gunshot wounds. Carjackings were common; rumors of home invasions were rampant. The British estimated that the city of 1.5 million people needed five thousand to six thousand police officers on the ground and one thousand in administrative and support roles. But by mid-May, the British had only between fifty and one hundred armed British military policemen on street patrol in Basra, along with a hastily organized unarmed auxiliary police force composed of five hundred to nine hundred former and new police.[56] Another group of up to one thousand were authorized to be a "guard service" to protect banks, government buildings, and main crossroads; the service was to be composed of people deemed unsuitable for actual police work, to be paid by the institutions they were to protect.[57] Paul Kernaghan, a British chief constable, visited Basra in mid-May and noted that nearly all official buildings in the United Kingdom's area of responsibility had been destroyed. He reported, "Looting does not do justice to the level of destruction inflicted and I can best liken the outcome to the progress of locusts across a field of corn."[58]

Life without a Leviathan

In short, Iraqis found themselves in a complex and confusing reality after the state collapsed and it became clear that the occupation authorities were not going to quickly reconstitute order. In the absence of the state, order broke down. Uncollected trash rotted in the streets, and after people stole collection bins for the metal, many people dumped their trash wherever it was convenient. Without sufficient electricity and experienced civil servants to maintain it, infrastructure quickly failed. Raw sewage flowed into the streets and further fouled the canals that cut across Basra and empty into the Shatt al-Arab. Underground piping, heavily damaged from multiple wars, leaked polluted brackish water that formed expanding pools in streets, empty lots, and between homes. There were no longer municipal workers to fix these problems, not even ones you could bribe to do it.

The lack of order was most obvious in terms of security, and a dominant theme in my interviews was the overwhelming sense of uncertainty that Iraqis felt in "the situation," as they called it. Everything seemed to them to be fluid and unpredictable. Gunfire could be heard both day and night, and it often was unclear if they were hearing a gun battle, a crime, or a celebration. Perhaps most often, gunfire in the middle of the city simply indicated that a group of men felt like firing assault rifles into the air. Guns were everywhere; the regime distributed them to supporters before the war, and additional supplies and ammunition looted from military depots flooded markets.[59] Saddam had released thousands of criminals prior to the war, and they now roamed freely. Members of a particularly notorious "marsh Arab" tribe, the Garamshi, who had purportedly been banned from the city by the Ba'th, now entered to settle old feuds and create new ones. Strangers seemed to be everywhere, which dramatically impacted Basrawis' notions of safety. Many people who feared being targeted due to old grudges and score-settling fled to other cities; Basrawis fled north, but others came to Basra to hide in anonymity. Exiles and Iraqis living abroad returned, including rebels who had fled in 1991 or 1999. Carjackings became common, and I frequently was warned that the model of vehicle I drove while in Iraq (a Mitsubishi Pajero) was a preferred target. In the first few months after the war, thousands of used cars and SUVs made their way from neighboring Arab states to Iraq. Without a system to register and license vehicles, stolen cars were easy to sell and impossible to track. Enterprising Iraqis manufactured and sold fake Iraqi license plates. Assassinations and kidnappings occurred regularly. Social disorder reigned, and the challenge for Iraqis was how to substitute for the Leviathan and create some modicum of order in their daily lives.

4
THE EMERGENCE OF LOCAL ORDERS

When the Iraqi government was toppled in April 2003, the provision of public goods by the state in Arab-majority areas of the country suddenly ceased. Trash piled curbside after municipal collection stopped. The state-led distribution of fuel, fresh water, and food ended. Police went home or fled. Some individuals looted offices and warehouses, and armed gangs quickly occupied deserted government buildings. The court system disintegrated overnight. Yet, within a few weeks of living under anarchy, some localities were able to begin to substitute for the state, such as by coordinating trash disposal and implementing basic measures to improve security in their neighborhoods. Other localities failed to do so. This chapter argues that the distribution of and control over information at the local level helps explain this variation in the production of order.

After the invasion, Iraqi Arabs faced many new situations where working with their neighbors was the only or the most efficient way to cope with local issues. Individuals were willing to participate in some joint actions if others also participated, such as dumping trash in a single location—instead of in the street—or helping to keep a watch for suspicious activity around the neighborhood. These are situations in which people coordinate together, and doing so requires correctly anticipating how others will act. Solving such problems requires a particular kind of shared information: *common knowledge*, or knowledge of others' knowledge. Other situations required people to make costly contributions in terms of time or money; solving those problems usually requires individuals to be rewarded for participating or punished for free riding.

In the immediate aftermath of state collapse, local clerics in Iraq controlled the most accessible and reliable way to induce neighbors to work with one another. Ritual aspects of the Friday mosque sermon make it an institution with a substantial capacity for producing common knowledge. As attendees came to believe that others would follow through on sermon messages, Friday mosques began to be able to coordinate residents of localities on priorities and basic behaviors, like how to dispose of trash and how to behave toward known looters. People produced and sustained order in many neighborhoods by hearing and coordinating around the content of sermons.

But local social orders generated by Friday mosque sermons were constrained by two factors. First, the set of behaviors on which local preachers could induce compliance was limited. Clerics could coordinate listeners effectively and foster contributions when the actions required of followers entailed relatively small costs, but as those costs increased, the effectiveness of clerics diminished. Second, messages in a mosque's sermon only reached those who heard it (or later heard of it). Thus, the cooperation that sustained local order was confined to the geographical catchment areas of individual mosques.

Why, in the aftermath of state collapse, did Iraqis turn to Islam to reestablish social order? Chapter 2 explored pre-2003 factors that contributed to Iraqis' willingness to "turn to religion": rising levels of piety in the 1990s and the traditional authority that clerics held were contributing factors. But these factors alone offer an insufficient explanation because Iraqis could have turned to any of a wide gamut of institutions and actors associated with Islam, such as respected families descended from the Prophet Muhammad, organizers of religious commemorations and festivals, local preachers, senior clerics in shrine cities in Iraq or elsewhere, pious lay notables, leaders of religious movements or orders, or leaders of religious parties. Why did they turn to some Islamic institutions and authorities instead of others? In particular, why did they come to rely on the Friday sermon, a ritual that Iraqi Shi'a had not undertaken en masse in decades and Sunnis had come in the 1990s to closely associate with Ba'thist propaganda? This begs for additional explanation.

Dilemmas under Chaos

After the collapse of central authority, perhaps the most natural thing for someone to do is safeguard their family and simply wait, either for a state to be reconstituted or for someone else to provide order from which they might benefit. This is what a majority of Basrawis did in the months after state collapse: they coped with disorder by fending for their families, keeping their heads down and waiting for a government—any government—to begin to govern.

But many of the negative effects of social disorder have a spatial quality: they tend to affect people near each other in similar ways. This is true for both nonexistent municipal services and other problems that arise in the absence of a state. The smell and risk of disease from a pool of raw sewage in a street affects everyone nearby. Cars speeding through a neighborhood endanger families living there. Celebratory or random gunfire into the air poses a risk of dangerous—potentially deadly—"gravity shots" raining down in the vicinity. Neighbors would all benefit (albeit perhaps not all equally) if they could somehow substitute for lost services and address problems and risks caused by the absence of a state. Successfully doing so, however, is often too costly or ineffective to do alone or with only a few others. Dealing with these problems requires collaboration with people who live nearby. People's decisions to work to resolve these problems are based on if and how their neighbors will also work to resolve them; in that sense, decisions about how to respond to disorder are interdependent. If neighbors can collectively act, they can achieve mutually advantageous outcomes. The question then becomes, under what conditions can individuals create regular and recurrent patterns of interaction with one another to address these issues of shared concern?

Social order involves two different kinds of collective action problems, which differ in the incentives facing potential participants: *coordinating* together and *contributing* together.[1] Coordinating together describes situations in which individuals will participate in a group endeavor if they believe that a sufficiently large number of others will also participate. If enough others are doing something, you therefore want to do it. The classic example of a coordination dilemma is which side of the road to drive on: if everyone else is driving on the left side, it is in one's interest to also drive on the left (even if one prefers that everyone drive on the right). Contributing together is different: it captures situations in which an individual's participation is costly—often in terms of time or resources—which creates an incentive not to participate, regardless of how many others are participating. These costs can vary across situations, solutions, and individuals. Even if others are doing something, any particular individual might prefer to sit back and enjoy the benefits of others' efforts. This is often called a "free-rider problem" because each person prefers to let others pay the cost of participation while enjoying the benefits, leaving the group endeavor unsuccessful or underprovided when enough people make a similar decision.

"Solving" each of these collective action situations requires different things. Successfully cooperating together, unless groups are small, often requires coercion—that is, external enforcement—or some form of individual reward to induce individuals to act in the common interest.[2] Third-party enforcement is the classic solution. Thomas Hobbes argues that under anarchy, individuals coordinate on selecting a sovereign, who is then (somehow) empowered to enforce cooperation. Cooperation can also occur when an entrepreneur pays the up-front costs in the hope of greater rewards in the future. Finally, cooperation can occur when individuals repeatedly interact and develop ways to monitor and enforce rules through sanctioning, although this is most likely to occur when society is small and socially homogenous. Preexisting trust in society, associational involvement, and the nature and strength of social ties between individuals have all been linked to cooperation. If the costs of contributing are small, the risk of being shunned by others might be enough to induce compliance, but the question then becomes, how do people coordinate on shunning noncompliers, or who pays the costs to punish if it is costly?

Successfully coordinating together is something different. It entails a lot of people doing things in a coherent way and knowing what others are doing. Once people "agree" on a solution, it is in their interest to follow through if others also do. In that sense, such solutions are self-enforcing. Coordination dilemmas are foundational and ubiquitous. They are foundational because coordination is causally prior to cooperating together; for example, the archetype prisoners' dilemma game presupposes that players have coordinated on what actions constitute "defection" and "cooperation."[3]

Coordination is ubiquitous because it can account for an extremely wide array of behaviors and features of human life, including what are commonly called "conventions," "norms," and "culture." Russell Hardin finds numerous coordination problems in the work of the philosopher David Hume: monarchical succession; rules of property, inheritance, incest, murder; rules of justice; traffic rules; language; what counts as money. Hardin adds additional examples: standardized time; the QWERTY keyboard; slang; markers of group identification.[4] Much of what we call "culture" is coordinated behavioral expectations: "appropriate" clothes, greetings and responses, when and how to display emotions, rules of spelling. In many, perhaps most, interactions, people want to do what they think others will do.

Yet, despite its centrality, there is relatively little theoretical and empirical work on how coordination occurs. It is so overlooked that many scholars incorrectly use the expression "collective action problem" as a synonym for the free-rider problem of contributing together. But coordination is a type—a different type—of collective action problem. One reason coordination problems are overlooked is because their solutions are often taken for granted: once they have been "solved," they tend to remain solved because solutions are self-enforcing and costly to change.[5] In contrast, many solutions to free-rider problems require costly external enforcement that can end, leading to an identifiable failure of collective action.

A central challenge of coordination problems is that there are often multiple ways to solve them. There are three basic solutions to this problem of indeterminacy.[6] Sometimes individuals observe, learn, and adjust their behavior in dynamic ways until solutions are selected in an evolutionary process.[7] The second way coordination can occur is if there is something focal that makes individuals' expectations converge. One solution might be prominent, similar to a known precedent, or otherwise "obvious" in a way that people would expect others to also select it instead of alternatives.[8] The third way coordination can occur is through a purposeful process of explicit communication that creates common knowledge. Common knowledge is knowledge of others' knowledge, knowledge of others' knowledge of others' knowledge, and so on. Common knowledge implies meta-knowledge—knowing that others know something—which distinguishes it from merely widespread knowledge.[9]

Common knowledge alone, however, is insufficient for a group to coordinate together; individuals must also believe that enough others will act on that knowledge. There is little extant theory on where such beliefs come from. Michael Chwe's influential work largely ignores this aspect of coordination.[10] Avner Greif identifies and emphasizes the importance of beliefs that others will act on information, and he links the origins of such beliefs to precedent and the source of a message. If a source has a history of providing information that is obeyed, individuals are more likely to expect others to act on future messages from that source.[11] History and precedent might matter for such beliefs, but there might be no precedent for certain situations—or there might be several. It is tempting to call such beliefs "legitimacy," but this risks a tautology. The origins of coordination are usually ignored or subsumed under the often near-mystical headings of "spontaneous" or "emergent."[12] Michael Hechter calls this the "problem of institutional genesis."[13] He writes, "What is most challenging to account for theoretically is just how institutions emerge out of anarchy, that is, from a state of nature."[14] This book traces how such beliefs, which can support preexisting institutions, initially emerged in postinvasion Iraq, a case of anarchy that is similar in several ways to an idealized state of nature.

Traditional rational-choice approaches to institutional analysis takes institutions as exogenous and looks at the effects of institutions (e.g., agenda-setting rules, veto powers) on individuals' behavior.[15] In contrast, the analysis in this book treats individuals' motivations to follow rules as endogenous: individuals' willingness to follow the rules of the game cannot be taken for granted.[16] Avner Greif, for example, argues that when a claimant to authority issues a "rule" or guidance for a new situation, individuals will comply when three conditions are met. First, the announcer must have the organizational capability to disseminate the rule and render it common knowledge. Second, a sufficient number of people must believe that others will actually act on the announced guidance. Third, the message must specify self-enforcing behavior—that is, a behavior that is in an individual's best interest to follow provided that they believe (correctly) that others will follow it. This book builds on Greif's approach using evidence from a specific empirical setting.

Coordinating together does not require that all people have the same interests or preferences; it merely implies that each person's motivation to participate increases (or, at least, does not decrease) the more others participate.[17] People differ. Some people will participate when only a few others are participating (they might be called "first movers"); others will want to see a larger number of participants before they join; and there likely will always be a few people who will not join, no matter how many others have done so. The dynamics of coordinating together, therefore, might take on a "tipping" quality if the incentives to participate increase as a function of the number of others already participating or if people differ in how many others need to be participating before they will join.[18] Finally, cogent information, even if widespread, is insufficient for a group to coordinate together, because individuals must still believe that others will act on that information.[19] Contradictory pieces of information can be equally cogent; for example, someone might hear two equally compelling but incompatible solutions for how to discourage people from discharging guns into the air.

Coordinating together is challenging. If a group of people has not coordinated before, how do they self-assemble? Until they do, the group exists as a group only in potential. How do they even come to understand the possibility that they *can* coordinate together? A small group of a dozen or so people can talk to one another, but, once the group grows sufficiently large—several dozens or hundreds of people—gossip and "phone-tree" networks of communication tend to fail to generate either common knowledge or the necessary belief that others will act on that information.

Problems of Coordination and Cooperation in Postinvasion Basra

Following state collapse, the most immediate problems Iraqis faced were local, and many of those problems affected neighbors in similar ways. Which of these issues might have been addressed by coordinating with neighbors, and which ones required them to cooperate together in costly ways? There are no hard and fast rules for classifying issues other than carefully considering the incentives and costs facing potential participants in any situation.[20] A surprisingly large number of issues could have been addressed by groups of neighbors coordinating together at particular points in time.[21] Clearing a street filled with trash might require cooperating together because the tasks of shoveling and then transporting away refuse are costly for individuals in terms of time and effort: it is unpleasant and even potentially dangerous. In contrast, successfully coordinating together can prevent trash from accumulating in the street in the first place. If neighbors know that most of their other neighbors will walk a short distance and throw their trash in a designated spot, then most of them will have an incentive to join in the group action. The costs of doing this are low, particularly if everyone else is doing it. Similarly, when the British military came along and occasionally cleared a trash-strewn street on a one-time basis, that community might then be able to coordinate together on a way to keep it clean, despite having been unable to cooperate together to clean it in the first place.

Managing trash might seem like a minor issue, but its impacts compound with climate. Summers in Basra are long and brutal; daily high temperatures typically exceed 100 degrees Fahrenheit in May and October and 120 degrees from June through September. Winds and dust storms sweep through the city, especially in early summer. The smell of rotting trash or fetid water, particularly in the summer heat, can be overwhelming. Autumn and spring in southern Iraq each last only a month. Winter is cold and rainy, and rivers sometimes overflow and produce stagnant pools of muddy water mixed with sewage. Public health has been a long-standing concern in Basra; the city saw six major outbreaks of plague from 1690 to 1800 and numerous minor outbreaks between and after those major ones.[22] The historian Thabit Abdullah quotes a verse from a medieval Basra poet, Ibn Lanak:

> It seems that life in Basra can be very funny
> If the north wind blows it feels like paradise or the countryside
> But if the south wind blows it feels as though we were in a toilet.[23]

A British officer who had previously served as a peacekeeper in Kosovo shared a similar thought—albeit less poetically—after his first ride through Basra in June 2003: "The rubbish, the pot holes, the sewage, all of it reminded me of Kosovo—only ten time worse. In particular, the smell of all that rubbish and waste in the heat had to be experienced to be believed. It was truly, hideously, vile."[24] This was not an exaggeration; during my fieldwork, I encountered several streets that were difficult to walk down without gagging.

There are other situations that would require neighbors to contribute together: pooling resources to buy a generator; providing labor and money to dig out an adjacent canal that was blocked with rubbish and sewage; mobilizing to stop a gang stealing a community water tank or kidnapping someone off of the street. The costs of participating in these efforts vary but typically are not low enough to be inconsequential. When the water distribution system collapsed, Iraqis were dependent on water purified via reverse osmosis (always labeled "RO" and sometimes in Arabic as *ma' hulw*) and distributed via tanker trucks. A year after the invasion, 73 percent of Basra's residents still relied on such deliveries for their fresh water supply.[25] In fact, only 23 percent of households in Basra Governate had drinking water piped to their dwellings, and this water was not clean enough to safely consume. The house in Manawi al-Basha where I lived, for example, had an irregular supply of piped, brownish water that we sometimes could use for bathing and cleaning, but like all our neighbors, we only used tanked RO water for cooking and drinking.

A family acting alone could fetch water from often-distant RO supply locations or they could pay someone to deliver it to their home. But a group of neighbors could save considerable effort and money if they pooled their resources and bought a large plastic water tank for storing RO water and contracted for regular deliveries directly from a tanker truck. The initial purchase of such a storage tank requires costly contributions, and individuals would prefer that others paid the costs. International NGOs and the British military sometimes gave poor neighborhoods such tanks, but resupplying them, regulating how much water each family takes, and protecting the tanks were all tasks that demanded people make costly contributions and therefore were subject to free riding. When provided to neighborhoods, these tanks were often stolen and sold on secondary markets (such tanks could be put onto roofs to store hot water and increase water pressure, or they could be used by people selling gasoline on the black market). A group of neighbors could coordinate to keep an eye on "their" tank, but they were rarely able to prevent it from being stolen because guarding it was costly in terms of time and potentially dangerous. I met residents in one quarter of the neighborhood of al-Tannuma, on the east bank of the Shatt al-Arab, who were thrilled to have recently received a large water tank from Save the Children. When I returned a few weeks later, it was gone—stolen.

Elsewhere, NGO-supplied water tanks sat empty after residents could not devise a system to pool money for its regular resupply and maintenance. Similarly, Save the Children distributed metal bins for neighborhood rubbish collection. They were often promptly stolen. When the NGO realized this, it began to construct trash boxes out of concrete blocks for neighborhoods. But poor families would sometimes occupy and claim these structures for homes, and the intended beneficiaries were unable (or unwilling) to prevent this or force out squatters.

Friday Mosques and Common Knowledge

In the absence of sufficient preexisting interpersonal trust in society, deep and meaningful social ties, and grassroots associations, under what conditions could sufficient common knowledge be generated to help Iraqis coordinate together? And to what extent could they cooperate together? This section describes how Friday mosque sermons create common knowledge among attendees, helping each know what the others know. This common knowledge can help congregation members coordinate together—to act like, and thereby become, a *group*—if they expect others to act on sermon messages.

Friday Sermons

The Friday mosque sermon is consequential for group behavior because it allows individuals to know what other attendees know; Friday sermons are social practices that generate common knowledge.[26] Every Friday afternoon, Muslim men typically gather together in designated mosques for special communal prayers and to listen to a sermon delivered in two parts or as two consecutive sermons (*khutba al-jum'a*). The ritual can be traced to the eighth century, but there are reports that the Prophet Mohammad and his early companions preached in a similar manner.[27] For followers of most schools of Islamic law, attending Friday congregational prayer is a religious obligation for all able-bodied Muslim men: the Quran (62:9) explicitly commands believers to put aside other business during this time.[28] Many otherwise ritually nonobservant Muslim men attend the Friday afternoon prayer and sermon. Arabs often distinguish between two types of mosques: mosques where Friday congregational prayers are held (*jami'*, plural *jawami'*; literally, something that gathers, unites, or brings together) and mosques where they are not held (*masjid*, plural *masajid*; literally, a place of worship).[29]

The physical layout, norms, and rhetorical style of a Friday sermon increase its ability to reliably generate common knowledge. During the sermon, attendees sit in parallel straight lines facing the direction of prayer. The preacher (*khatib*) stands on a small pulpit (*minbar*) facing the congregation as he delivers two sermons, with a brief pause between them, before leading the congregation in prayer. In Iraq, some Shi'i Friday mosques had two preachers each Friday—one who discussed a Quranic verse and another who delivered a political or social sermon; Sunni mosques typically had the same preacher deliver both sermons. Talking and disturbing others during the sermon is forbidden, a norm enforced both by congregation members and by religious injunctions.[30] The repetitive language, the layout of ritual space, and the organized sequence of ritual actions that characterize Friday sermons increase each individual's confidence that others did not miss a message.[31] Although the structure of Friday prayers is ritualized, the sermon's purpose of delivering pious counsel is flexible enough to allow preachers to address a wide variety of issues relevant to the local community.[32] Islam also provides a shared symbolic system that helps Muslims know how other Muslims—at least, those with the same theological interpretations—understand sermons' messages.[33] Attendees know that other attendees heard the same message, and they know that others know that they received it. Men who miss a sermon have an incentive to learn what messages they missed if they believe that attendees will condition interdependent behavior on those messages.

Congregations

The typical religious congregation in the United States is, in the words of Robert Putnam and David Campbell, "an all-purpose association with members who choose it, belong to it, and make contributions to it." They say this form and function are a consequence of America's Protestant heritage and they note that immigrants

> adapt to the American religious ecosystem upon arriving in the United States. Even faiths that are not organized around the congregation in other nations come to adopt a congregation-based structure here in the United States. From there, it is a small step to adopting many of the same practices as American, especially Protestant, congregations. For example, Islamic mosques in the U.S. often hold Sunday school, or provide a social hall for community events—not what they typically do in other nations. In the U.S., imams are frequently called upon to serve as counselors and to engage in public relations, responsibilities outside the purview of imams elsewhere, but common for many congregational leaders in the United States.[34]

The 2006 Faith Matters Survey indicates that religious congregations are the most common form of association in the United States, more than groups formed around hobbies or sports, professional or business associations, service organizations, or neighborhood or ethnic or political associations.[35]

Putnam and Campbell are correct: mosque congregations in most of the Muslim world, including Iraq, do not resemble religious congregations in the United States. In Iraq, people do not "affiliate" with a mosque, and mosques do not have membership lists or formal organization. Large mosques often have a receiving room for the imam to meet with people, but mosques in Iraq do not play the community center role that many do in the United States and, perhaps, in Muslim-minority communities around the world. Being a "member" of an Iraqi mosque congregation means you attend and listen to the sermon; it does not translate into a form of association similar to American congregations. Iraqis always told me that I did not need anyone's permission to attend prayers or listen to a sermon; mosques were open to all.

Few social scientists have studied Friday sermons.[36] Although insightful ethnographic work exists on preaching in Egypt and Jordan, there is little theoretical or comparative work.[37] Existing studies emphasize the role of sermons in the acquisition of religious knowledge, not the acquisition of knowledge of others' knowledge. Preachers have been described as "cultural brokers" and authorities who affirm existing orders. Previous work on the Islamic sermon as a channel of political communication emphasizes its emotional role.[38] Even fewer studies have focused on the role of Friday sermons in Shiʿi communities, with the important exception of work on the role of sermons in channeling antigovernment protest during the Iranian Revolution and in consolidating and legitimizing the Islamic regime after the reinstitution of Friday sermons throughout Iran in July 1979.[39]

Shiʿi Islam and Friday Prayers

Various schools of Islamic thought have different requirements for the holding of Friday prayers, but the issue has been particularly complex for Imami Shiʿa.[40] Shiʿi scholars agree that Friday prayers are one of the religious and political duties of the infallible Imams. Imam Ali (also caliph at the time), is said to have held Friday sermons, such as the one he delivered outside Basra just after the Battle of the Camel in 656.[41] Those scholars disagree, however, on who—if anyone—can assume the Imam's duties in his absence during the ongoing period of the Greater Occultation (*ghabya*). The Greater Occultation is when the messianic Mahdi is alive but has disappeared from the world and is no longer in contact with his followers through designated deputies; it began in 939 or 941 and continues today. The holding of Friday prayers, therefore, has been an issue of debate among Shiʿi scholars for over a thousand years. The lack of Friday prayers helps explains why some heterodox Shiʿi groups, such as Alawis in Syria and Alevis in Turkey, do not have mosques or traditions of Friday congregational prayers; if groups do not hold Friday congregational prayers, large and conspicuous mosques are unnecessary.

In the classical period of Shiʿi thought (1000–1300s), some jurists prohibited performing the Friday prayer in the absence of the Imam, while others said they were permissible but not obligatory.[42] The issue became associated with the Usuli-Akhbari debate over whether legal scholars as a group can serve as representatives of the Imam in his absence and thereby assume some of his duties; Akhbaris saw it as usurping the Hidden Imam's authority.[43] When the Safavids made Shi'i Islam the official religion of their empire, they saw Friday prayers as a way to legitimate their role and establish their authority vis-à-vis the Ottomans.[44] In Iran, Friday sermons played a role in disseminating the 1891 fatwa prohibiting the use of tobacco—which came after protests were underway—but their prominence declined as Reza Shah's regime became more authoritarian and attempted to take powers away from clerics. After 1979, Friday prayers in Iran became bureaucratized and preachers essentially became civil servants, part of the state apparatus.

In contrast, Shi'a living in majority-Sunni areas rarely held Friday prayers. Because the leader's name is traditionally invoked during the sermon Shi'i scholars have been hesitant to hold sermons that might be construed as approval of rule by Sunni leaders.[45] This was particularly true in Iraq, where they have rarely been held. In the mid-nineteenth century, Sheikh Murtadha Ansari, widely credited as being the first supreme clerical exemplar (*marja' taqlid mutlaq*), ruled that Friday prayers could only be performed with the authority of the ruler and in his presence.[46] Sheikh Muhammad Mahdi al-Khalisi sought to revive the practice of Friday prayers among Shi'a and wrote a book in the 1930s (published in 1949) boldly reinterpreting the Friday prayer as a Quranic religious duty applicable in all times for all Muslims—a duty not conditioned on the presence of the Imam.[47] He held Friday prayers in Kadhimiya, and his followers continued the practice in that one mosque. Other than there, formal Friday prayers in Shi'i mosques in Iraq have been held only on rare occasions. Grand Ayatollah Mohsin al-Hakim issued a fatwa in the 1950s (sometimes dated to 1958) prohibiting the Friday prayer under a secular regime, and except for the one mosque of the small al-Khalisi movement and perhaps a few other specific groups, Shi'i mosques in Iraq did not hold Friday prayers for forty years.[48]

Thus, historically there have been relatively few mosques for Shi'a in Iraq. In general, Shi'a there rely on hussainiyas instead of non-Friday mosques (*masajid*). Hussainiyas are prayer halls designed primarily for use during the first ten days of Muharram, the first month of the Islamic calendar, when they serve as sites for the distribution of charity and communal lamentations for the martyrdom and suffering of Husayn and his supporters at Karbala in 680. They are also used for religious lessons during Ramadan, for mourning visitations after a death, and for daily prayers. But weekly Friday sermons are not held in hussainiyas. In this way, they are analogous to Sunni non-Friday mosques. Under the Ba'th, it was very difficult to get approval to construct a hussainiya or use an existing building as one; I was told by several Basrawis that only influential Shi'i members of the Ba'th Party were given such approval. The vast majority of the mosques in Basra, including the Friday mosques, were for Sunnis, who constituted perhaps

15 to 20 percent of Basra's population in 2003. After 2003, a few Sunni mosques, notably those in homogenous Shiʻi areas, were taken over by Shiʻa and used for Friday prayers.

During the height of Saddam's Faith Campaign, and with at least tacit approval from the Baʻth regime, Grand Ayatollah Mohammad Mohammad Sadiq al-Sadr reinstituted Friday prayers and sermons beginning in 1996 in several mosques affiliated with his clerical network.[49] In an interview, Sheikh Adnan Silawi, who had been one of Sadr's wakils in Basra in the 1990s, told me that Sadr sent a delegation from Najaf around to each city in the south (and also to Kirkuk) to try to consolidate Friday prayers if they were being held in different places.[50] While other grand ayatollahs in Iraq often shared wakils in a city, Sadr's wakils were allowed to represent only him. Shiʻi Friday congregational prayers and sermons began in al-Kut in 1996 and in al-Nasiriya and Baghdad's al-Thawra neighborhood (known then as Saddam City and later as Sadr City) in 1997.[51] One Sadrist cleric told me that the first sermons for Shiʻa, in 1996, occurred as a commemoration of the birthday of Fatima, which fell on a Friday, which led to sermons and prayers being held in the fashion of a Friday congregational prayer. After then, they continued weekly and spread to other towns.

A resident of Nasiriya told Patrick Cockburn in 1998, "People came to see this strange event. They had not seen Friday prayers. Most of those who came to pray were young people who stood in lines and held hands with each other."[52] Silawi, Sadr's wakil, told me that before this time, Friday prayers were only held in Sunni, "Akhbari," and Yazidi mosques in Iraq. He said the Shiʻa rhetorically asked, "Why not us? Why did Saddam not permit us to pray like this? He [Saddam] was scared."[53] Silawi said when he began giving sermons, "the people heard my words. When I spoke, thousands listened."

Sadr himself delivered sermons on forty Fridays in his mosque in Kufa, from 17 April 1998 to 19 February 1999.[54] This was two years after his wakils began holding them. Silawi told me that Sadr did not initially give sermons himself for two reasons.[55] First, he wanted to examine the people and test them, to see how they would respond to the new (for them) ritual. Second, he did not want to insult other Shiʻi clerics who had long rejected the practice. Sadr's first sermons focused on justifying Friday prayers, which might have seemed like a politically dangerous—or even blasphemous—innovation to many Shiʻa in Iraq.[56] Sadr emphasized that he was preaching in the same mosque where Imam Ali preached when he ruled as caliph and Imam in the seventh century (the only Imam to hold political power). Sadr's first sermon, not coincidentally, was timed to coincide with the day after Eid al-Ghadir, the anniversary of what Shiʻa believe to be the Prophet's appointment of Ali as his successor.[57] Although—or because—Friday sermons were such a novelty for Iraq's Shiʻa, large crowds began to attend

Sadr's sermons; according to reports from the Baʿth Party's Najaf branch, ten thousand to twelve thousand people attended.[58]

Sadr did not talk about contemporary events in his sermons until his last few. He and his preachers focused on large-scale "social problems" and emphasized proper Islamic behavior and values.[59] He forbid followers to watch the popular al-Shabab television station, which was owned by Uday Hussein, because it showed Western movies. He told taxi drivers not to pick up unveiled women.[60] But on 15 January 1999, Sadr addressed the nationwide problem of electricity blackouts and demanded the provision of uninterrupted service.[61] Some of his followers were subsequently arrested, and Sadr's sermon two weeks later called for them to be released. He also discussed the selling of "stolen" hospital medicines in the black market and blamed it on insufficient salaries for hospital workers. He authorized the taking of medicine from hospitals by employees, and he did so in a way that could be understood as implying that the Baʿth government was illegitimate.[62] His final sermon said that if his arrested followers were not released, all Friday preachers throughout Iraq should call for their release.[63] He was assassinated the following week, and his network was severely repressed.[64]

In our interview, Adnan Silawi emphasized that Friday preachers never mentioned Saddam in their sermons. He said that the Basra head of the General Security Service (*al-amn al-ʿamm*), Mahdi al-Dulaimi, had instructed them to bless Saddam in their sermons but that he and the other Sadrist preachers refused to comply.[65] Silawi said that in not hearing Saddam's name, "the people began to feel what was going on."

Friday sermons in Shiʿi mosques ended soon after Sadr's assassination in February 1999, and the vast majority of Shiʿi mosques, including those affiliated with Grand Ayatollah Sistani, had never held sermons under the Baʿth. The overwhelming majority of adult Iraqi Shiʿa, therefore, had never attended a Friday sermon before April 2003. There was not a tradition of using mosques for discussing events of the day, and sermons did not have a tradition of mobilizing Iraqis. Friday sermons were a new institution for Iraq's Shiʿa, and how and why mosque sermons became influential in 2003 is a puzzle that must be explained.

Mosques and the Emergence of Local Social Order

Lacking immediate alternatives, Iraqis in many places after the invasion quickly came to rely on sermons to coordinate together and reduce harmful effects related to the loss of state services. Where this occurred, Iraqis began to expect other Iraqis who lived in their immediate area to look to mosque messages to know how others would act. Messages from these Friday mosques gradually became consequential for more complex endeavors: the range of behaviors they could affect increased, and preachers' authority ratcheted up. Preinvasion, many clerics were respected locally and were looked to for guidance on religious and spiritual issues. But postinvasion, this preexisting authority was augmented; clerics became authoritative on a wider set of issues. Iraqis might have begun attending postinvasion Friday congregational prayers to be closer to God, but there is no precedent in Iraq for mobilization around sermon messages.

Mosque sermons became an efficient way for Iraqis to know what other Iraqis knew. This provision of common knowledge—and the belief that others will act on this knowledge—helped rational, self-interested actors to coordinate their behavior under conditions of anarchy. But as we will see, clerics were much less successful at helping communities to solve contribution problems because common knowledge alone is insufficient as a solution—some form of coercion is generally required. Religious edicts were less likely to be obeyed when the costs they imposed on individuals was higher.

Disorder and Preachers' Response

Urban areas in postinvasion Iraq demonstrated tremendous variation in their ability to compensate for the sudden collapse of the state. In some localities, residents dumped trash haphazardly onto streets, sewage drains clogged, and criminals roamed freely. Residents in other areas, however, dumped and burned trash in designated spots, contributed modest efforts to keeping drains open, and improved safety through coordinated efforts to keep an eye on their area. In the neighborhood where I lived during fieldwork, residents threw their garbage wherever they wanted, often in the middle of the street. Neighbors did not even share the idea that they *could* coordinate together to solve such problems; one man, who lived around the corner, dismissed the notion of local action, telling me that order and services were the sole "responsibility of the sovereign power (*sulta*)."

What explains this variation in localities' ability to provide order? When I asked Basrawis why residents in one area could coordinate together while those in another area—facing similar challenges—could not, the most common response was that it had to do with differences in the quality of people in various areas. If people throw garbage in the street, they are "uncultured." If they do not, they are "good" people. Save the Children, the most prominent foreign NGO in Basra at the time, implemented a community action program to engage communities in projects. I asked their field-workers what distinguished neighborhoods where residents cooperated from those where they did not. The head of the program could not name systematic factors that differentiated communities and simply told me that "people are different."⁶⁶ They later shared with me their baseline assessment coding sheets for neighborhoods they considered for projects, and the raw data they collected showed no clear patterns.

On 18 and 25 April 2003, the second and third Fridays after the US-led coalition took Baghdad and toppled the regime, many Shiʻi mosques began to hold Friday prayers and sermons. The possibility of using mosque sermons for mobilization was a new phenomenon for Iraqis. Under the Baʻth, the government tightly regulated who could give sermons, and sermons in Sunni mosques reflected regime messages.⁶⁷ For most Shiʻa it was a new institution, and how and why mosque sermons became influential is a puzzle. Presumably, most of those preachers in April 2003 were preaching their first-ever Friday sermon.

After coalition troops entered Baghdad, followers of the late Mohammad Mohammad Sadiq al-Sadr—who had been quiet, in hiding, or in exile since a fierce regime crackdown on them in 1999—quickly emerged and took control of many mosques, including those that had been closed since the crackdown, such as al-Muhsin Mosque in the area of Baghdad they rechristened Sadr City.⁶⁸ A Sadrist told the journalist Patrick Cockburn that in the days leading up to the overthrow of Saddam, Moqtada al-Sadr had been in touch with twelve to fifteen clerics, presumably his father's former students and lieutenants.⁶⁹ This network of preachers moved to quickly restart Friday prayers, holding them in a few mosques on 11 April, two days after Saddam's statue was pulled down in Baghdad's central Firdos Square. Sheikh Mohammad al-Yaqoubi, a student of Grand Ayatollah Sadr who would soon split the Sadr movement by declaring himself a marjaʻ and heir to its spiritual mantle, led prayers that first Friday in Kadhimiya. He claimed to speak for "the hawza," referencing the collective leadership in Najaf of Iraq's most senior Shiʻi clerics. Moqtada al-Sadr preached that day in the Grand Mosque of Kufa, from the same pulpit of Ali where his father had preached on forty Fridays, urging his late father's followers to undertake the Arbaʻeen pilgrimage to Karbala later that month and to follow the rulings of Grand Ayatollah Kazem al-Haeri in Qom.⁷⁰ Sadrists prepared to organize prayers in all major Iraqi cities for the following Friday, 18 April. Some of these first sermons condemned the occupying powers and called for Islamic government to be instituted.⁷¹

Once it became clear that Sadrist clerics were claiming to speak on Fridays in the name of the hawza, Grand Ayatollah Sistani made the surprising decision to authorize his clerical representatives in each city to hold Friday prayers and disseminate a statement on the situation facing the country. In the lead-up to the invasion and before Baghdad fell, Sistani had remained fairly quiet. At the behest of the Baʻth regime, he had issued a fatwa calling on Iraqis not to cooperate with occupation authorities, but after the invasion, this fatwa was cast aside and it does not appear in the official compendiums of Sistani's rulings and statements.⁷²

During the invasion, his office issued a few brief responses to questions about his safety, looting, and law and order. But on 18 April—a week after the Sadrists—Sistani's representatives held Friday sermons to disseminate a statement, a close version of which was released by his liaison office in London.[73] The statement addressed a number of issues, including assurances that the Shi'i clerical establishment would not seek to rule or select a government, the concern that former regime and intelligence members might "creep back into" posts, and a warning about foreign rule. But the statement also authorized Friday sermons to be held in Shi'i mosques and laid the foundation for the role they would come to play in Iraq. These portions of the statement, as disseminated from London, read,

> In these crucial times and the absence of a central authority to govern the country—leading to widespread anarchy and breakdown in law and order—we urge the active participation of our pious brethrens everywhere, including those living the unfolding events in our beloved Iraq, to fill the current vacuum with suitable and devout people.
>
> ...
>
> The Supreme Marja'iyya in Najaf has ordered all its Wakils (representatives) throughout Iraq to implement this matter urgently before it is too late. It is everyone's responsibility, with no room for excuses, no matter the circumstance.
>
> ...
>
> Implement the principle of "enjoining good and discouraging evil," for this is the criterion in Islamic Law that safeguards Muslim society from going astray.
>
> ...
>
> Just and reliable Wakils (representatives) must convene Friday prayers in all areas in accordance with Shari'a standards and invite everyone to abandon violence and discord and search for secret prison sites and detentions centers and return all looted goods and volunteer to serve society whilst relying on Allah the Almighty for victory and support.[74]

Sistani's office likely intended for only one or two of his wakils to hold Friday prayers in each city, but by the following Friday, 25 April, Friday prayers were being held in most Shi'i mosques. It is highly doubtful that Sistani intended for multiple Friday prayers and sermons to be held in each city because their proximity to one another violates his own religious rulings on the conditions under which such prayers are valid. Shi'i religious law says that the distance between places where Friday prayers are offered should be no less than one *farsakh*, which Shi'i religious authorities variously define as between 4.8 and 5.5 kilometers.[75] If the distance between Friday prayers is less, prayers offered in whichever mosque begins first (i.e., marked by the prayer's first *takbir*, the expression "God is great" in Arabic) are valid and those offered in other mosques within one *farsakh* are void. If both begin at exactly the same time, both are void. Since April 2003, I estimate that Friday prayers have been held in at least seventeen and up to thirty-one Shi'i mosques or outdoor prayer areas in Basra City. Based on distance, prayers at four of them, at most, could have been valid. Other cities also saw multiple Friday sermons. According to Sistani's own fatwas, therefore, the Friday *jum'a* prayers of most of his Iraqi followers since 2003 have not been valid. During interviews, I separately asked several Shi'i clerics in Basra about this in 2004 and again in 2011. The first cleric I asked, in 2004, became defensive and angrily questioned my motivations for raising such a topic. After that experience, I broached the subject carefully. One of Sistani's wakils engaged in linguistic gymnastics in Arabic and argued that only four Shi'i mosques in Basra hold Friday prayers (*salat al-jum'a*) while the others hold the regular midday congregational prayers (*salat al-jami'*) but with a sermon. This is inconsistent, though, with how people pray those prayers: the number of prostrations (two *rak'a* instead of four) and other differences in ritual clearly designate a Friday prayer from a *dhuhr* prayer done in congregation. A third Sistani-affiliated cleric in Basra agreed with my observation and spatial analysis, simply saying, "Yes, from a religious point of view, this is not correct."

How did Friday prayers come to be held at so many Shi'i mosques? In my earliest interviews with preachers, in late 2003, preachers did not emphasize or sometimes did not even mention Sistani's authorization. When I asked clerics to explain how they began to hold sermons, they described their responsibility to provide education (*al-ta'lim*) and guidance (*al-irshad*) to believers and referred to a need at the time to restore social services. Most mentioned the looting and insecurity of the time. One preacher, for example, said he began including a sermon on Fridays "because of problems that began in the community or in the society."

My interviews suggest that Shi'i clerics unaffiliated with Sadr independently began to hold Friday sermons on 18 or 25 April after seeing crowds of young Shi'a flock to sermons by their Sadrist rivals the previous Friday. This suggests that Sistani preemptively "authorized" a practice that was already about to occur. Clerics might have concluded that al-Hakim's 1950s-era fatwa was no longer valid because the (now nonexistent) state was no longer secular; at the least, this could have been an acceptable justification for holding sermons, even without an authorization from Sistani. Perhaps Sistani's statement was meant to authorize sermons in only one or two mosques in each city, but other clerics seized the opportunity and began to hold prayers. Friday sermons were a clear break from a precedent that had lasted for at least forty-five years—arguably, for centuries—so some degree of confusion among preachers about who was authorized to hold sermons was to be expected, particularly in the weeks following the fall of the regime. Or perhaps Sistani did intend to give imams tacit or even explicit authorization to hold Friday prayers, despite the distance between locations. The Sadrists claimed to be speaking in the name of the hawza, a move that must have certainly troubled senior clerics in Najaf. It is possible that Sistani and his wakils conveniently ignored the "necessary conditions" for valid Friday prayers in order to flood the spatial landscape with alternative sermons read in his name to dilute the Sadrists' reach.[76]

Sistani's pronouncements in late April, May, and June 2003 were few, limited, and often focused on looting and the vigilante killings of Ba'thists. For example, he condemned the theft and seizure of "government property," said that individuals must consult "the relevant department" before retaking property stolen by the previous regime, and ordered artifacts to be returned to Baghdad's looted Iraq Museum.[77] In mid-May Sistani prohibited vigilante killings of Ba'thist officials until the establishment of a "legitimate court" (*mahkama shari'ya*).[78] Some of these early edicts were ignored. On 20 April he issued a fatwa warning clerics against seeking political office, but this did not stop a number of clerics—including some of his own followers—from taking up such offices or running as candidates in later elections.[79] Two clerics—Ayatollah Mohammad Bahr al-Uloom and Abdul Aziz al-Hakim—accepted appointments to the Iraqi Governing Council in July 2003 and served terms as its rotating president (technically making them prime ministers of Iraq). Although it is difficult to measure its effect, Sistani's prohibition on vigilante killings of Ba'thists did not stop hundreds—perhaps thousands—from being murdered over the following months.

Before and in the first months after invasion, most Iraqis considered Sistani a political quietist and did not expect him to be involved in political developments.[80] In late 2003, a pious and usually well-informed follower of Sistani in Basra, whom I interviewed on several occasions, told me that Sistani simply was following the precedent set during the 1991 uprisings by his predecessor and mentor, Grand Ayatollah Khoei, and that he had copied verbatim Khoei's two fatwas from the time (I later checked; he had not). That follower of Sistani never expected his marja' to become as interventionist as he soon became.

Sistani's fatwas and statements did not address local issues—such as how to collect trash, organize security, regulate traffic, or share scarce resources—which naturally vary from locale to locale. Preachers acted on their own initiative regarding local affairs, and these messages were uncoordinated across mosques in the months immediately following the US-led invasion. By 20 April, when Sistani issued his first fatwa on looting, many mosque preachers had already condemned looting and called on believers to return looted items. What looked like compliance with Sistani's fatwa can be understood as the grand ayatollah sanctioning already established patterns of behavior toward looters, which varied by locality. Were the Sadr sermons coordinated at this point? The Sadrists held sermons in only a few mosques, but permanent divisions among Sadrists developed during these first few Fridays. Sheikh Mohammad al-Yacoobi preached in Kadhimiya on either 18 or 25 April, while another Sadrist cleric spoke in Baghdad's towering but unfinished al-Rahman Mosque. Within a week or two, Yacoobi would fully split from the Moqtada-led Office of the Martyed Sadr II network and organize independently, from al-Rahman. From that point on, rival Sadrists in Basra held two, and later three and then four, different Friday prayers and sermons that were uncoordinated and often contradicted one another. They all claimed to speak in the name of Moqtada's father, but the son could not shape the messages of many of his father's former students and wakils.

Figure 4.1 shows graffiti on a wall in Basra, dating from April 2003, that announces the initiation of Friday prayers at a Shi'i mosque. The wording suggests the novelty of what was occurring. The first line reads, "Yes yes to Islam," which was a common chant of banned Islamist parties, but it then continues with the phrase "Yes yes to Friday," a phrase associated with Sadr's resumption of Friday prayers in the late 1990s. In retrospect, it is surprising that the widespread initiation of Friday congregational prayers did not spark bitter controversy among Shi'a who did not follow Sadr and had never participated in the ritual. The graffiti

FIGURE 4.1. Graffiti in Basra announcing the initiation of Friday prayers

identifies the neighborhood where the mosque is located, which is perhaps meant to signal that this is where residents of al-Husayn should gather. It is worth repeating that except from 1997 to February 1999 at one mosque where the preacher was affiliated with Sadr, Shi'i Friday prayers had not been regularly held in Basra since the 1950s, and even then it is not clear how often they were held or in how many mosques. Attending Friday congregational prayers and hearing a sermon was a new ritual, previously forbidden, for the vast majority of Iraq's Shi'a. Many of them might have begun to attend Friday prayers for the first time in April 2003 to be near God, but others would have been unwilling to go unless a sufficient number of others also began to attend this new ritual. The initial decision to attend necessitated coordinating together, but once they did, they found an even more powerful space for further coordination.

Sermon Content

I attended ten Friday congregational prayers in Basra from October 2003 to March 2004. In Shi'i mosques, the two sermons were sometimes given by different preachers, but the first almost always focused on a Quranic verse or religious instruction and the second on social and political commentary. The most common theme in the sermons was the Friday prayer itself, which is unsurprising since this was a novel ritual and preachers had to normalize it and reinforce its norms and rules. We were told to listen attentively to the *khutbahs* and to straighten and tighten up our rows; one preacher said not to allow children to sit next to each other during the Friday prayer. In two sermons I attended the preachers expounded *al-wajib al-takhyiri*, the idea that an obligatory act can have one or more substitutes and that the believer is free to choose between them. The preachers used this concept to justify why the Friday congregational prayers had always been an obligatory act, yet for decades they had been neglected and replaced by a different prayer. In a November 2003 sermon in a Shi'i mosque, I and other attendees were told that attendance at Friday prayers was now compulsory and that it is okay to come late—if, for example, you are stuck in traffic or "your mount dies"—but that you cannot leave early "to buy and sell." In several sermons, preachers meticulously instructed us on how many series of ritual prostrations must be performed for a valid Friday prayer (*salat al-jum'a*) as opposed to the substitutable regular noon prayer (*salat al-dhuhr*). This always took the form of strict instruction in ritual, with no explanation for why it was that way. My postsermon discussions with fellow attendees would often turn into impromptu lessons on ritual practice or history, such as the importance of *Du'a' Kumayl* (the Prayer of Kumayl), a supplication the sage Khidr revealed to Imam Ali and then passed to a follower named Kumayl, which is often recited on the evening before attending Friday prayers. These associated rituals likely helped Friday sermons become quickly accepted and embedded in Iraqi Shiʻi society because they fit with what Haddad identifies as the Shiʻi myth-symbol complex.[81]

Sermon messages and their social meanings were embedded in discussions of morals and ethics, often using stories from the lives of the Imams as models of proper behavior. I was surprised at how often Imams other than Ali and Husayn were discussed—not only how they died but also characteristics Shiʻa associate with them. For example, referencing the ninth Imam, known as Muhammad al-Jawad (the Generous), in a sermon would be understood as implicitly instructing listeners to help people who asked for help.[82] Because I was unfamiliar with many specific details of Shiʻi narratives of the Imams, I did not fully understand all the messages in sermons I heard. During one sermon I missed the significance of the preacher's brief reference to "Shimr" (bin dhul Jawshan), the Umayyad soldier who killed Imam Husayn or cut off his head or both, until I heard his name in a Shiʻi lamentation session several weeks later. Without knowing why Shimr is such a reviled figure for Shiʻa, the political message embedded in the sermon was difficult to parse.

Coordinating through Sermons

Why did individuals begin to change their behavior in response to messages from the mosque? Although clerics had been looked to for religious guidance long before state collapse, why did Iraqis now look to them for guidance on an ever-wider set of issues, seemingly unrelated to ritual and transactions? Coalition forces, emergency relief organizations, exiled Iraqi political groups, tribal authorities and other local notables, and nascent civil society movements tried to address social order, and they sometimes succeeded, albeit on an ad hoc and irregular basis. But compared to these alternatives, local mosque preachers had geographic and informational advantages, in addition to some amount of preexisting religious authority. They were physically embedded in localities and had firsthand information about local conditions and possible solutions. The two-part format of Friday sermons made it easy for preachers to both provide religious instruction (in the first sermon) and discuss public and political issues (in the second sermon); sometimes the two parts were related, other times they were not.

When local preachers began to address local problems in their sermons, all attendees knew that all other attendees heard the messages. But how did they come to expect others to act on those messages? This is the particularly undertheorized aspect of coordination: the origins of "authority" and "legitimacy." While preachers did have some preexisting religious or traditional authority, that authority was augmented. It is that expansion in authority that is puzzling.

In their first postinvasion sermons, many preachers condemned the rampant looting and called on followers to return stolen goods. A number of preachers in Basra independently told their congregations that looting public buildings is wrong. They added, however, that mistakes can be rectified and looted property can be returned anonymously to designated locations. The BBC reported one such case on 15 April 2003, five days before Sistani's anti-looting fatwa. Sayyid Ali Hakim al-Mosawi, a preacher in Basra's Junayna District, decreed that it was illegal to steal or keep looted items and that looters would be shunned by other Muslims.[83] The mosque's yard allegedly filled with "a bizarre array of looted items," including paint cans, streetlights, and desks.

Why did the sermon, in the words of the BBC reporter, give some looters "second thoughts about their booty"? One man who stole a trailer from a local oil company says that he turned it over to the mosque because "we were told by the imam [preacher] that what we had done was illegal. I now believe my actions in taking the abandoned trailer were wrong." But what the sermon message really did was coordinate listeners on a way to punish looters—by shunning them. There is a cost to shunning someone, but it is relatively low, especially if everyone else is also shunning them for the same reason. Looters who heard this message knew they faced a choice: hand over their looted goods or keep them and risk being shunned. But they also knew that more severe punishment was unlikely because no one would bear the costs of providing it; some amount of shunning was all that the mosque could get people to do. Unsurprisingly, the BBC story says much of what was returned "can only be destined for the dump," such as a half-melted globe and fixtures irreparably damaged after being ripped from their original locations. People acted on the preacher's message—to return looted goods and to shun looters who did not—when the cost of compliance was low. The man who took the trailer admitted that he "had no use for it," and he knew that he could not hide the fact that he had stolen a noticeable trailer. Perhaps he was happy to be interviewed by the BBC because he could publicize his change of heart. But people who took valuable items likely kept them, even at the risk of being shunned by some of their neighbors. The BBC story admits that looting in Basra continued, "despite the response to the imam's decree."

Sistani's fatwa the same week telling people to turn over looted items had similar limited effects.[84] Two "Ali Baba" markets for looted goods continued to see brisk business when I arrived five months later: one was in a chaotic northern neighborhood and the larger one was in the center of the city, in the mixed Sunni-Shiʻi area known as Old Basra. Residents in both areas did not approve of the nearby markets specializing in stolen goods, but they were unable to cooperate together to shut them down because doing so would have been costly. Iraqis spoke publicly about looted goods, calling them *hawasim* goods after Saddam's name for the 2003 war, Um al-Hawasim (Mother of the Decisive Battle). In May, the Sadrists circulated a fatwa saying that looters could keep their loot as long as they donated one-fifth of its value to the local Sadr office.[85] A Sadrist cleric told Cockburn that the fatwas came from Grand Ayatollah al-Haeri in Qom, who was nominally the marja' for most Sadrists at that point, but Cockburn thinks it was more likely to have come from Moqtada. Moqtada may have been applying a 1999 ruling by his father that effectively authorized the stealing of medicines from hospitals on the grounds that the owner was unknown.[86] It is an example of a fatwa providing religious authorization for something that would have occurred regardless.

After sermons helped neighbors coordinate together to act on simple but pressing dilemmas, it was intuitive for residents to look to them to resolve other issues, including what could be considered more complex ways of coordinating together or engaging in relatively low-cost efforts to contribute together: where and how to dispose of trash, how to keep sewage ditches clear, basic traffic regulation, and, in some instances, which militias to tolerate in the neighborhood and which to shun. Individuals expected their neighbors to continue to act on these mosque messages, making it in their interest to do likewise provided a sufficient number of others participated. In many areas, an individual's best prediction of what his neighbors would do came from information disseminated in his local mosque's sermons. In this sense, coordination ratcheted up and cooperation was possible when the actions required of followers imposed relatively small costs. In early October 2003, I attended a sermon in al-Hooda Mosque in central Basra in which the preacher announced that a suggestion box would be set up in the mosque for people to put in questions or suggestions for the community. Despite having lived in Iran for years, this particular preacher had an ability to identify local issues of concern to residents and a means by which to broadcast his preferred solutions to them.

Local preachers were the first on the scene in the immediate aftermath of state collapse and were better informed about local conditions than foreign organizations, and they had an ability to create common knowledge that other aspiring leaders and social organizations lacked. After Iraqis saw others act on these messages, they expected others would follow future messages if they specified self-enforcing behavior. If state-provided social order had not broken down, clerics would have been significantly less influential in postinvasion politics. Iraq's clerics had preexisting traditional authority, but that had historically been limited to religious issues. That classical authority was augmented and broadened by the infrastructure of common knowledge generation—Friday prayers, clerical statements, mosque loudspeakers—and Iraqis' need to work with one another after looting destroyed the state.

But the authority of preachers was limited to issues that people had an interest in obeying. In October 2003 I attended a sermon in which the preacher talked about the importance of using your eyes and ears to avoid doing wrong. He instructed members of the congregation not to give or take bribes, and he specifically addressed "doctors, nurses, and bank workers." He said bank employees should not demand or be given a "tip" to exchange money. We all heard this message, and some attendees with whom I later spoke said that they agreed with it. But they also said they would continue to give bribes when they had to. When I asked a doctor from the community about that particular sermon message, he became agitated and revealed how little he was paid, saying that of course he will continue to ask and expect to be "tipped" by patients and their families. He compared himself favorably to other Iraqi doctors who left the country, "even last week," for higher salaries in the United States or Dubai. On a different Friday, that same preacher appeared to become frustrated and even angry during his sermon as he relayed that people were not obeying him when he instructed them to do (costly) things. He spoke about what it means to be a true Muslim and then shifted to admonish the congregation, saying, "You pray, fast, and go to the Friday prayer, but as soon as you leave, you steal, lie, and cheat. This is not Islam." Like other preachers in Iraq at the time, he was learning the limits of his ability to induce compliance among his audience.

Consequences: Islam Appears Ascendant

Mosque preachers couched their messages and proposed norms and sanctions in religious terms. As Iraqis conditioned their behaviors on these messages, Islam appeared ever-more ascendant in society. Religion and religious markers of identity had gained prominence throughout the sanctions era, but the analysis here suggests that the additional "turn to Islam" after the invasion may have been based as much on Iraqis' rational responses to immediate problems as on increased religious devotion. People sometimes coordinate on solutions that they prefer less than other plausible solutions; for example, if everyone dumps their trash in the empty lot next to your house, you will too, even if you would have preferred that everyone had "chosen" to dump their trash in a lot farther down the street. Preachers embedded social and political messages in exhortations to comport oneself and one's community with Islamic values. Sistani's own authorization of Friday sermons mentions "the principle of 'enjoining good and discouraging evil' for this is the criterion in Islamic Law that safeguards Muslim society from going astray."[87] In the sermons I attended, we listened to messages about local issues and then, as each of the two sets of prayer movements (*rakat*) finished, we rubbed our right hands on the clay *turbah* stones in front of us and shook the hands of nearby congregants. Those hands, warmed by Shiʻi symbolism, would then jointly act on those messages. The sermon as a source of coordination and the ways people acted on mosque messages and later talked about coordinating together made it seem as though the turn to Islam was natural, instinctive, or even primordial.

The overarching substantive norm that emerged among Iraqi Arabs in such localities is that one should be a "good Muslim" and "command right and forbid wrong," but the specific workaday norms that flow from this overarching substantive norm varied from locality to locality, as shaped by local preachers.[88] Islam appeared to be ascendant. A June 2006 cable from the US embassy in Baghdad to the secretary of state in Washington reflects such variation. Describing challenges faced by Iraqi embassy staff members, it reads, "If they must travel outside their own neighborhoods, they adopt the clothing, language, and traits of the area." Such differing traits include "ethics," "dress code," and "a particular lingo." It continues, "Our staff—and our contacts—have become adept in modifying behavior to avoid 'Alasas,' informants who keep an eye out for 'outsiders' in neighborhoods. The Alasa mentality is becoming entrenched as Iraqi security forces fail to gain public confidence."[89] Religious discourses flourished in post-Saddam Iraq, but what that meant—the specific norms it engendered—varied from place to place. One implication of this book is that the diffusion of those norms can be spatially understood.

Consequences: Inadvertent Sectarianism

Sunnis and Shiʻa attend separate mosques, and many likely would find it awkward to pray in each other's mosques. There are a host of differences in prayer (and the call to prayer) between Shiʻa and Sunnis that are discernable, but a few stand out. First, Imami Shiʻa pray touching their forehead to small, matchbox-sized pieces of dried mud from Karbala (called a *turbah*, literally "soil"; plural *turab* or *atriba*); this would strike Sunnis as odd, or even a heretical innovation.[90] Second, Shiʻa are permitted to combine daily ritual prayers and thereby pray only three times a day. This is possible because Shiʻa say that the mid-afternoon prayer (*ʻasr*) can be prayed as soon as it is possible to complete the noon prayer (*zuhr*), so the two prayers can be performed as a continuous sequence or with a short interval between them. Similarly, the evening (*ʻisha*) prayer can be done as soon as it is possible to do the sundown (*maghrib*) prayer. Most Sunni schools of Islamic thought disagree with Shiʻa on these timings. This means that the length of prayers and the sequence of prostrations vary. When Sunnis and Shiʻa in Iraq pray together for much-publicized interfaith prayer events, Shiʻa inevitably adapt their usual prayer cycle to match Sunnis' by not combining prayers. Finally, Shiʻa prayers invoke blessings on the Imams, and sermons often include verbal and physical expressions of grief at the Imams' fates. The most frequently mentioned difference between Sunni and Shi'i prayer—where to place one's hands—is arguably the least important difference in terms of praying together.

Because Sunnis and Shi'a attend different mosques, they hear different sermons. Sermons create common knowledge within the geographically bounded catchment area of a particular mosque, but only if the community is sufficiently either Sunni or Shi'a and the mosque is from the same group. Iraqis, who came to rely on mosques to coordinate together, would disagree with the implication that this collective action was sectarian or distinctly either Shi'i or Sunni. And Sunnis living in majority Shi'i areas (and vice versa) found themselves left out of neighborhood endeavors or brought in after "decisions had been made," as one such Basrawi phrased it to me. Hence, a reliance on sermons led to an unintended rise in the saliency of sect-based identity.

Churches could have played a similar role for Basra's small but vibrant Christian community, but I was told by regular churchgoers that the priest in the city's operating Chaldean church never talked about social problems or politics during his sermons.[91] One interviewee said that the priest did so before the 1991 Gulf War but has not since that time, perhaps to avoid any problems between Christians and Muslims. I attended one mass at the church, and as interviewees predicted, the sermon focused on the Bible and the interpretation of biblical stories. The priest did not make any announcements about contemporary issues or distribute any information.

Local Alternatives to the Mosque

Other local actors and organizations lacked the capability to consistently and reliably render messages common knowledge, or Iraqis did not expect other Iraqis to act on those messages. The main conduit of information in Iraqi society in 2003 was simple word of mouth, which was severely limited by the previously mentioned social network structure of Ba'th-era Iraqi society. Cell phones were not yet available in Iraq, although Basrawis discovered that they could sometimes get intermittent coverage on a Kuwaiti cell phone network.[92] Once word of this spread, Basra was flooded with cheap cell phones and Kuwaiti SIM cards, overwhelming the limited network and, ironically, making them useless. Most Iraqis at the time lacked a home landline; these had been tightly controlled and monitored during the Ba'th era. Home Internet penetration in 2004 was effectively zero. Internet cafes quickly sprouted up around Basra, but inexperienced Iraqi IT technicians were often unable to cope with the barrage of pop-ups and computer viruses. Young Iraqis quickly abandoned the cafes that could not keep their computers operational. This early Internet use, however, reached only a tiny fraction of Iraq's population. Cell phone coverage and access to the Internet increased as the years went on, of course, particularly after 2005. Other conduits of information appeared. But in 2003 and 2004, there was no WhatsApp or Facebook or YouTube.

Societal trust in Iraq was low in 2003. From what I was able to learn about Basrawi society from my ethnographic observations, in social network terms, clusters of strong ties were small and connected by only a few weak ties. This is a network structure that hinders the generation of wide common knowledge.[93] However, there were other potential leaders in Iraqi society, such as tribal sheikhs and local notables. Why did these alternative forms of leadership fail where the mosque sermon succeeded? Amid anarchy, imams of Friday mosques in cities had critical advantages over rival claimants to authority: they had a preexisting religious legitimacy that got people to attend sermons and a pious public receptive to their messages, but they also had an unparalleled ability to render messages common knowledge among people living in a specific geographic area, on a routine and predictable schedule.

The way Basra developed over time meant that although the city looked like it was divided into discrete neighborhoods, the spatial boundaries between named neighborhoods often had little meaning for residents. Municipal services such as street cleaning and trash collection were organized at the district level, not by neighborhood. The only significant neighborhood-level state institution was the *mukhtar* (literally, chosen one); this is the preexisting local authority that Iraqis may have been most likely to turn to amid anarchy. Historically, in Iraq and the Levant a mukhtar is a village chief, mayor, or respected elder who might settle local disputes and often served as a community representative with (or for) higher authorities. In Iraq, the historical relationship between individual mukhtars and state institutions was often ambivalent and occasionally conflictual. For example, when Basra's mukhtars "went on strike" in the early 1930s to protest tax burdens imposed by the Municipalities Law of 1931, the municipality (*baladiyya*) replaced some of them with more pliant headmen.[94] The importance of mukhtars in Iraq as a political institution declined over time, perhaps in parallel with the growth of mass party politics, and under the Ba'th the mukhtar became yet another instrument of state control. Basrawis told me that mukhtars in the city were vetted by the General Security Directorate and cooperated with intelligence agencies to track and monitor residents in their area of responsibility. Some government, military, and educational forms required the signature of an individual's mukhtar to establish one's identity and residence. Mukhtars updated these personal records for the state, recording births, deaths, marriages, and activities in their neighborhoods. Dina Khoury says they were "the linchpin" in the party's series of school surveys because they provided information on the reputations and virtue of students' families.⁹⁵ After 1996, mukhtars became involved in the distribution of ration cards for the Oil-for-Food Programme. Several Basrawis told me that they believe their mukhtar recorded every visit made to every home in the neighborhood. Mukhtars were considered part of the Ba'thist regime and were widely despised; they received $40 annual gifts from Saddam—not from the Iraqi state, but from Saddam Hussein himself.⁹⁶

When I asked Iraqis about their neighborhood's prewar mukhtar, or mukhtars in general, interviewees almost always began by associating them with the Ba'th Party or the security apparatus (*al-Amn*) or both. Following the invasion, many mukhtars, perhaps dozens, were killed by Basrawis settling scores. Despite efforts, I was unable to interview any Ba'th-era mukhtars from Basra; by late 2003, they had all fled the city or made themselves difficult to find. Partly because of the mukhtar system, preinvasion neighborhood identity was weak in most localities, at least in Basra. No significant prewar local institutions or gatherings existed.⁹⁷ Under Saddam, central authorities maintained tight control, and this was reflected in formal institutions. Members of governate councils were unelected, and they generally were filled with local directors general of central government ministries and offices and other members selected by Ba'th Party officials. They advised the governor, who was appointed by the regime and the Ministry of Interior. Such municipal officials had no local standing postinvasion.

Many local notables, who in other contexts might have emerged as neighborhood leaders, were incriminated by the mukhtar system. The Sadah or sayyid families—those who claim descent from the Prophet through Ali and Fatima—traditionally held a special status in Shi'i society, often served as arbitrators of disputes, and played important roles in mobilizing Shi'a in the 1920 revolt.⁹⁸ As late the 1950s, some Sadah families remained dominant in local politics and commerce in Basra and even helped arrange public security in the city when the local government withdrew from advancing British troops in 1941.⁹⁹ But their status declined after the 1958 revolution, and they are no longer looked to as a distinct group within localities. Many other potential notables, particularly urbane liberals and intellectuals (*mosaqaf*) such as doctors, lawyers, and professors, had been low-level members of the Ba'th Party or were wary of being labeled and targeted as Ba'thists if they tried to assume prominent roles in their neighborhoods postinvasion. But even those who did try to organize their neighbors failed more often than not. In my neighborhood in late 2003, for example, one respected resident named Abu Haitham, a well-known judge, went door to door and tried to speak to each family living on our street about the security situation and the danger of cars cutting through our neighborhood to bypass a busy nearby intersection. I heard him discuss joint solutions to these issues with several people; someone suggested we build and paint speed bumps or erect and maintain makeshift barriers to force drivers to slow down. But nothing tangible came from his efforts. Even after Abu Haitham sent his children and nephews to place large branches and bins in the street, others in the neighborhood did not participate and the endeavor quickly fizzled. He lacked an ability to generate sufficient common knowledge among his neighbors, and he certainly lacked an ability to make us believe that others would act on his ideas or to induce us to make even minimally costly contributions. Although he is only one example, Abu Haitham is characteristic of a broad class of actors who failed to mobilize their neighbors, even when they could offer compelling solutions to issues of mutual concern. Certainly, some neighborhoods found non-mosque ways to solve problems, but these were often ad hoc solutions or via an institution unique to that one place.

Other political organizations including tribes, coalition forces, and nascent and exile political parties lacked an immediate ability to consistently generate common knowledge in a specific geographic area. Even if organizations had developed this ability, though, Iraqis would not have expected other Iraqis to act on those messages.

My participant observation and interview data suggest that the social networks Iraqis maintained or developed in the 1990s were hierarchical and overwhelmingly focused on securing basic needs such as food, employment, and security from the state. International sanctions against Iraq in the 1990s bit hard because the economy was heavily reliant on imported goods and oil sales. By 1991, about 40 percent of Iraqi households were directly reliant on government payments.[100] Per capita income declined from $3,510 in 1989 to $450 in 1996. Iraq's GDP went from $66.2 billion to $10.8 billion over that period.[101] The generous Iraqi state welfare system collapsed, and Iraqis had to find new ways to access ever-declining state resources.

As mentioned in chapter 2, the Oil-for-Food Programme strengthened the Iraqi state vis-à-vis society after 1996. A stunningly large percentage of Iraqis had long been dependent on the state, either as civil servants, state-sector employees (e.g., teachers, police officers, health workers, employees in state-owned companies), or pensioners. In Basra, twenty-five different Iraqi ministries paid people through 168 different utility companies and state organizations.[102] And this does not include groups that were paid through the Ba'th Party, including unions, some security networks, and martyrs' families. What vibrancy existed in society was intertwined with the state apparatus and the Ba'th Party.

By the late 1990s, a reconstituted or newly manufactured form of tribal order had become important for maintaining law and order in urban areas of

Ba'thist Iraq. As crime increased, Iraqis looked to local tribal or kin groups to guarantee their personal protection. As Faleh Jabar points out, however, this new form of tribalism had little in common with older forms of tribes.[103] These new tribal authorities were middle class, educated, and based in city apartments (instead of the traditional tribal meeting hall, or *mudhif*, characteristic of southern Iraq). This new tribalism did not constitute a territorially marked community. Therefore, even if these urban tribal institutions could have generated common knowledge, they could not have provided geographic public goods. They might be effective, however, in providing private goods, such as personal security for tribesmen. But historically, various Iraqi governments—as well as foreign occupiers—empowered tribal structures to distribute patronage and maintain order.[104] Without state largesse, tribal leaders in 2003 had little ability to get tribesmen to obey. Despite the perceptions of journalists and coalition officials, prominent tribal sheikhs appeared to be less influential over individual tribesmen than sub-tribe clan leaders, who often can affect members' marriage prospects within extended families and access to the clan's burial plots in Najaf and Karbala.[105] Many tribal figures were Ba'thists and became targets for assassination, such as the head of the influential Saadoun tribe, who was assassinated in Basra on 6 June 2003.

Basrawis generally differentiate between the city's "original" tribes and the tribes of migrants who moved to the city from rural areas near Amarah and Nasiriyah in the 1960s and 1970s, but particularly after 1991. Members of the former—such as the Saadoun, Dosairiyyi, Benu Tamim, al-Batat, and large families like the al-Ghanim—were spread throughout the oldest neighborhoods of Basra (e.g., Old Basra and al-'Ashair) and the planned neighborhoods immediately surrounding them. The pejoratively labeled "marsh Arab" tribes that migrated to the city largely settled in neighborhoods developed as housing schemes after 1951, such as al-Jumhuriyya, al-Asma'i, and Hayyaniah. I expected to find tribesmen living in close proximity to one another in these areas, particularly in the so-called slums of Hayyaniah and Khamsa Meel, but surprisingly I found little concentration of tribe or place or origin, aside from extended families sometimes living in nearby houses.[106] Parts of Hayyaniah are locally referred to by the clans and sheikhs that initially settled there, but residents in the ones I visited now constitute a wide mix of tribes and clans. The most compelling explanation I heard for this lack of tribal concentration in Basra's dense housing blocks relates to the real estate market. Demand for housing in the city has long exceeded its supply. The development of Iraq's oil industry led many to move to Basra, but the Iran-Iraq War devastated the city's infrastructure and housing stock. One study of reconstruction in Basra estimates that "almost 95% of all homes, offices and shops were either demolished or badly damaged and entire areas of traditional architecture were destroyed and subsequently left to deteriorate during the eight-year war."[107] We lack important socioeconomic data on Basra, but my interviews suggest that many residents sold or rented out their homes in the "slums" because it was extremely profitable to do so. In other words, even if members of particular clans migrated together to parts of Hayyaniah decades ago, over time members of the clan moved to other parts of the city or subdivided their homes to sell or rent portions of them.

I interviewed about a dozen tribal "sheikhs," and every one of them owned or was associated with a contracting company.[108] I met periodically with a Sheikh Salim from the Albu Darraj, a large and influential clan originally from al-Amarah, and we usually met in his office in a commercial—not residential—part of the city. There were hundreds, perhaps thousands of members of Sheikh Salim's clan in the city. Although concentrated in six neighborhoods, they were scattered throughout those large neighborhoods and lived among members of many other tribes and clans. Sheikh Salim was in the business of manpower contracting, and he would periodically tell me that if I helped him obtain a contract with the British military or CPA that he could provide "5,500 men tomorrow morning." What we both understood, however, is that those men would follow him only if he could offer them jobs. His "authority" was based on his ability to provide goods and services to his tribesmen, and he desperately needed new forms of patronage now that the Iraqi state had vanished.

I had many conversations, both formal and informal, with Basrawis about what "their tribe" meant to them and the situations in which they would obey tribal leaders' orders. Tribal sheikhs often could provide private goods to members of the tribe, including personal protection. But there is a price to be paid for such goods. A number of doctors, lawyers, and engineers in Basra were nominally members of the Halaf tribe, but like many urban migrants, they had lost any significant tribal connections. If one of them got into a dispute over a car accident, they could go to the sheikh of their clan, who most likely was a businessman and owner of a construction company. He might be willing to arrange to have someone threaten the other driver or protect the individual if the other party involved their tribe or hired a militia. But such benefits of tribal membership are restricted to those who participate. The person would then owe the sheikh and could expect to be called on in the future, perhaps to help the sheikh's company procure a contract. Elements of the Halaf tribe had an ongoing feud with another tribe, the Garamshi, over land far from Basra. If (perhaps, when) the feud turned violent, the tribesman might be expected to show up armed, or if he was a lawyer or businessman, send money or vehicles. If he was a doctor, he would be expected to facilitate medical care for tribal members in the city's hospitals. Most accounts of tribalism in Iraq emphasize the primordial aspects of tribal identity and ignore the political, social, and economic transactions that sustain kinship ties—transactions in which many Iraqis choose not to engage because of their costs. One Basrawi whom I knew well was nominally a member of a large and influential tribe that had members throughout southern Iraq and in Kuwait. I asked him why he and his brothers did not use those kinship ties to obtain valuable jobs or better their family's situation. He emphasized the dangers of associating with your tribe. He said that going to his sheikh or relying on his tribe for help opens up the risk of him or his sons being abducted by another tribe that was in a dispute with his tribe. Although a member of the tribe, he was outside of both its disputes and benefits.

Tribes are hierarchical and consist of a federation of clans, usually based on some real or imagined descent from a common ancestor. The highest levels of the tribal organization, mentioned in books, seem to have no salience for most urban Iraqis today. Iraq's great tribal confederations (*al-mashaikha*) are a thing of the past. The vast majority of Iraqis whom I interviewed had met the sheikh of their overall tribe (*al-'ashira*) a few times, and usually only in passing. Tribes divide into branches or clans, called *fakhaths* (literally, thighs).[109] More Iraqis knew the sheikh of their fakhath, and this is what Iraqis usually meant when they referred to their sheikh. The Banu Tamim is often referred to as Basra's most important tribe; it currently consists of 157 distinct fakhaths plus dozens of smaller tribes and families linked to (*murtabit bi-*) the tribe.[110] The Bani Malik, another important tribe, has 161 fakhaths.[111] Even the al-Ghanim in Basra, often referred to as a "family" and not a "tribe," consists of 139 fakhaths.[112]

When I asked Iraqis to remember the last time they saw their sheikh, the most common response by far was that it was at a *fat-ha*, a three-day wake where extended kin and acquaintances meet a deceased man or woman's immediate family.[113] The sheikhs I met seemed to spend a disproportionate amount of their time rushing between fat-has, and I had several meetings postponed or cancelled because of such events. I went to fat-has and saw people interact—superficially and briefly—with their sheikh.

Other organizations such as the CPA, political parties, and NGOs had different means to get their messages out, but they all lacked a reliable way to consistently generate common knowledge, which, again, is not just "everyone knows a message" but "everyone knows everyone knows a message." Parties and movements tended to rely on word of mouth or banners hung on buildings and at intersections. This latter strategy might generate common knowledge among those who see it, but it is unlikely to lead people to expect others to act on that message, a necessary condition for successful coordination. Parties had a difficult time mobilizing people to attend their rallies, even if they were well advertised, unless they distributed incentives to attend.

The failure of the United States and its coalition allies to plan for postinvasion Iraq has been well documented. The first Office of Reconstruction and Humanitarian Assistance had little presence in Basra, and the first senior CPA official in Basra, the Danish ambassador to Syria, Ole Wøhlers Olsen, resigned after less than three months and left Iraq on 28 July 2003, complaining that his team had received insufficient support from the United States.[114] His replacement, Hilary Synnott, arrived in Basra on 30 July and later described his initial staff as overwhelmed with basic day-to-day challenges. At the time, the United Kingdom had approximately one hundred officials seconded into the CPA, including thirty in CPA South.[115] Synnott quotes a British official as calling the coalition effort in the south "the bastard red-haired godchild of the CPA."[116]

Despite its efforts, CPA South was relatively unsuccessful in getting its messages out to Basra's residents. Few Iraqis attended its poorly announced press conferences. The press and public affairs adviser told me that sending Iraqis out—sometimes on bicycles—to distribute leaflets at cafes, mosques, banks, and other locations was the most effective way CPA South had found to get its message out in society.[117] Some parts of the city, though, were no-go zones for CPA's Iraqi messengers; one told me that they stopped going to Hayyaniah and several other neighborhoods after being attacked by stone-throwing children or needing British military protection. The content of some CPA messages put the Iraqi deliverers at risk; one recalled being surrounded and berated by an angry crowd as he distributed leaflets about back pay for soldiers.[118] It was clear from my interviews that the Iraqi messengers sometimes discarded CPA leaflets with controversial messages but led CPA officials to believe that the leaflets had been handed out. The messengers did occasionally deliver copies of leaflets to Friday mosques specifically for preachers to read out in their sermons, but it was then up to preachers to decide if and how to deliver the information. CPA Basra, located at the time in the centrally located old Electricity Accounts Building, had closed its gates to the public by mid-July 2003 and became virtually inaccessible to Iraqis after moving to the isolated and walled-off Basra Palace in mid-October.

One of CPA's rarely discussed successes was the demonetization of Saddam-era Iraqi currency and the introduction of a new currency that Iraqis called "Bremer dinars." This complex effort was carried out over three months, from 15 October 2003 to 15 January 2004, and it was a rare instance in which the coalition wanted to explain something to the Iraqi public that the Iraqi public was extremely interested in hearing. Details of the currency exchange—the timeline, process of exchanging bills, rules, and locations—were explained in flyers, press conferences, billboards, newspapers, and mosque sermons. One of CPA's biggest fears at the time was the prospect of tens of thousands of Iraqis gathering outside of banks on 15 October with bags full of cash. The main messages that CPA wanted to disseminate were that (1) the old currency would still be valid throughout the three-month period of the exchange, (2) the exchange rate from old to new dinars would be fixed and constant throughout that time, and (3) people should not accept any allegedly new currency before 15 October because it would be fake. Some of these messages were meant to get Iraqis to coordinate on patterns of behavior regarding the exchange, but despite being common knowledge, the messages failed to induce coordination because Iraqis did not expect other Iraqis to follow them. For example, Iraqis were uncertain whether partially torn currency would be accepted by banks during the exchange. If banks refused such currency it would soon be worthless, and no one wanted to be stuck with it. This seems like a minor issue, but a huge percentage of bills in circulation were ratty and torn. Authorities assured people that torn bills, as long as they were in one piece, would be accepted, and everyone knew everyone else heard that message. Despite this, for months it was almost impossible to get an Iraqi to voluntarily accept a torn bill for face value, no matter how slight the tear. Everyone would have been better off if everyone had just accepted torn bills, but instead, every transaction entailed a thorough inspection of each bill and a damaged bill prompted either a rejection or prolonged haggling over the discount required to accept it. Everyone's time and energy were wasted, although some likely made fortunes through arbitrage.

It is true that dozens of newspapers flourished in postinvasion Iraq, but many went days or even weeks without publishing an edition. In Basra, *al-Manarah* was the most prominent and reliable high-quality newspaper that covered local events, but I met only one Basrawi who told me that he read it regularly (and he worked for the CPA's media office, and part of his job was to read every newspaper in the city every day, a seemingly impossible feat). The only radio station in Basra before the fall of the Baʻth regime was the state-controlled and low-quality al-Ahwaz. Soon after, five substantive stations appeared, most of which were affiliated with a political actor: the British Army's al-Nahrain (eventually transferred to the Iraqi Media Network and renamed Basra Radio), the Supreme Council for Islamic Revolution in Iraq (SCIRI)'s al-Nakheel, the Iraqi National Accord's al-Mustaqbal (The Future) station, the BBC-supported al-Mirbad, and the independent but inconsistent Shatt al-Arab. None of them were listened to on a regular basis by any of my Iraqi friends or contacts. The most popular radio station by far during my time in Basra was a sixth station: the music-only Shanasheel. None of these media stations generated common knowledge and certainly not within specific neighborhoods.

Some political organizations, including the police, tried to create order by directly punishing people. This failed partly because it was easy to avoid new authorities with limited organizational capabilities and information. Traffic order exemplifies this. Used cars from neighboring states quickly poured into Iraq postinvasion; sanctions and state regulations previously had made car ownership prohibitively expensive for most Iraqis. Without a functioning bureaucracy or enforcement, however, drivers could not (and need not) register vehicles. Shops sold unofficial, outdated, and stolen license plates, but many cars simply went without. Attempts to reconstitute traffic police in Basra failed to control the rapid increase in vehicles, and many police feared confrontations with armed motorists. Drivers in Basra knew they could ignore traffic police without consequences, but they often slowed down and were cautious in neighborhoods where militia enforced traffic norms.

Throughout Muslim history, mosques often directly provided public goods such as hospitals, schools, orphanages, and soup kitchens. These are usually supported by self-financing religious endowments (*waqf*, plural *awqaf*) and religious alms. Outside of the shrine cities, Shi'a *awqaf* in Iraq are relatively rare and modest compared to those typically found in Shi'i communities in other countries or to those established by Sunnis in Iraq. The Ba'th-led state tightly controlled Sunni *awqaf*. I heard of only a few instances of mosques in Iraq directly providing services, and it was always on a small scale (for example, a doctor might provide free assessments for a few hours each month).

Perhaps people did not need a sermon to coordinate; maybe they could talk and network around the mosque and figure out ways to jointly provide order. As mentioned earlier, Shi'a are more likely to use hussainiyas for daily prayers, and I often found men—albeit older-than-average men—sitting and talking in fan-cooled or air-conditioned hussainiyas between prayer times. But such gossip is insufficient to generate common knowledge among a medium or large group of people, even if they live near each other. Some Friday mosques in Basra held nightly sermons during Ramadan. I attended several in October and November 2003. The attendance was a fraction—maybe 10 percent—of the mosque's usual Friday attendance, and there was no praying, just a sermon followed by ritualized lamentations about Imam Husayn. Although these sermons also addressed social and political issues, they did not coordinate or induce low-cost cooperation because too few people attended and heard them. And they only occurred during a single month.

But perhaps information posted around the mosque can generate common knowledge: signs and banners are often placed on the outside of mosques and can easily be seen and read by people walking by or entering mosques. I spent a significant amount of time during my first few months in Basra documenting the ubiquitous black banners that political parties and groups hung outside mosques and at busy intersections. I expected these messages to be impactful, particularly those hanging outside Friday mosques. To my surprise, no one I asked could remember or summarize a message on a banner outside the Friday mosque near their house. This included men who attended the sermon in the mosque and whom I knew walked by or even under the banners as they entered. A few interviewees recalled seeing signs that I knew were not there, perhaps remembering a sign they saw elsewhere or simply guessing at what might be there.

One explanation for mosque banners' lack of saliency comes from Paco Underhill's study of the science of shopping.[119] Underhill and his team found that there is a transition area, what they call a "decompression zone," in the entryway of stores where people tend not to pay attention to marketing or messaging. Underhill argues that entrants are preoccupied as they physically transition from the parking lot to the store, adjust to changes in lighting and temperature, and regain their bearings. His team found that shoppers are unlikely to read anything posted on the outside of stores, and he advises merchants to place information ten feet inside the door, not outside or at the threshold.[120] I suspect something similar happens as people enter the mosque to pray. Many are focused on performing their ablutions, and some are already engaged in preparatory prayers. The only thing most entrants are focused on is the required ritual washing (*wudhu* or *ghusl*) or, if they did that at home, securing a good space in the prayer area—perhaps one where they can see the preacher, enjoy air circulation from a ceiling fan, or leave quickly once the prayer ends. In several sermons I attended, the preacher emphasized the meaning and importance of an intention (*niyah*) to offer prayer. People often enter mosques silently, softly announcing their intention or reciting remembrances of God. The outside of the mosque is not the most effective place to hang banners and convey messages; placing them directly above ablution stations would likely be more effective.

5

THE GEOGRAPHY OF ORDER

Order eventually emerges after state breakdown, but it does so unevenly across time and space. This chapter provides empirical evidence about the importance, effectiveness, and limits of mosque sermons in creating order. Other things equal, localities with a single Friday mosque in postinvasion Basra exhibited greater levels of social order than localities that have either no Friday mosque or more than one Friday mosque. But having one Friday mosque provides an advantage only in resolving coordination issues and low-cost contribution dilemmas; it does not help residents undertake costlier collective actions. Mosques helped create order, but only of a particular type.

Clerics have an ability to make information common knowledge in areas where residents all hear a single sermon and know that everyone else in that area also heard the sermon. This chapter develops the idea of a Friday mosque's "catchment area": the geographical area from which a mosque attracts a population to use its services. If an area is not served by any Friday mosque, then there should be lower levels of common knowledge among residents there. And in areas where residents are distributed across multiple sermons because two or more Friday mosques are close by—meaning their catchment areas overlap—sermons will not create widespread common knowledge because residents will not know if or how many of their neighbors received the same information they did. Common knowledge among and coordination by residents will be lower in such areas. More trash, for example, should litter streets near the border of two Friday mosques' catchment areas than near either of those Friday mosques. Since men attend Friday sermons in Iraq and fewer women (particularly Shiʻa women) attend, Friday mosques are less likely to be related to the ability of women in a locality to coordinate or resolve low-cost contribution dilemmas.[1]

This chapter first presents ethnographic evidence that shows political processes playing out in a manner consistent with these conjectures. The evidence includes ethnographic observations and interviews conducted in Basra over seven months from late 2003 to early 2004 and two weeks in 2011, as well as journalistic accounts, surveys, and data from NGOs. The second part of the chapter complements this by using maps and geographic information system (GIS) techniques to demonstrate, insofar as available data allow, a spatial relationship between mosque location and murders in Basra. But such a relationship could be a result of mosques having been built in areas that already had more order. The final part of the chapter explores the history of urban geography in Basra and explains why mosques in the city are located where they are.

A Tale of Two Neighborhoods

Al-Asmaʻi—named for a renowned eighth- to ninth-century philologist and Arabic grammarian of the Basra school—is a planned residential neighborhood in Basra populated largely by poor and lower middle-class Shiʻa. It was conceived by the Ministry of Housing from 1955 to 1959 in an attempt to solve some of the city's housing problems.[2] To purchase one of the 1,776 detached homes, the head of the family had to be a government employee, and many who initially moved there were semiskilled and manual laborers. A 1970 survey of seventy houses in al-Asmaʻi found that 72 percent of the families were from other parts of Iraq, including rural areas of Basra Governate, Maysan, Wasit, and Baghdad.[3] That same study concluded that the al-Asmaʻi housing scheme, barely a decade old at the time, "has not been a success." It was crowded (twenty-five homes per acre), houses were too small for growing families, paved streets were "in a bad condition," and the neighborhood lacked "many of the basic urban amenities that should have been considered in a modern housing development."[4] But what the planned neighborhood of al-Asmaʻi did have, then and now, was a single central mosque in each of its sections.

When state-provided public services collapsed after the 2003 invasion, the Sahlani Mosque in al-Asmaʻi al-Jadid began to hold Friday prayers and sermons in which the preachers addressed local issues, including trash and security concerns. Al-Asmaʻi's residents began to look to the mosque for cues on how they should jointly tackle these shared challenges; when residents acted on these messages, a precedent was established. They coordinated their dumping of trash at specific sites, and compared to much of Basra, al-Asmaʻi's streets were relatively clean and safe in late 2003 and early 2004. Residents had positioned concrete barriers to force vehicles to slow and swerve as they entered the neighborhood. And although the neighborhood could not produce anything like a standing militia, residents watched out for strangers. If you parked your car in al-Asmaʿi, you did not need to worry about someone siphoning its fuel to sell on the black market (queueing at the city's few operating gas stations could take hours). The influence of the mosque began in April 2003, months before the mosque's namesake and family patriarch, Sheikh Muhammad Jawad al-Sahlani, returned in October from over twenty years in exile.[5]

When Sahlani, his sons, or designated preachers addressed other issues in sermons that required coordinating together, residents expected other residents to act on those messages. The Friday sermon became a source of information for al-Asmaʿi's residents about what they both *could* and *should* do. According to Abu Dhar al-Sahlani, Jawad's son and brother of the primary preacher, up to five hundred men and boys from the neighborhood could be called on to act half an hour after the sermon ended. Such sermons addressed things like cleaning and how to treat residents of the area (*musakin*).[6] Yet, the authority of the preachers in the mosque was limited. Al-Asmaʿi is bordered on several sides by water canals that at the time were clogged with refuse and sewage. Everyone knew that clearing the canals would have benefited the community. But the preachers never asked residents to donate their time or money to clear the waterways; they knew that there were limits on what pronouncements would be obeyed. Enough people could be counted on to respond immediately after a sermon to achieve a collective endeavor that imposed low costs on participants. But few—if any—would obey a request that demanded high-cost contributions, such as time-consuming maintenance projects or dangerous tasks. Furthermore, if such requests went unheeded, residents might begin to doubt whether others would act on any future sermon messages, even the low-cost ones. By only issuing requests that they knew would be followed, preachers maintained a key component of their local authority—namely, individuals' belief that others will act on sermon messages.

The locality to the west of al-Asmaʿi al-Jadid, in comparison, reeked of rotting trash, and sewage clogged and overflowed from narrow ditches that ran directly in front of people's homes. Neighbors there pursued their own trash disposal strategy, and throughout the seven months of my field research in Iraq, the area was considered unsafe, especially after dark. Two neighbors with whom I separately spoke could not even agree on the name of their area: One called it Hayy al-Khalij al-ʿArabi, the other said its name is Hayy al-Asdiqaʾ (both are names of nearby areas with unclear borders). Later, a third person told me that both names are incorrect; he claims the area is Hayy al-ʿAbbas. All three, however, agreed that their locality was part of neither al-Asmaʿi to the east nor sprawling Hayyaniah to

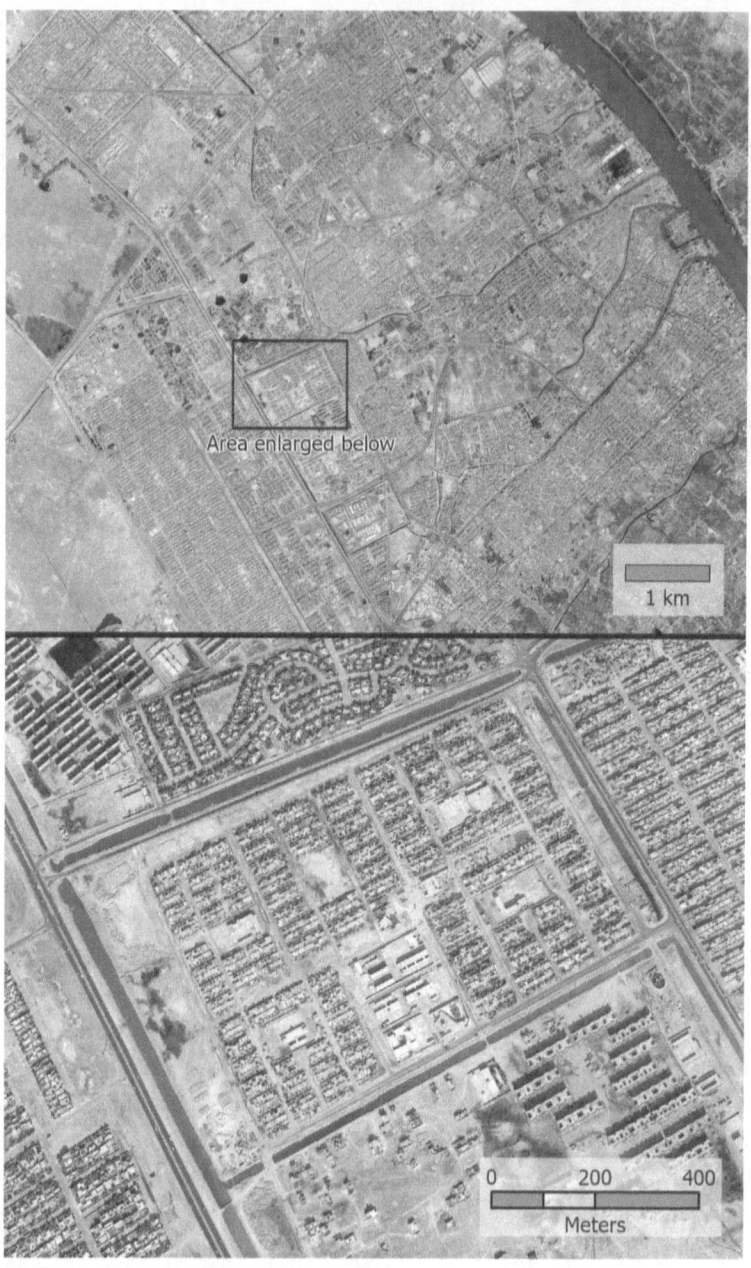

FIGURE 5.1. Al-Asmaʻi al-Jadid, Basra

the west. No "community" existed there, and neighbors did not share an understanding of how they might solve local issues of mutual concern. The locality did not have its own Friday mosque at that time, and residents who attended Friday sermons went to different ones nearby. Some residents went east on Fridays to al-Asmaʻi al-Jadid's mosque, others went west to one of Hayyaniyah's mosques, yet others headed south to a Friday sermon in Hayy al-Jamiaʻt. Residents heard different sermons in different mosques and did not know what their neighbors heard. The contrast between the order in al-Asmaʻi al-Jadid and the disorder in the neighborhood west of it was replicated elsewhere in the city and throughout Arab-majority parts of Iraq. One place found a way for residents to develop shared understandings as the mosque became focal, facilitating coordination and relatively low-cost contributions. The other did not.

Security and the Limits of Sermon-Generated Order

Friday mosques had a limited capacity to help residents in localities to organize to provide security beyond rudimentary and low-cost endeavors. It could not create a neighborhood militia because participation in such an endeavor would be time consuming, perhaps boring, and possibly dangerous. At best, Friday mosques could mobilize volunteers for short, specific, and low-risk security tasks, such as to search and protect prayer-goers in the hour before and during Friday prayers. Many mosques began to do this by late 2003 as rumors swirled that insurgents might target congregational prayers.

In October 2003 I regularly attended Friday sermons in al-Hooda Mosque in Basra, and one week, all attendees had to pass through basic security. A block away from the mosque, young men wearing printed badges that identified them as a "servant (*khadim*) of al-Hooda Mosque" frisked prayer-goers. In the sermon, the preacher discussed the importance of these local guards, reminding us of the assassination of Mohammad Baqir al-Hakim two months earlier after Friday prayers in Najaf and ominously mentioning that similar bombing plots in Basra had been foiled. The preacher instructed us to be patient with the mosque guards and allow them to protect us. We knew, and we knew that everyone else in attendance knew, that the preacher had just told us to acquiesce to the authority of these particular guards, and it could have been a way for a neighborhood to select a militia to guard it.[7] But the willingness of individuals to participate in costly local security endeavors was limited. Several dozen local youths were willing to conduct Friday morning pat-downs—perhaps because they knew their neighbors would see them and they thought they would earn social status for contributing—but this Friday mobilization did not translate into a neighborhood guard or patrol during the rest of the week. Sermons were insufficient to induce people to volunteer to guard or patrol the neighborhood because similar work paid what was considered a good wage at the time: the police received between $90 and $125 per month, and private companies and NGOs paid guards between $100 and $180 a month (plus food and a weapon) to work twelve hours a day and five and a half days per week.

Similarly, I once heard a preacher in a different mosque tell the congregation not to allow lorries to dump their loads of debris in empty lots in the neighborhood, but this was a costly request—who wants to confront a truck driver?—and the neighborhood's open spaces continued to be occasional dumping grounds for trucks. Some preachers tried to motivate congregations to organize as a neighborhood watch, but these efforts largely failed to launch or slowly fizzled because they demanded (ongoing) costly contributions. And these efforts failed despite tremendous demand for improved local security. At best, neighbors might coordinate together to simply keep watch for suspicious individuals or vehicles and thereby slightly reduce the risk of kidnapping or crime in an area. Hayder al-Mohammad, an anthropologist studying Basra, calls this "existential security" and writes, "The phenomenon of kidnappings was so widespread after the invasion that within a few years I never met a person in Basra or Baghdad who had not experienced at least one kidnapping of a close family member, friend, or neighbor."[8] One person told Hayder that nine people who lived on his street had been kidnapped.[9] Fear of kidnapping—particularly of their children—was one of the most commonly expressed concerns in my interviews with Basrawis in 2003 and 2004.

Inducing people to engage in collective endeavors that were more than minimally costly required external forms of punishment and reward. In a few places, Sadrists combined sermons with militias to coordinate and coerce residents, respectively. Anthony Shadid of the *Washington Post* describes how after the invasion Ali Shawki, a forty-seven-year-old cleric in Baghdad's Sadr City, declared an 8:00 p.m. curfew, demanded that all gunfire cease, and ordered clinics to reopen.[10] These injunctions were broadcast in sermons and by loudspeakers outside the Prophet Mohammed Mosque. Shawki's commands went beyond coordination or requests for low-cost contributions, such as his imposition of a curfew and demand that clinics reopen. Those are costly actions for individuals. Yet they were obeyed, but not solely because of the sermon. People obeyed his costlier instructions because of his power to have already-established militiamen punish noncompliance. In his area of Sadr City, Sheikh Shawki assigned a group of 200 armed men to enforce order among its 60,000 to 120,000 residents. We do not know for certain, but these men likely were paid for their efforts.

They established permanent roadblocks in the neighborhood and collected piles of looted goods after Shawki condemned looting in sermons. He told Shadid, "We order people to obey us. When we say stand up, they stand up. When we say sit down, they sit down.... With the collapse of Saddam, the people have turned to the clergy."[11] He also reportedly sometimes preached with a handgun holstered on his hip.

Without the militiamen (who would soon be rebranded as part of the Mahdi Army), Sheikh Shawki's writ would have extended only to the geographic catchment area of the Prophet Mohammed Mosque and would have been limited to edicts to coordinate together or make low-cost contributions. His public exhortations alone might have induced residents to cease celebratory gunfire if they created norms whereby residents would jointly confront shooters in their neighborhood. Instead, he could rely on the two-hundred-strong "neighborhood militia" to enforce the curfew, race to the site of any gunfire, and reopen clinics by running a protection racket. Without the militia, Shawki (and residents) would have seen drastic limits to his authority. He can motivate residents to stand and sit, but he could not get them to do things that they would rather not do, even if everyone else was doing them, without the coercive capacity of the militia.

One notable mosque-based group in Basra could induce people to participate in the provision of local security and other costly collective endeavors, but their organization could not be replicated elsewhere. The neighborhood to the east of the commercial district of al-Jaza'ir Street, which was often called al-Saymar despite being labeled al-Fursi on many maps, was perhaps the safest neighborhood in Basra after the invasion because it was dominated by the Shaykhiyya, a heterodox Shi'i religious group whose leadership controlled significant financial resources. The Shaykhiyya branch of Shi'i Islam emerged from the teachings and ideas of Sheikh Ahmad al-Ahsa'i (1753–1826) after his death.[12] Many of Basra's most prominent Shaykhiyyas are said to be descended from families who emigrated to today's Kuwait and Iraq in the late 1700s and 1800s from al-Hasa, in today's Saudi Arabia. As Toby Matthiesen notes, this coupling of a common geographical origin with a minority heterodox religious movement helped Basra's Shaykhiyya retain a well-developed group identity.[13] This explains why the Shaykhiyyas' enormous mosque in al-Saymar—officially named al-Musawi Grand Mosque, after the clerical family that has led the community for several generations—is known throughout Basra as al-Hasawiyya Mosque (for the "Hasawis" who pray there).[14]

Despite the collapse of the state, residents of al-Saymar enjoyed numerous public goods, such as regular trash collection, organized night guards, and electricity from generators attached to the mosque and to a large hospital that was under construction in the neighborhood. The impetus for these costly local goods was Sheikh Ali al-Musawi, the Shaykhiyyas' religious leader. The community's elite families became extremely wealthy after 1979. Although the Shaykhiyyas in Basra no longer have strong clerical and religious links with Shaykhiyyas in Kuwait and al-Hasa, Basra became the headquarters of the Kermani school of Shaykhiyya Islam when it was forced to relocate from Iran after the revolution there.[15] The clerical families in Basra, therefore, collect and allocate religious dues from followers of that sub-tradition, mostly in Iraq and Iran. For several reasons (including historical tensions between them and Iraq's orthodox Twelver Shi'a), the Shaykhiyya have long cultivated a reputation for being apolitical, and to an extent that is perhaps unique among social groups in southern Iraq, they enjoyed relative freedom under the Ba'th without being deeply coopted into its patronage networks. Since 1979, wealthy Shaykhiyya families expanded their economic activities—including real estate, agriculture, and trade—and developed the adjacent al-Jaza'ir Street as one of Basra's centers of commercial activity.

After the invasion, the Shaykhiyyas cooperated with the British military and coalition officials and also reestablished family and business ties with Hasawis/Shaykhiyyas in Kuwait. The Shaykhiyyas' religious leadership, within-group solidarity, and financial resources all carried over from the preinvasion period. At night, groups of neighborhood men—all Shaykhiyya—stood at the entrances of al-Saymar and also provided security along al-Jaza'ir Street. They were paid, and the religious leadership also paid for the streets to be cleaned and for the generators. The Iraqi Ministry of Health approved the construction of the private al-Musawi Hospital in 1999, and work on the project was ongoing when the invasion occurred. The provision of order in the area protected the hospital site, the mosque, and Shaykhiyyas' businesses, as well as residents.

By September 2003, the British military had de facto endorsed the Shaykhiyyas' provision of security in this central part of Basra after a series of violent confrontations along al-Jaza'ir between the Shaykhiyyas and members of the Garamshi tribe. By November, neighborhood guards wore bright orange vests, badges, and whistles that were provided by either the British military or by a police fund for auxiliary guards.

The Shaykhiyya were the only religious group in Basra capable of consistently contributing together; one non-Shaykhiyya Basrawi told me that when they act, "they are like one man." But they did not do this through mosque sermons. Instead, they relied on preexisting dense networks that were not disrupted by the collapse of the state, a preexisting leadership endowed with enormous financial resources, and a group that was sufficiently small that valuable goods could be offered to members in exchange for obligations. The few non-Shaykhiyya who lived in the area benefited from the provision of geographical public and club goods: clean streets, security, backup electrical supply. One told me that he was asked to join the community but declined. Without hassle, he was able to free ride on the local provision of order, but this was tolerated only because of how few non-Shaykhiyya lived there.

The British military and CPA South saw the Shaykhiyyas' impressive local organization as a model that should be emulated, and they regularly met with Sheikh Ali al-Musawi or his son. Several attempts were made to spread this model of a "neighborhood watch with attitude" (in the words of a British officer) to other localities, including through a formal local security force organized under the Nineteenth Brigade, but these efforts failed. The head of CPA South, Hilary Synnott, admits in his memoirs that they took a "nuanced view" of neighborhood militias that CPA Baghdad would not have approved of. He writes, "Community leaders were asked to recommend and vouch for men who might help the coalition to guard the neighborhoods from whence they came."[16] The deputy governor for local government in Basra told me in October 2003 that there was money in the local police budget for areas to pay night guards, who were to be attached to the police and organized through local councils.[17] But the Shaykhiyya model of cooperating together could not be reproduced because it was based on factors that did not exist elsewhere: dense networks, preexisting authority, a leader who could pay, and a small enough group. Elsewhere, orange vests were distributed to groups of young men whose names were often provided by local mosque preachers. But those groups lacked a capacity to cooperate together; they soon melted away, and there was little evidence of these efforts in the streets of the city. Most of the designated funds likely were misappropriated.

Stray Gunfire

Insecurity affected the basic ways Iraqis dealt with their environment. As temperatures rise, Basrawi families traditionally socialize in open courtyards or on their front porches and, at night, sometimes sleep on their rooftops. Basra's houses are designed to take advantage of these methods of dealing with the climate. This traditional way of beating the heat, however, came to be seen as dangerous after the invasion because of risks associated with gravity shots—bullets falling from the sky. Under the Baʻth, police and local security punished unauthorized weapon discharges; although guns were widely owned, gunfire was prohibited. After the invasion, however, discharging firearms into the air, especially AK-47 assault rifles and Tariq semiautomatic pistols, became a staple of wedding celebrations and a popular pastime in some areas but not in others. Localities exhibited vastly different norms about discharging weapons. A full year after the invasion, the United

Nations Development Programme (UNDP) found that 37 percent of Iraqi households reported weapon shots in their neighborhood every day, 23 percent reported it several times a week, 19 percent less than several times a week, and 21 percent never.[18] On Thursday evenings, wedding celebrations in Basra seemed to compete in lighting the sky with tracer fire and noise.[19] Several Iraqis I knew told me that falling bullets are not dangerous. To an extent, they are correct: an AK-47 bullet falling straight down possesses about 1 percent of the energy it did when it was fired, but falling at approximately 150 miles per hour, it can still break skin, and bullets fired at an angle can descend much faster and be lethal. So what explains variation in neighborhood conventions regarding such gunfire?

Save the Children tried to discourage shooting by distributing information about its consequences. The organization posted a sign, shown in figure 5.2, at a major intersection one block from my house.

The sign shows a drawing of a child bleeding from his head, a crossed-out silhouette of an AK-47, a Quranic quote, and the message "Share your happiness with others, and do not kill them in your overenthusiasm." Because the sign uses an Arabic word (*afrah*) that is often used in the context of weddings, a local would interpret the sign's message—and know others would interpret the message—to imply that shooting AK-47s in the air for celebrations is dangerous and can kill

FIGURE 5.2. Save the Children sign in Basra, late 2003

innocent children. Additionally, the sign contains a well-known Quranic injunction against the killing of innocents: "Whosoever kills a human being, except (as punishment) for murder or for spreading corruption in the land, it shall be like killing all humanity."[20] Above the quote, the sign begins with the well-known phrase "In the name of God, the Benevolent, the Merciful," which begins 113 of the 114 chapters in the Quran.

The placement of this sign at a busy intersection near my neighborhood generated common knowledge among my neighbors. I saw the sign almost every day, and I knew that my neighbors saw it. I asked two neighbors if they knew the sign, and both said they did. Furthermore, the message on the sign seems like it would be cogent, vividly showing the potential costs of celebratory gunfire and invoking one of the Quran's principal edicts.

Norms regarding celebratory gunfire can be understood as a coordination dilemma. If a resident knows that other residents never discharge their firearms in the locality, he probably would not discharge his. Yet there is no reason to believe that the sign's message changed the behavior of residents in my neighborhood. Common knowledge alone is insufficient for coordination; receivers must also believe that others will act on that knowledge. Nonviolent gunfire was common in the area where I lived, and I frequently heard and several times witnessed neighbors shooting into the air. Guns were fired to commemorate weddings, holidays, school exams, the purchase of a new weapon, or seemingly any occasion that could warrant a celebration. Although the sign's message was common knowledge, residents did not act on that message because they did not expect other residents to act on it.[21]

In contrast, I attended celebrations in other neighborhoods in Basra where I was explicitly told (sometimes apologetically) that, regarding such gunfire, "we do not do that here." In two localities, residents told me that preachers in their local mosque had condemned such shooting in sermons and warned of its risks. In some neighborhoods, celebratory gunfire occurred only on coordinated dates. Gunfire rang out, for example, in almost every neighborhood in Basra after sunset prayers on 28 October 2003, marking the beginning of Ramadan by Iraq's Shi'a. But residents in some neighborhoods knew that they all would do such things only on certain occasions (e.g., beginning of Ramadan), while in other neighborhoods the gunfire on that day was merely more intense than usual. This was a convention. There might be mild repercussions for discharging a gun in a neighborhood where they "do not do such things"; perhaps neighbors will shun someone who goes against the grain, or gossip about them. But these norms of not shooting seemed to be more a coordinated response—a convention—than a behavior induced by the threat of sanctions.

The Spatial Ordering of Urban Violence

Thus far, this chapter has described the process by which sermons contributed to ordering areas. It now asks whether or not there was a more general relationship between Friday mosque location and the production of order.

Mosque Catchment Areas

A mosque's catchment area can be understood as the geographic area from which it attracts a population. But does geography represent who attends a nearby mosque? I found that Muslim men in Iraq in the year after the invasion generally attended sermons in the Friday mosque of their sect (Sunni or Shi'i) that was closest to their homes.[22] This is partly for convenience: Iraqi families often gather at home for a family meal following Friday afternoon prayers. Weather, poor public transportation, safety concerns, and the relative newness of sermons in Iraq might also be factors that help explain why people prefer a mosque close to their home. There were exceptions: Shaykhiyyas would travel to al-Saymar's al-Hasawiyya Mosque, and some men who had moved away from home would return to their parents' neighborhood to attend with their father and brothers. But the vast majority of Basrawis whom I interviewed did not travel farther than necessary to attend Friday prayers; they did not select sermons based on preachers' ideology or political affiliation. Several Shi'i preachers in Basra emphasized that all Friday mosques are open to all Muslims and formally unaffiliated with parties or groups, unlike hussainiyas, which sometimes have such explicit affiliations. At the time of my fieldwork, three Friday sermons in Basra were affiliated with three different Sadrist clerical networks—the Office of the Martyred Sadr II, Kazem al-Haeri, and Mohammad al-Yaqoubi—reflecting the splintering of the movement.[23] But surprisingly, I found that many followers of the late Mohammad Mohammad Sadiq al-Sadr attended Friday prayers in mosques affiliated with Sistani when those mosques were closest to their homes. I also knew Shi'a who emulated Sistani and disagreed vehemently with Moqtada al-Sadr's politics but attended his wakil Bahadali's fiery Friday sermons simply because they lived near the mosque where he preached, in al-Tamimiya. Finally, as people came to condition neighborhood collective endeavors on local sermons, it created additional incentives to stay local on Friday afternoons and hear what their neighbors heard. The catchment area of a Friday mosque, therefore, is also a geographic space in which people might come to develop common knowledge via a sermon.

This geographic regularity in mosque choice allows us to visualize and map the catchment areas of Friday mosques. The top map in figure 5.3 shows the

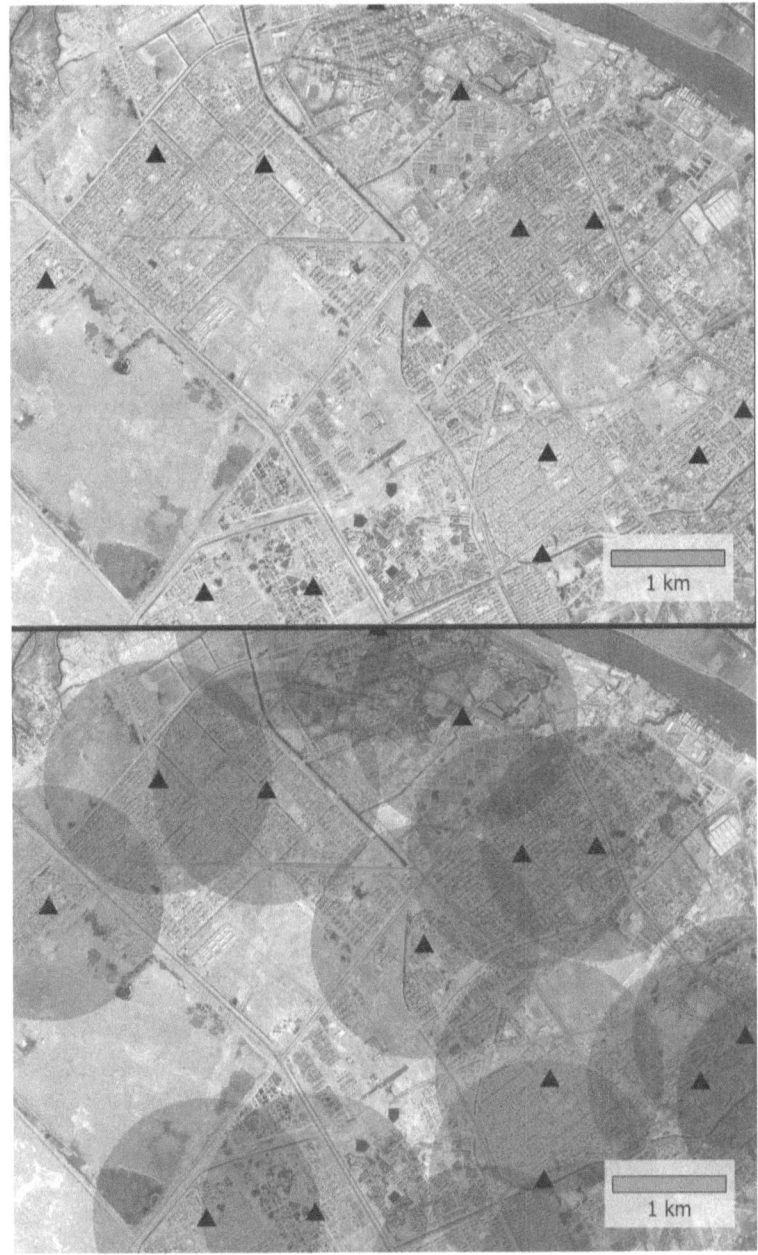

FIGURE 5.3. Friday mosques and catchment areas

locations of mosques that held Friday sermons in early 2004 in a portion of Basra. The bottom map depicts a circle of one-kilometer radius centered on each of those mosques, representing a stylized catchment area. These circles overlap wherever mosques are less than two kilometers apart, and the resulting overlap in the catchment areas is shaded a darker color. Some areas fall within three mosques' catchment areas. Unshaded areas are outside of the (one-kilometer) catchment area of any mosque.

But what is the geographic size of a Friday mosque's catchment area? One kilometer? Half a kilometer? There is no obvious answer.[24] If catchment areas are assumed to be large, then the percentage of the city falling into overlapping catchment areas will also be large, and a smaller portion of the city will be in one and only one mosque's catchment area. To address this uncertainty, the analysis examines a range of differently sized catchment areas.

Equally sized circles assumes that all Friday mosques have both the same carrying capacity and the same "pull."[25] These are reasonable assumptions. There is little relationship between the internal size of a mosque and the number of people who can attend its Friday prayers; congregations at Friday mosques in Iraq (and elsewhere) often spill out into courtyards and adjacent streets. Some mosques rely on Friday morning volunteers to block nearby streets, lay down extended prayer mats, and even erect temporary shade for attendees to hear sermons conveyed via loudspeakers. Other mosques let such spillover occur spontaneously and without accommodations. Assuming that all mosques have the same "pull" ignores factors, such as the charisma of a particular preacher or which marjaʻ he speaks for, that might lead someone to travel farther than necessary to hear a sermon. In other places or times, these characteristics of particular mosques and preachers might matter more for the size of catchment areas than they did in Basra in 2003.

Murders as an Indicator of Disorder

Residents in areas with a single Friday mosque should have a greater capability to coordinate and solve low-cost contribution problems than people living either in areas with no Friday mosque or in areas with two or more Friday mosques. Where there was no such mosque, residents lacked a way to develop common knowledge. In areas close to two (or more) mosques, residents did not know what messages their neighbors had received. But having one and only one Friday mosque should help people coordinate on issues like trash disposal and, over time, higher levels of order and collective behaviors that, to some extent, make violence in the locality less likely.

During most of the occupation of Iraq, coalition forces maintained and added to a database of field reports that document a wide variety of events they defined as "significant activity" (SIGACT). Many of these are attacks by coalition forces, Iraqi security forces, and insurgents. Each report includes the date, time, and location of the incident. After removing sensitive information—such as coalition casualties, units involved, and many coalition-initiated events (e.g., targeted killings)—the US military released versions of this database to scholars, most notably those involved with the Empirical Studies of Conflict Project (ESOC). And in October 2010, WikiLeaks released the full dataset of 391,832 SIGACT reports that span the period from 1 January 2004 to 31 December 2009 (except for May 2004 and March 2009), calling it the "Iraq War Logs." These reports chronicle 109,032 deaths, including those of 66,081 civilians. A number of scholars have used SIGACT data to examine spatial and temporal variation in insurgent and counterinsurgent operations in Iraq.[26]

Murder events from the SIGACT dataset are an indicator of social order, albeit a limited one. There are several reasons why murders might be lower in areas where residents coordinate and make some low-cost contributions to collective endeavors but are unable to engage in high-cost collective actions. Many studies on crime assume that criminals calculate costs and benefits when deciding whether and where to commit a crime.[27] Areas that have coordinated on ways to watch out for suspicious people or vehicles might deter murders from occurring in those areas, even when residents would not collectively respond to an attack. The mere sense that a locality has "eyes on the street" would make it riskier to kidnap or kill people there. A criminal targeting someone who lived in an area where residents coordinated together might choose to attack the person outside the neighborhood, perhaps on their way to work or at the market. Another possible link between murder events, common knowledge, and coordinating together relates to the idea that physical disorder in an area—such as trash and sewage in the street—is a signal of low community control and invites crime. Hence, removing signs of disorderliness is thought to deter crime. Such "disorder effects" are often associated in the United States with the so-called broken windows theory of policing, but the logic that disordered areas are particularly vulnerable to criminal invasion could apply broadly.[28]

I adopt a conservative approach to identify murders in the SIGACT dataset that indicate local order. I remove any deaths involving coalition forces, including obvious insurgent or counterinsurgent operations, improvised explosive devices (IEDs), and suicide attacks. The goal is to identify deaths that indicate local disorder, not insurgent or terrorist activity. I dropped assassinations of security officials because they could be related to insurgency. I retained the few events labeled in the dataset as tribal disputes. According to these criteria, the dataset includes 1,031 murders of Iraqis that occurred over the 2004 to 2009 period within the boundaries of Basra that I analyze (again, not including deaths from terrorist, insurgent, or counterinsurgent activities).[29] The data for Basra do not include murders that occurred during Operation Charge of the Knights in late March 2008, when the SIGACT reporting system appears to have broken down or otherwise been paused.

Based on information in the dataset and cross-checking some events with news reports, Iraqi sources, my knowledge of Basra, and what we know about violence in other contexts, many murders in this sample likely involve personal vendettas or score settling, such as in business or property disputes. Some murders may be political in nature, but there is no reason to expect that some mosques were more likely than others to provoke political murders nearby. In contrast, hussainiyas may have been more likely to attract violence than Friday mosques for two reasons. First, some buildings were designated as hussainiyas because of property disputes; one party in an inheritance squabble over a house may have designated it as a hussainiya to prevent the other party from living there. Second, several Islamist militant groups operated out of specific hussainiyas in Basra, such as TharAllah, whose hussainiya was demolished by the Iraqi military during Operation Charge of the Knights in 2008. These groups were responsible for many assassinations and kidnappings in the city, and retaliatory attacks could be expected near their headquarters.

This count of 1,031 murders in the SIGACT dataset is a severe undercounting of the murders that actually occurred in Basra over those seventy months. The dataset includes only murders recorded by Multi-National Forces Iraq, and many murders either were not reported to coalition forces or were not included for one reason or another.[30] The Iraqi Body Count project (IBC) uses press reports to track the deaths of noncombatants, and IBC data document 2,374 deaths perpetrated by "unknown attackers" in Basra Governate (larger than Basra City) over this time period.[31] Although the IBC data and reports are not spatially precise enough to be useful in testing the relationship between Friday mosques and murders, they do suggest the size of the undercount.[32] We will never know how many actual murders occurred in Basra; even Iraqi authorities do not have a full accounting. According to police officials in Basra with whom I spoke in June 2011, no comprehensive murder records exist for the 2005 to 2008 period in the city. And, of course, gangs and militias operating under the guise of the police were responsible for many murders during that period.

But to assess the relationship between mosque location and this indicator of order, we do not need a record of every murder that occurred. This dataset provides a *sample* of murders that occurred, and although we do not fully understand the criteria that determined which murders were reported and which were ignored, there is no reason to believe that those criteria were related to mosque location.[33] The goal here is not to account for all murders that occurred or to fully explain where and why murders occurred; that is a worthwhile but different research endeavor. The sample of murders is sufficient to estimate a basic relationship with a reasonably low risk of making a biased inference.

Figure 5.4 shows the location of the sixty mosques that I identified as holding Friday prayers in Basra in 2003 and 2004 (twenty-nine Shi'i and thirty-one Sunni) and the 1,031 murders in Basra from the SIGACT dataset. Eyeballing the map, no obvious spatial relationship between mosques and murders jumps out. Ethnographic evidence suggests the two are related, but how would we know?[34] Spatial analysis is one way to further identify patterns and explore relationships in the data. In figure 5.5, circles of 0.75 kilometers have been drawn around each of the sixty Friday mosques, and different shades indicate areas that are within only one mosque's catchment area, within two or more mosques (overlapping) catchment areas, and not in any mosque's catchment area. Are murders more common where catchment areas overlap?[35] And how large should we assume catchment areas to be?

The x-axis of figure 5.6 graphs different sizes of mosque catchment areas, ranging from a radius of two hundred meters to sixteen hundred meters. That refers to the radius of the circle centered on each mosque. The two lines show the number of murders per square kilometer in areas within only one mosque's catchment area and in the overlapping area of two or more mosques' catchment areas. For any assumed size of mosque catchment area, the murder rate (by area) is higher where those catchment areas overlap than in places near one and only one mosque.[36]

Although these findings support the argument, we do not have sufficient population or other demographic data for more comprehensive tests. The Oil-for-Food Programme's population data enumerates households, not individuals, and was increasingly inaccurate over time for large parts of Basra because of migration into the city. Although Iraqi censuses are supposed to be held every ten years, the most recent one occurred in October 1997. The instruction form for that census asked respondents for their precise address (boxes 5–9), including neighborhood (*hay*) or quarter (*mahalla*) or district *muqat'a*, zone (*majal*), street or lane (*zukak*), and "house census number."[37] But the dataset released by the Central Statistical Organization does not include those responses; publicly available versions only go down to the district (*qadah*) level, making them unhelpful for spatially precise analyses. A lower-level geographic identifier for the data would be needed. The Ba'th Party archives contain disaggregated data on Basra from October 1984, but population figures from 1984 cannot be extrapolated to 2003. Iran began to deliberately shell the center of Basra City with artillery in February 1984 and continued until 1988.

FIGURE 5.4. Friday mosques and murders in Basra

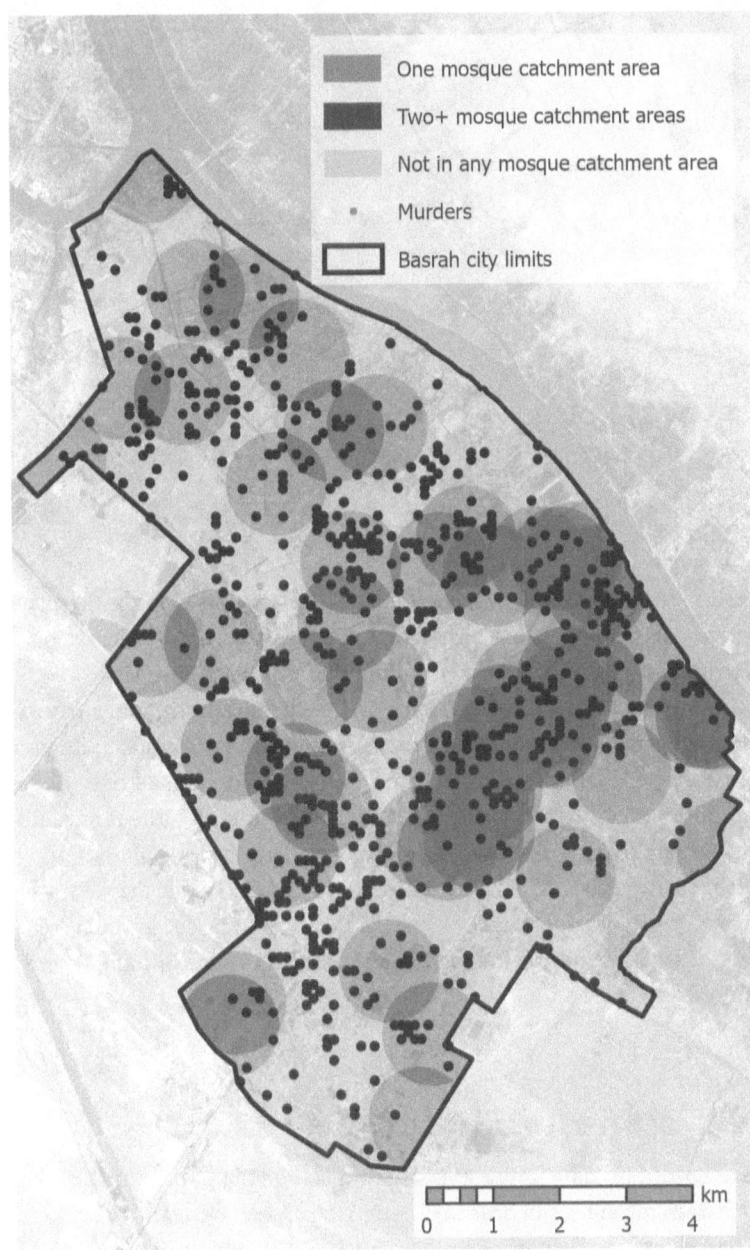

FIGURE 5.5. Catchment areas and murders

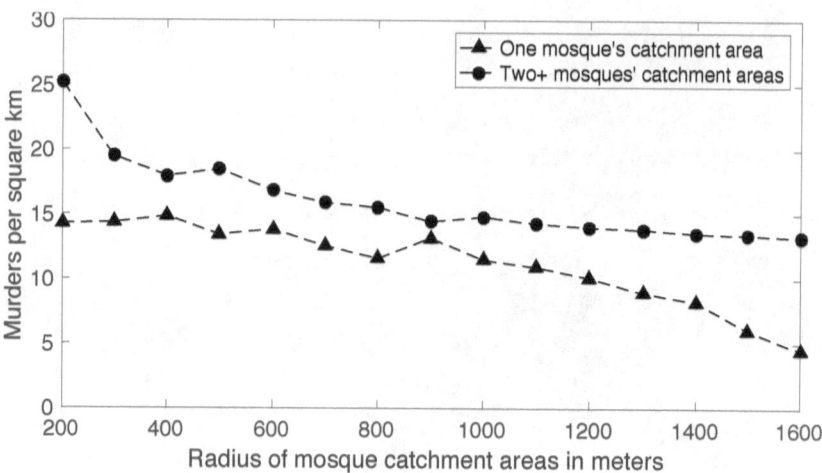

FIGURE 5.6. Murder rates by the size of catchment area

One estimate found that 95 percent of homes, offices, and shops in the city were demolished or badly damaged. The only other available and reliable population data at the district level or lower is from the 1957 census.

Even if we find a statistical association between mosque catchment areas and murders, though, we cannot jump to interpreting that correlation as a causal effect of mosque location on order. Maybe an omitted variable provides some communities forms of solidarity that allow them to both build a mosque and provide order. Perhaps the location of Friday mosques reflects underlying social divisions (which, in turn, affect coordination in a locality), or maybe the building of a mosque by a community is itself a form of public goods provision. This requires us to ask what determined where mosques were built and where they were not.

Basra's Spatial History

Despite significant data limitations, Basra is a good place to study the relationship between mosques and order. Although it has an ancient and illustrious history, Basra in its modern incarnation is a young city; its neighborhoods do not reflect tribal settlement patterns; and central planning diktats, not local influence or social characteristics, determined the location of its Friday mosques.

Basra moved. The original city of Basra is said to have been founded in 638 by Utbah bin Ghazwan, a companion of the Prophet, on orders from Omar bin al-Khattab, the second caliph, on the site of an old Persian settlement about twelve miles to the west of the Shatt al-Arab and the future site of the modern city of Basra.[38] This original Basra was the famed city of Islamic history, which Louis Massignon described as "the veritable crucible in which Islamic culture assumed its form, crystallised in the classical mould, between the first and fourth century of the *hijra* (from 16/637 to 311/923)."[39] In the eight to ninth centuries, Basra was a center of commercial, financial, religious, and intellectual activity. Arab grammar was codified there, and the city was famous for its poets and religious development (Ibadi theology, for example, developed there). Today, little is physically evident of that city: a half dozen tombs, a reproduction of a renowned mosque, and unexcavated ruins adjacent to the town of al-Zubayr, named for the companion who fell just outside of Basra during the Battle of the Camel in the first Muslim civil war (*fitna*) in 656.

The original city of Basra declined because of its location, the rise of Baghdad, and political instability. Insufficient drinking water had always been a problem at the site; Baghdad's expansion under the Abassids led to Basra being eclipsed as a political and religious center; and a series of internal revolts and raids by foreigners and nomads repeatedly ravaged the city. The city's decline was exacerbated after the Mongols entered Iraq in 1258; the Il-khanate government largely ignored Basra, which continued to be plagued by uprisings and raids.

When the famed traveler Ibn Battuta visited Basra in the mid-fourteenth century, he found that the city had shrunk and the population had shifted to the point that the Grand Mosque of Ali, originally in the center of the city, was by then two miles to the west of it.[40] Ibn Battuta continued his journey ten miles east to the bank of the Shatt al-Arab and the village of al-Ubulla, which now sits under or near the 'Ashair district at the heart of the modern city of Basra. The original location of Basra was abandoned around 1397, and a town with the august name developed on the navigable river. Members of the Sadah Bash'ayan family claim that their ancestors, along with the head of the al-Mughamis tribe, led the migration of the old city's population to the new site in 1407.[41] The Ottomans took Basra by 1548, but except when tribal or urban notables became too independent, they paid little attention to the area until the mid-1800s. Throughout the Ottoman era, tribal raids were recurrent, as were malaria and plague.

The modern city of Basra—its urban pattern, streets, public buildings and services—did not truly begin to take shape until after the British occupied the city in 1914. The creation of the port during World War I began the transformation and attracted migrants looking for work. Oil was discovered near al-Zubayr in 1948 and first exported by pipeline in 1951 or 1952, further increasing migration, dramatically expanding the city, and giving it its contemporary shape. The city grew from a population of about 25,000 in 1900 to 200,000 in 1955, to 450,000 in 1977, and over one million by 2000.[42]

All of this is to say that the "old" parts of the city of Basra are not that old, certainly not like Cairo's, Damascus's, Aleppo's, or even Baghdad's older districts. The number and character of Basra's quarters change over time: visitors identified twenty-eight quarters in the mid-1500s; eighty-eight quarters were listed in the census of 1689; and a visitor named seventy-two in 1764.[43] The historian Thabit Abdullah notes, "Interestingly, in both the Ottoman census of 1689 and Niebuhr's list [from 1764], there are hardly any quarters named after a religious, ethnic, or tribal community."[44] In fact, there were two: a Jewish quarter and what might have been a Sabian quarter.[45] Most quarters in the seventeenth and eighteenth centuries were named after a neighborhood notable, usually a religious figure, and several others were named after markets, including the Slave Market (*Mahallat Maydan al-'Abid*). Only a few of those names continue to be used today; the laying down of a modern road network, housing schemes, and public buildings in the twentieth century wiped away many characteristics of the city's historic quarters. The oldest parts of the city are Old Basra and 'Ashair; the former remains largely residential and dense, while 'Ashair has modern homes for the wealthy and a large commercial area. Aside from a few small neighborhoods that essentially were villages surrounded and incorporated relatively untouched by the expanding city—such as Subkhat al-Arab—few neighborhoods in Basra today are characterized by narrow winding lanes and families who have lived near each other for generations.

A 1972 study of urban development in Basra emphasized that "recent development in the city has been almost completely unplanned."[46] The modern city of Basra developed around three centers: Old Basra, about three kilometers west of the Shatt al-Arab; 'Ashair, on the western edge of the Shatt; and al-Maqil, a village 6.4 kilometers north of 'Ashair where the British built a new port in 1914. Development was haphazard; much of it was initially reed huts along the roads connecting those three centers. The layout of today's Basra is largely defined by public housing schemes developed and implemented by officials in Baghdad in repeated attempts to solve the "problem" of housing, settling, and regulating the huge number of migrants to Basra from rural areas, such as al-Amarah and al-Kut. From the 1930s onward, Iraqis flocked from rural areas to Basra and Baghdad for several reasons: British efforts to extend the reach of the Iraqi government empowered sheikhs as landowners vis-à-vis tribesmen; drought made agriculture unsustainable in some areas; and the port and, later, oil revenues created jobs in cities.[47] Iraq rapidly urbanized during this period, despite post-1958 land reforms. The census of 1947 shows that 71 percent of Iraq's population lived in the countryside and 29 percent was urban; the census of 1980 showed those numbers had reversed—by then, only 31 percent lived in the countryside and 69 percent lived in cities.[48] Municipal housing projects have existed in Basra since at least 1931, when local authorities began constructing residences to rent to migrant laborers from the countryside, partly to discourage them from setting up *sarifa* huts.[49] In the 1950s, the Basra branch of the Iraq Petroleum Company (the Anglo-Iranian Oil Company/British Petroleum Company) requested large-scale housing projects for workers.

Large parts of Basra today consist of these planned areas, including Khamsa Meel (1946–1950), al-Jumhuriyya (1951), al-Asma'i (1955–1959), and the enormous project established in 1958 as Hay al-Husayn but known to Basrawis as al-Hayyaniyah, named after the governor at the time, Muhammad al-Hayani.[50] These districts vary in size and density of blocks, as well as whether the state built individual houses or terraced-housing or allocated plots for families to build their own homes. Much of the rest of the city filled in piecemeal, often slowly because speculative investment in land has long been an important part of the city's political economy. The municipality built roads, and neighborhoods gradually developed around them.[51]

I found little evidence in 2003 that neighborhoods could be characterized as being predominantly settled by distinct and meaningful tribal groups. Yet, the stereotype of Hayyaniyah (and other so-called slums or flats) as tribal persists. There are several reasons for this. Although members of tribes may have settled near one another within these projects in the 1950s and 1960s, housing shortages made land very valuable and many families subsequently sold or subdivided their parcels. Rising prices gave families incentives to sell to the highest bidder, often outside of the tribe. Second, some interior roads in these areas are known for the names of tribal elders who once lived there. But those markers do not reflect enduring tribal influence; they merely mark the road on which wealthy or influential people once lived. Finally, tens of thousands of refugees from the southern marshes moved to Basra in the 1990s, but they did not settle together in cohesive areas because of the lack of new projects and dearth of space in existing ones. Clans such as the Albu Darraj, Albu Hamid, and al-Suwa'ad each have hundreds or thousands of members in Hayyaniah, Jumhuriyya, and Khamsa Meel, but they are spread throughout those dense and sprawling neighborhoods and are not concentrated in particular sections of them.

Basra's outward expansion largely ended in the 1980s. Few, if any, new housing projects got off the ground during the Iran-Iraq War. And, writing on post-1991 reconstruction in Basra, Sultan Barakat quotes a senior planner at the Ministry of Local Government in Baghdad: "A decision was taken in August 1988 to limit the size of Basrah to the existing city's boundary and only to develop new zones within this as and when needed."[52] What expansion that did occur in the 1990s seems to have been efforts at Ba'th resettlement schemes. As with elsewhere in Iraq, some Ba'th Party members and retirees from certain military units were given grants of land or the right to purchase land cheaply. This was partly to compensate loyalists during the austere sanctions period, but the regime also likely intended to establish loyalist redoubts near strategic intersections, bases, and public facilities. Although Basra has neighborhoods named for such groups—such as "Neighborhood of NCOs" and "Naval Officers"—these areas often have more undeveloped plots than occupied homes, and many of the grantees seem to have sold their plots or the rights to their plots to persons not in the group. These neighborhoods were "Ba'thi" in name only.

One important result of this pattern of urban development is that Basra has relatively few Friday mosques for a city of its size; most mosques date from the late twentieth century and were built according to central planning guidelines.[53] Since Shi'a did not traditionally attend Friday prayers, there was no need to reserve space for large Shi'i mosques. This partly explains why, under the Ba'th, many of the sole Friday mosques in almost homogenously Shi'i areas were for Sunnis. Before 2003, Friday prayers at these mosques might have consisted of only the Sunni imam and a few custodians. After 2003, several of these mosques were taken over for Shi'a to use.

Few of the city's mosques are old. A visitor to eighteenth-century Basra found ten large mosques and over forty smaller ones.[54] A 2006 book on Basra's mosques and my fieldwork suggest that few of those survive today.[55] Basra's older mosques, situated along east-west roads or near the creeks jutting into the city, were torn down in the early twentieth century to make way for wider roads and modern buildings. One notable and conspicuous exception is the circular tomb of Sheikh Muhammad Amin al-Kawaz, the head of the Shadhili Sufi order who died in 1547, which sits in the center of one of Basra's main thoroughfares. Only a handful of religious buildings in the city are more than a century old, such as the Maqam Ali (said to contain Ali's footprint) and the tomb of a son of the seventh Imam.

Many of Basra's mosques were damaged or destroyed during the Iran-Iraq War, and postwar reconstruction was headed by the Supreme Committee for the Reconstruction of Basrah and Fao, established by presidential decree and headed by Saddam Hussein himself.[56] A 1989 postage stamp commemorating the completion of the Basrah Re-construction Great Campaign shows Saddam (with a holstered gun on his hip) using a shovel next to a nearly completed project. The stamp accurately reflects the extent to which planning and reconstruction under the Ba'th was a top-down process. The same thing occurred after the 1991 war, when the Reconstruction Supreme Committee oversaw individual ministries repairing buildings in their charge.[57] Even after the regime stopped investing significant resources in Basra in the 1990s, residents were not permitted to repair or build mosques without permission.

The Baʿth carefully controlled who was allowed to build, rebuild, or even rename a mosque. Permission needed to be obtained from the Ministry of Endowments and Religious Affairs, and the individual would be vetted by the local party branch and security services.[58] After passing a background check, a few individuals were given permission to build private mosques, but these rarely operated as Friday mosques. Importantly, the regime did not allow communal funding of mosque construction, presumably because the regime wanted it to be clear whom to hold responsible if the mosque was used for unauthorized activities.[59]

In general, the locations and building of Friday mosques in Basra were planned in Baghdad without input from citizens or much consideration for need. The planning and building was overseen by the central Ministry of Endowments and Religious Affairs in cooperation with the Department of Local and Regional Planning in the Ministry of Local Government.[60] Few Friday mosques were built by the Baʿth regime (although they allowed several Sunni mosques in Basra to be built or started after the commencement of the Faith Campaign in 1994); one official in the Awqaf Directorate in Basra in 2004 told me that Saddam built only three mosques in Basra during his reign. Friday mosques, therefore, do not reflect neighborhood characteristics.

Unlike Friday mosques, however, non-Friday Sunni mosques and Shiʿi hussainiyas might reflect demographics and other social characteristics of a locality. Sunnis have Friday mosques (*jawamiʿ*) and mosques in which Friday prayers are not held (*masajid*). Shiʿa in Iraq have non-Friday houses of prayer called hussainiyas. Many Shiʿa go to hussainiyas for their thrice daily prayers, but Friday sermons are reserved for the much fewer *jawamiʿ*. Hussainiyas play special roles during the commemorations of Ashura and can serve as tribal or party gathering places, but they otherwise serve a similar purpose as *masajid* and are important places for Iraqis to hold a fat-ha, a three-day reception or wake where people go to express condolences to the deceased's kin. Traditionally held in temporary tunnel-shaped tents outside homes, the proliferation of hussainiyas in post-Baʿth Iraq quickly brought the fat-ha to more comfortable indoor surroundings.

Few hussainiyas existed in Basra under the Baʿth, which rarely gave permission for them to be established. In the months after the invasion, however, dozens were established in the city for a wide variety of reasons. Most often, a prominent individual built or designated an existing building as a hussainiya. In several cases, a building with disputed ownership or inheritance was turned into a hussainiya by a party to the dispute. This might entail as little as hanging a banner or sign and designating places for ablution and prayer. Some buildings were later converted to other purposes. Other hussainiyas were built by sheikhs to be tribal gathering places. Political parties and militias expropriated a number of homes of Baʿthists and converted them into hussainiyas for their own use;

one such building was around the corner from my house in Basra and was reportedly used by Ali Hassan al-Majid, also known as "Chemical Ali."

The existence of multiple hussainiyas in an area might reflect underlying social divisions, but the number of hussainiyas in an area appears to be unrelated to the number and locations of Friday mosques. Unlike with mosques, there is no formal oversight of hussainiyas by either the Directorate of Religious Endowments or the marjaʿiyya. Men may gather and gossip in hussainiyas, but this is insufficient for the dissemination of common knowledge and widespread coordination.

Sectarian Distribution: A Missing Factor

Much research associates higher levels of ethnic diversity with lower provision of public goods.[61] The informational approach presented here offers an underlying mechanism for such a relationship and suggests that some types of diversity should have greater negative effects on the provision of public goods than other ones. Sunnis and Shiʿa in Iraq do not dislike mixing, and they could have coordinated behaviors and provided low-cost public goods for mutual benefit (e.g., trash collection, order and safety, reliable supply of water). Instead, Sunnis' and Shiʿa's reliance on sermons from different mosques for common knowledge and behavioral norms suggests that we should see less coordination and social sanctioning across these groups, especially if neighborhoods are sufficiently diverse.[62] Ethnic or religious differences that do not affect Friday mosque choice, such as tribal divisions or which marjaʿ is followed, should have less of an effect on neighborhood-level coordination. But a relatively homogenous Shiʿi neighborhood with two Friday mosques should have similar low levels of public goods provision as a neighborhood roughly split between Sunnis and Shiʿa with either one Friday mosque (either Sunni or Shiʿi) or one Friday mosque for each community. Other social divisions, such as tribal allegiances, ethnic affiliations, or regional affiliations, should not influence the provision of public goods because they do not affect mosque choice.[63]

The Limits of Sermon-Based Social Orders

Sermon-generated social orders were constrained by two factors: the set of behaviors on which local preachers could induce compliance and the geographic catchment areas of individual mosques. In October 2003, Basra's deputy governor for local government told me that after the war, more than 120 local councils were set up in Basra City and were "largely self-forming."[64] He thought some of the councils were nominally elected by locals but implied that others were set up by political parties or mosques. Could sermons generate order in a neighborhood that might develop into or spawn formal governance structures that municipal authorities could interact with or even incorporate? Can a "state" be stitched together from the fabric of mosque catchment areas?

Figure 5.7 shows the location of Basra's Friday mosques and divides the city into polygons depicting the areas closest to each of those mosques. These shapes, known as Thiessen polygons, compose a Voronoi diagram of the city based on mosque location. Local councils presumably would need to represent mutually exclusive territories and cannot geographically overlap. Figure 5.7 is a geography of institutional Islam. Figure 5.8 overlays that Voronoi diagram of exclusive Friday mosque territories with the boundaries of the 120 local councils that continued to exist, at least on paper, as of February 2004.[65] There is no correspondence between mosque location and the councils that allegedly emerged spontaneously. In fact, almost none of them appear to match any Friday mosque's exclusive territorial zone.

Why could the local orders generated by mosque sermons not develop into formal governance structures, ones that might be "visible" to municipal planners and provide the backbone for larger districts and even citywide order? Why did it not scale up? There are several reasons. First, these local orders did not need to formalize to achieve much local success. Mosque-centered coordination was a self-enforcing equilibrium: it did not require the creation of external enforcement or sanctioning to induce compliance. And formalization might have been resisted. Preachers would be reluctant to attempt to formalize this order because doing so could reduce their power and undermine the very reasons that they were influential in the first place (people listen and obey because they have come to expect that others will listen and obey). Finally, mosque catchment areas rarely correspond to roads and state-drawn neighborhood boundaries. They are oddly shaped and cut across infrastructure.

In early 2004, the Research Triangle Institute's (RTI International) Local Governance Program, funded by USAID, attempted to fashion a pyramidal system of local government in Basra. They started with a spatial grid of the city and an intention to form neighborhood advisory councils (NACs, *majales al-hayy*), which would then be aggregated up into district advisory councils (DACs, *majales al-qat'a*) and a Basra city council (*majlis al-baladiyeh*). An institutional geography of Islam made little sense as a map of neighborhood boundaries to RTI's municipal planners. They understood infrastructure and physical manifestations of neighborhood boundaries; they could not even imagine a delineation of space based on

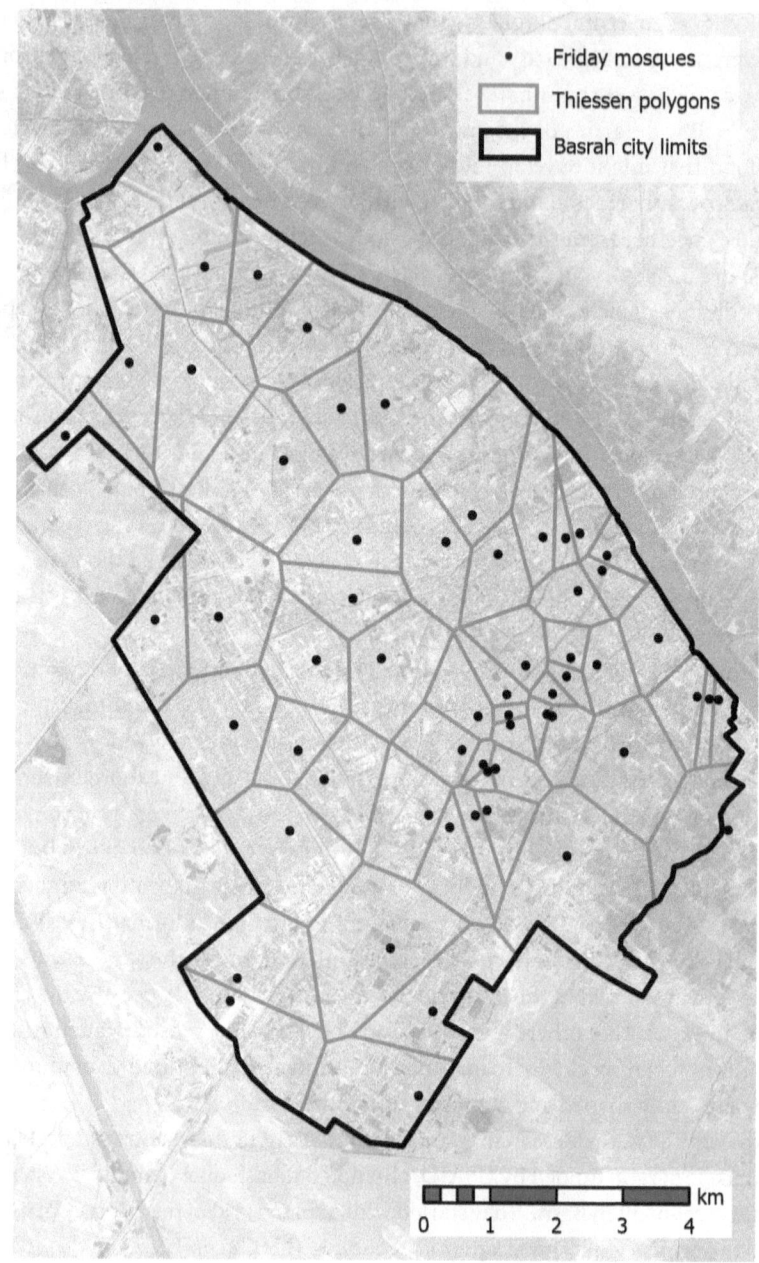

FIGURE 5.7. Dividing Basra by Friday mosques

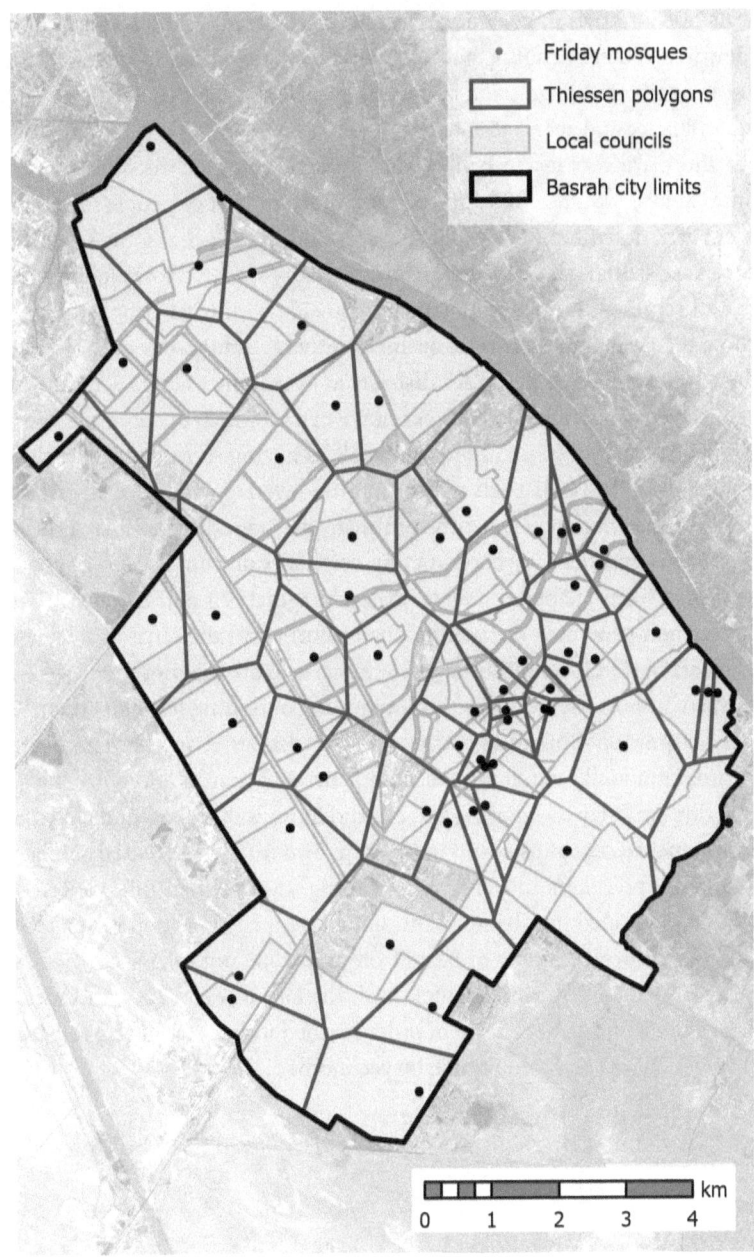

FIGURE 5.8. Friday mosques and local councils

patterns of coordination generated by sermons. Instead, militias and local notables dominated these fledgling NACs because they were a way to interact with coalition and military officials and because they believed that they would eventually lead to influence and access to money.

But there are reasons to believe that a partitioning of the city into Friday mosque "zones" would have captured an important part of people's lived grassroots experiences, if not their explicit understandings of geographic space. Social processes are spatial, but they also are productive *of* space.[66] How planners design space and represent it on a map may not coincide with what people do in space and how they imagine their relationship to others. In his work on how a city is perceived, Kevin Lynch describes districts as "medium-to-large sections of the city, conceived of as having two-dimensional extent, which the observer mentally enters 'inside of,' and which are recognizable as having some common, identifying character."[67] Those districts may or may not overlap with other districts, and they may or may not coincide with administrative boundaries. The relative locations of Friday mosques, by coordinating neighbors on conventions and ways of doing things, likely shaped residents' spatial imaginations of their city.

But sermon-generated orders remained informal in the sense that they were based on self-enforcing equilibria; conventions held because once they were were established, almost everyone had an interest in continuing to follow them. They were geographically limited to catchment areas. In Basra, an alternative form of social order gradually supplanted sermon-generated coordination. Roving gangs and religious militias could grow and expand in ways that geographically bound sermon-generated groups could not. Gangs and militias threatened or assassinated many preachers in the city—including several I had interviewed—and intimidated, defeated, or absorbed mosque-based neighborhood groups. Gangs and militias controlled much of Basra from mid-2006 until the security services of the central Iraqi government took back the city in early 2008 in Operation Charge of the Knights. One form of order reached its limits and was replaced by another, which was replaced in turn by yet another.

6
AYATOLLAHS' NETWORKS AND NATIONAL AUTHORITY

Why was Shi'i political identity both salient and relatively cohesive in post-Ba'thist Iraq while Sunni Arabs remained fractured? Why was it Ali Sistani and Moqtada al-Sadr who unexpectedly emerged as Iraq's most influential political entrepreneurs, instead of richly endowed elites, both religious and secular? The answer to these questions lies partly in the past; the rise of religious actors and the saliency of sectarianism postinvasion have roots in changes in Iraqi society in the 1991 to 2003 sanctions era. But those roots grew in particular ways because of Iraqis' need to order their world after the state collapsed and the tools they used to do it. The distribution and control over information at and then above the local level is a missing factor. Some postinvasion political organizations were able to coordinate Iraqis beyond localities while others were not.

Recognizing the influence of local preachers, a number of political entrepreneurs tried in mid-2003 to organize messages across mosques. Two Shi'i clerics—Grand Ayatollah Sistani and the much more junior Moqtada al-Sadr—were particularly successful. Sunni clerics and other Shi'i clerics, including several other grand ayatollahs, were less successful. Imams and preachers in Shi'i mosques are part of preexisting hierarchical networks connecting grand ayatollahs to their followers. These networks allowed the most senior ayatollahs to disseminate similar messages reliably and consistently in different mosques, generating common knowledge and shared behavioral beliefs across geographically dispersed Shi'i congregations within each network. Shi'a know that other Shi'a living far away but attending mosque sermons within the same ayatollah's network will know what they know on particular topics, a key feature of sharing an identity and imagining being part of a community. This common knowledge allowed Shi'a to coordinate together and act collectively above the local level on national-level issues such as electoral strategies and constitutional bargaining positions. It helped augment Sistani's authority, which was critical as he moved away from an established tradition of relative clerical quietism.

Sistani and Sadr emerged as Iraq's most prominent political entrepreneurs because they controlled Iraq's two largest clerical networks. From late 2003 until February 2006, Sistani coordinated Shi'a on a number of stances regarding post-invasion political processes while under occupation, including the November Fifteenth Agreement, the Transitional Administrative Law (Iraq's interim constitution), the desirability of UN involvement, and electoral strategies. His network coordinated voters on one electoral list for parliamentary elections in January and December 2005, which inadvertently made sectarian divisions more salient in Iraqi politics by creating incentives for Shi'i parties and political figures to cling together electorally instead of competing against one another in cross-sectarian electoral alliances. But Sistani did not tell Shi'a how to vote in governate council elections held concurrently in January 2005, resulting in a wide disparity in vote fractionalization in Shi'i areas across the two January elections. His authority also was limited to instances of inducing followers to engage in low-cost endeavors.

Moqtada al-Sadr, despite being a twenty-nine-year-old seminary student in 2003, controlled a sizable remnant of his late father's clerical network, which he tried to use to mobilize Shi'a attending affiliated mosques on joint positions of nonparticipation and resistance to the political process. But Sadr overreached by calling on congregations to go beyond low-cost endeavors and to engage in costly actions, such as boycotting the inchoate government and resisting occupation authorities. This undermined his authority to induce coordination, such as his call to support a shadow government to occupation authorities. He came to rely more on his militia to coerce compliance. Sistani's influence was damaged in mid-2006 after his calls to end sectarian violence went unheeded, and he consequently sought to preserve his remaining authority by being more selective about his interventions and calls for action, until political and security crises in 2014 brought him back to prominence. Other ambitious Shi'i clerics, including some with sizable followings, did not control large clerical networks and lacked an analogous ability to get Iraqis to coordinate together.

Sources of Clerical Authority

Grand ayatollahs hold a special position in the Usuli Twelver Shi'i religious landscape. They are uniquely empowered religious authorities charged with elucidating God's laws for the untrained laity, who according to doctrine are supposed to follow their rulings. History and tradition, particularly in Iraq, grants grand ayatollahs a cultural capital and emotional currency that makes their messages resonate with followers. Yet the emotional and symbolic aspects of their authority are insufficient to explain when and how their authority expands to encompass new issues as well as the limits on that expansion of authority. In 2003, there was a long tradition—dating from 1925 and particularly pronounced since 1969—of the Najaf marjaʿiyya remaining apolitical and restricting the writ of clerical authority to ritual and transactional rules. In late 2003 and early 2004, Sistani dramatically and surprisingly expanded the set of issues on which Najaf's most senior clerics might intervene. If Sistani was a traditional authority in a Weberian sense, his authority should have been limited by the tradition that legitimates it. How did this expansion of authority come about, and what were the limits—if any—on that newly augmented authority?

According to the perspective developed in this book, grand ayatollahs' messages are influential not solely due to their standing and preexisting authority. Instead, Sistani's authority was reinforced and augmented by his ability to issue messages in such a way that they influence listeners to coordinate with one another. It is widely acknowledged that a grand ayatollah's mandate comes from the laity.[1] But the informational argument implies that the standing of a grand ayatollah is not just about the relationship between an authority and an individual who looks to him for guidance. Instead, it is just as fundamentally about the relationship between people who need to reach agreement and their reliance on a source to provide cues that help them know what others know. The relationship between clergy and laity is a circular one. The sermon generates common knowledge, but the sermon is geared toward the audience and what messages they need to hear to solve the problems they want to solve. In some regards, the audience determines the common knowledge that they seek and could receive. Authority, including in a Weberian framework, is often understood to imply acquiesce, an unconditional compliance with a legitimate superior. Here, however, it is a different sort of belief system—one based on common knowledge and beliefs that others will follow messages from a source—that not only socially legitimates the exercise of control but actually constitutes it.

The ability of religious authority to expand to new domains is rooted partly in a belief by each follower that a sufficient number of other followers will obey an injunction, often making obedience a best response for the individual.[2] As Iraqis saw other Iraqis following religious authorities' statements and rules, they formed expectations that others would also follow future statements and rules. Religious authority expanded into a sort of political authority; an authority became more authoritative.

An implication of the information approach, however, is that this expansion of authority has limits, and those limits are determined not by topic (e.g., ritual and transactions versus political) but by cost to the follower of following any particular edict. Grand ayatollahs' messages were not able to resolve costly free-rider problems among followers; their influence was limited to coordination dilemmas and low-cost edicts. Even if a follower knows that a message is common knowledge and expects others to act on it, it might not be in their interest to act on it—if, for example, participation was sufficiently costly and they could benefit from others' participation without doing so themselves. In such a case, the follower would not follow; they would not act on the message.

Restrained Authorities

According to Usuli doctrine, every follower (muqallid) of Sistani—which includes the overwhelming majority of Iraqi Shi'a—is religiously obligated to follow his rulings. When, however, does Sistani (or any grand ayatollah) choose to issue an edict? Western journalists often incorrectly refer to any message from an ayatollah's office as a fatwa, but the vast majority are not fatwas.[3] A grand ayatollah seeking to influence Muslims has four options. First, he could issue a *hokm*, a supreme edict that all Shi'a—including other mujtahids!—are obligated to follow.[4] Second, he could issue a fatwa, which his followers—and only his followers—are technically obligated to follow. Third, he could issue a *bayan*, an advisory opinion that is meant to guide his followers but is not strictly obligatory. Fourth, he could choose not to issue a written opinion but instead use his network to merely disseminate or suggest his preferences. In practice, the trump *hokm* is almost never used. Fatwas are also relatively rare, and grand ayatollahs frequently attach provisos or word them in such a way that followers can avoid the obligation if they so choose. Followers do not always follow fatwas, and, partly due to technological changes and the wide spread of literacy, some people argue that fatwas do not retain the binding power they had in prior centuries. Advisory *bayans* are more frequent, as are unwritten communications through a cleric's network.

Each grand ayatollah sits atop a hierarchical network that is in competition with other ayatollahs' networks for followers and religious taxes. Ayatollahs, therefore, are careful not to issue rulings that followers might not follow. If followers see other followers *not* obeying an ayatollah's command, it weakens the authoritativeness of his authority by lowering his followers' expectations that other followers will obey his rulings in the future. One becomes a grand ayatollah by attracting followers: the mandate comes from the laity. If followers stop following a grand ayatollah, his standing decreases. From this perspective, we should expect grand ayatollahs, even the most senior ones, to be hesitant to issue rulings that require people to make costly sacrifices. Instead, their rulings are more likely to focus on resolving coordination dilemmas and demanding only low-cost actions.

There is evidence that even the most influential grand ayatollahs worry about being disobeyed or losing followers. Grand Ayatollah Abu al-Qasim Khoei (1899–1992), the most prominent Shi'i cleric in Iraq after 1970 and the most followed globally, ruled that women should cover their faces. But he also said that his female followers were free to follow a different marja' on this one issue, which allowed any who preferred not to cover to heed Grand Ayatollah Ruhollah Khomenei's less restrictive ruling that women do not need to cover their faces. Khoei refused to declare jihad during the 1991 uprising against the Ba'th regime. Apologists say that he feared that most Shi'a would not participate, which would make them sinners if he had issued such a fatwa (the expected response by the Ba'th also clearly played a role in his calculations). Similarly, Grand Ayatollah Muhsin al-Hakim supposedly told Khomeini in 1965 that the people would not obey if the ulama called for rebellion.[5] Ayatollahs fear noncompliance by followers and strive to avoid putting them in situations in which they would choose to disobey. Followers are free to change their marja', and even the acknowledged head of the hawza can face potential challengers to his authority.[6] When al-Hakim (finally) issued his anticommunist fatwa in 1960, the second-most-senior grand ayatollah in Najaf at the time rejected it and argued that communists must still be treated as fellow Muslims.[7] Sistani lost hundreds of thousands of Iraqi followers in the late 1990s to the populist Grand Ayatollah Mohammad Mohammad Sadiq al-Sadr, who issued rulings and statements on contentious issues such as the compatibility between Islam and tribal customs.[8] Clerics might avoid controversial rulings, especially ones they know would be unacceptable to some followers. Grand Ayatollah Bashir al-Najafi, for example, has avoided addressing the issue of sayyids marrying non-sayyids, a controversial issue in Pakistan where he has many followers. Conveniently, clerics find such issues not so important to directly address.

Most mujtahids from Najaf's hawza disapprove of the self-harming rituals—which include flagellation and cutting of one's forehead—that occur during some Muharram processions (Shiraziyyin clerics, discussed later, often de facto support them). Yet, those Najaf-trained mujtahids refrain from officially condemning these rituals, for good reason. An early twentieth-century ayatollah from Najaf was attacked by his own followers when he spoke against it.[9] Similarly, many fatwas are worded in such a way that they do not bind followers to take costly actions. For example, regarding smoking, Sistani says that smoking is not forbidden per se, but any Muslim who knows that it is harmful to his or her health should refrain from smoking *unless* the harm in quitting is greater than the harm in continuing, or "the great difficulty that he will face in quitting is such that it cannot be normally tolerated."[10] Sistani's defenders would say that this judgment was arrived at by sustained engagement with religious sources or that it was based on current conditions (the "reputation of Islam" is often a consideration). There is truth to that. But Sistani's semantic gymnastics permit a follower to both smoke without violating the ruling and know that other followers know that smoking is permitted under conditions that no one except the smoker can judge. In contrast, an inflexible prohibition on smoking would be ignored by many, and followers, if and when they saw other followers ignore it, would know that others do not always expect commands to be followed.

Thus the authority of Shi'i clerics is self-fulfilling. It might appear that grand ayatollahs' fatwas are always followed, but this is at least partly because they tend to only issue those they are confident will be obeyed. The senior clerics in their network are their eyes and ears to ascertain what orders followers will and will not follow. Ayatollahs might issue fatwas when coordination is the issue, but they rely on *bayans* or informal messages if there is a sufficiently high probability of being ignored or of free riding by followers.

Successful clerics—both local preachers and grand ayatollahs—recognize and respect the limits of their influence. In uncertain situations, they might push— or test—the scope of their authority. But they would be wise to avoid issuing edicts that, if disobeyed, would result in lasting damage to their credibility. Since authority is self-fulfilling, those who do not recognize the limits of their authority lose what authority they have. In a 2014 interview with Reuters, Farhan al-Sa'adi, a cleric and professor in Najaf, described the reluctance of clerics to involve themselves directly in politics by recalling a scene from *Don Quixote*: "A ruler, the knight in the Cervantes novel tells his squire, should not make too many decrees, and those he does should be well-considered." Sa'adi elaborated, "If the *maraji'* as a group or any religious figure intervened in every crisis—about energy, about borders—they would turn into mere politicians."[11] What observers call a tradition of "quietism" in Najaf can be understood partly as a strategy to preserve authority. As we will see, when the Ba'th-era constraints suddenly vanished with the collapse of the state, Moqtada al-Sadr and preachers affiliated with the Sadr movement failed to recognize or respect the limits of their ability to induce compliance via sermons. They repeatedly overreached. Sistani, in contrast, used sermons to gradually coordinate public opinion and ask followers to engage in low-cost behaviors. But he was cautious in not asking his followers to do too much; he did not ask them to engage in costly actions. In early 2006, as the risk of sectarian violence dramatically increased, Sistani reached the limits of how far his authority had been augmented, leading to a retrenchment in how he used his authority in the decade that followed.

The Augmenting of Sistani's Authority

By early 2004, Grand Ayatollah Sistani had surprisingly emerged as the most important political entrepreneur in postinvasion Iraq. This stunned coalition officials, who repeatedly failed to recognize his growing influence in the months after the invasion. According to Larry Diamond, an ORHA employee encouraged Jay Garner to reach out and meet Sistani. Garner reportedly said, "Why? Who is this person?" Similarly, Bremer was "dismissive of Sistani's importance," despite a UN team encouraging him to take Sistani's objections seriously.[12] Analysts and academics were surprised too. Faleh Jabar, one of the leading scholars of Iraqi politics and society, published a timely book in 2003 on the Shi'i movement in Iraq. In it, he mentions Sistani only three times, all in passing: twice in the introduction (written postinvasion, in May 2003), in the context of how Moqtada al-Sadr was challenging his authority; and once more, where Sistani is described as "apolitical" and as having been in a rivalry with Moqtada's father.[13] Linda Walbridge's 2001 book contains one of the few published preinvasion discussions of Sistani. She says, "He is a man totally engrossed in his religious studies who has shunned all involvement in either Iranian or Iraqi politics. He has been portrayed as someone who does not even read the newspaper."[14] This is all to say that Sistani's involvement in postwar developments was unanticipated, and his influence increased gradually after April 2003. As late as September of that year, the International Crisis Group published a briefing, "Iraq's Shiites under Occupation," without mentioning Sistani by name.[15]

Iraqi Shi'a were also surprised at Sistani's shift and growing involvement in new affairs. The views of Ridha, a pious Shi'i in his late thirties in Basra with whom I occasionally discussed religion, are representative of what many Iraqis believed about Sistani in the months before and after the invasion. Ridha kept a small picture of Grand Ayatollah Khoei in his living room. When I asked him in September 2003 whom he follows now, he said, "the maraji' [plural] in Najaf." When I responded that I thought it was obligatory to emulate one marja', he first mentioned Sistani but also mentioned Grand Ayatollahs Muhammad Saeed al-Hakim and Muhammad Fayyad. When I asked him about the role those grand ayatollahs might play in Iraqi politics and the transition process, he confidently explained that the maraji' in Najaf always limit their "guidance and direction" (*irshad wa tawjih*) to ritual and social affairs, never politics. He said (approvingly) that "Sistani does not read a newspaper, he does not watch the television," implying that Sistani viewed such matters as beneath or outside of his concern. This particular conversation occurred four months after Sistani had begun to gradually involve himself in politics, but even at that late date Ridha believed that Sistani's involvement was ephemeral and that he would not—could not—become a player in what would transpire.

Sistani remained true to his quietist reputation and the modus operandi of Najaf's marja'iyya in the immediate postinvasion anarchy. He took—or solicited—questions from followers about events and issued rulings, often giving near-identical responses to similar questions. Although he issued a few fatwas and statements in April and May 2003 on looting, vigilante killings of Ba'thists, and the illegality of militias, Sistani appeared at the time to be following his mentor Khoei's example from 1991. He issued a statement calling on Iraqis not to resist coalition forces, but this appears to have been done in part to supersede a fatwa he had issued in 2002 at the behest of the Ba'th regime calling on Iraqis to resist the invaders.[16]

As described in the preceding chapters, local mosque preachers throughout Arab Iraq restarted Friday sermons in the first weeks after the invasion and began to actively enable and guide coordination and low-cost collective efforts related to the creation of order. On 20 April Sistani cautioned clerics against becoming involved in politics and encouraged them to confine their role to providing "general guidance" to followers. Seeing their effectiveness, though, Sistani gradually began to use his network of preachers to disseminate his own centralized messages on aspects of the transition process. Sistani's son-in-law and chief representative in Iran, Sayyid Jawad al-Shahristani, estimated in 2006 that Sistani had more than two thousand religious representatives (wakils) worldwide.[17] Sistani's agents are experienced, respected in their local communities, and adequately funded: Sistani continued a tradition stemming from a 1981 fatwa by Khoei of allowing representatives to collect religious dues in his name and spend them locally instead of conveying them to Najaf.[18]

Reider Visser identifies 26 June 2003 as the key turning point in Sistani's postinvasion activism.[19] Sistani choose this date, a Thursday, to formally respond to a follower's question about the legitimacy of the occupation authority's plan to appoint the members of a constitution-writing committee. Sistani's fatwa stated, "Those authorities have no mandate to appoint the members of the assembly charged with writing the constitution," and he called for a general election for all Iraqis to elect members to write the constitution. He added that "all believers" should insist on such a process.[20] As with many of his fatwas and announcements, Sistani released this message on a Thursday, which allowed it to be read in Friday mosques the following day.

Sistani tried to coordinate and mobilize Shi'i opinion on a range of critical postwar issues in the 2003 to 2006 transition period. This chapter focuses primarily on four issues during this period and a fifth one that occurred years later: US-sponsored plans for an unelected assembly to write the Iraqi constitution (the November Fifteenth Agreement); the Kurdish veto clause in the interim constitution (the Transitional Administrative Law); electoral strategies in Iraq's postwar nationwide elections in January and December 2005; how Shi'a should respond to insurgent attacks intended to provoke sectarian conflict; and finally, his fatwa in June 2014 calling on Iraqis to take up arms and fight the Islamic State in Iraq and Syria (ISIS) following the collapse of Iraqi security services in Mosul and ISIS's advance in Sunni-majority governates. This chapter is not meant to be a narrative history of Sistani's involvement in postinvasion Iraqi politics; those books already exist.[21] Instead, it examines a set of cases to show the augmentation of Sistani's authority, its limits, and some of its effects.

Altering the Roadmap of the Political Process

The Agreement on Political Process (November Fifteenth Agreement) between the CPA and the Iraqi Governing Council outlined coalition authorities' vision for an accelerated transfer of sovereignty to an interim Iraqi government by 30 June 2004. It consisted of five provisions, including details on the drafting of a "fundamental law" for Iraq; reaching an accord regarding the status of coalition forces in Iraq; and setting a deadline for reestablishing Iraq's sovereignty.[22] But the most controversial was the provision for selecting a transitional National Assembly. A complex system of caucuses would be selected in each governate by local, district, governate, and national councils. These unelected caucuses would then select each governate's representatives to a transitional National Assembly that would select a transitional government and make a constitution.[23] Sistani opposed the plan after hearing its details, stating that there is no substitute for a directly elected council to draft a constitution.

Sistani had issued a fatwa in June dismissing the legitimacy of any unelected constitutional body, and he reiterated this position in a late October *bayan*.[24] In response to a written question from the *Washington Post* reporter Anthony Shadid in late November, Sistani issued an official opinion calling the November Fifteenth plan illegitimate and suggesting that elections could be held based on UN ration cards.[25] The statement read,

> The [occupation] does not have any authority to appoint the members of the committee to write the constitution. Further, there is no guarantee that such a committee would draft a constitution according to the

supreme interests of the Iraqi people and their national identity, whose main pillars are the pure religion of Islam and noble social values. Hence, the project is categorically unacceptable. There is no alternative to starting with a general election, allowing all eligible Iraqis to elect their representatives to a constituent assembly to write the constitution, which in turn will be presented to the people to vote on it. It is the duty of all believers to demand this process and achieve it in the best manner.[26]

Preachers in Sistani's mosques delivered this message in sermons throughout Iraq on Friday, 28 November 2003, turning Shi'i public opinion against the caucus plan before the CPA and Iraqi supporters could make their case. In the weeks before and the first two weeks after the release of the November Fifteenth Agreement, the overwhelming majority of Shi'a knew nothing about it; those who did know about it expressed a range of opinions from positive to negative. Members of the Governing Council (GC), including most Shi'i members, accepted the broad outlines: they preferred caucuses to facing an Iraqi electorate.[27] In my discussions with Iraqis at the time, some Shi'a mentioned specific people on the GC and said that if they had approved it, the plan must be acceptable. Other Shi'a who opposed the plan suggested a range of alternatives, such as a new (perhaps elected) Governing Council or a mixed transitional National Assembly that is partly elected and partly appointed. I found initial Shi'i opinion on the plan to be all over the map.

Sistani had already stated his opposition—in June and October—to a constitution written by an appointed body, but it was not until sermons on 28 November that Shi'i opinion became entrenched both against the idea of unelected caucuses and for direct national elections for the entire assembly. During my conversations in Iraq after 28 November, Shi'a would respond with the specific reservations and alternative process they had heard in mosque sermons—they had coordinated on Sistani's critiques and alternative plan. For example, they said the resulting assembly might not represent the Iraqi people, a specific concern that I heard verbatim after the sermons but rarely before.

Perhaps to de-emphasize the US role in the constitutional process, Bremer instructed CPA South in December to arrange a nationally televised "town hall" public meeting in Basra to explain the caucus concept and have Iraqis discuss it. The meeting was held on 26 December, and I was able to attend. Afterward I found extremely few Shi'a who had watched it on TV and none who had changed their minds about the caucus plan. In contrast, my Christian and Sunni contacts were more likely to have watched it, and they continued to hold diverse views about the transition plan. The timing and content of the convergence of Shi'i opinion stood in marked contrast to the lack of convergence of opinion among Sunnis and Christians. And none of the Shi'a with whom I spoke saw themselves as having adopted a "Shi'i" opinion. They did not see themselves as choosing things that best served the interests of the Shi'a; they saw those things as being in the best interests of Iraq.[28] Despite this, through late November and December 2003, members of the GC and US officials tried to push ahead with the caucus plan and repeatedly sent dignitaries to discuss the issue with Sistani. A number of the Shi'a on the GC such as Abdul Aziz al-Hakim, Mowaffak al-Rubaie, and Ahmad Chalabi tried to assuage some of Sistani's concerns.

Finally, Sistani's network mobilized tens of thousands of peaceful Iraqis in mid-January 2004 against the November Fifteenth Agreement's caucus plan. On 13 January, Sistani's network released plans for a peaceful "election demonstration" to be held two days later at the mosque of Sistani's preeminent wakil in Basra. Diverse groups of followers from different classes, neighborhoods, ages, and political persuasions received similar messages and plans through their mosques and hussainiyas. Details on what would happen, when, and how were distributed on flyers. The plan was for people to organize locally—outside of Friday mosques, for example—and then move as groups to one of two locations: outside the naval base near the port or at the military hospital. From there, the groups would converge at the al-Abila crossroads and proceed north to al-Abila Grand Mosque. I participated and spoke to numerous Iraqis about the event before, during, and after.

Critically, the cost of participating in this event was expected to be low. We all knew what to expect and were confident that it would be peaceful. The mosque and the route were relatively secure areas, and it was far from any coalition forces or sensitive sites. The flyers and organizers made clear that the event would culminate with a speech by Sheikh Ali Abd al-Hakim al-Musawi al-Safi, Sistani's preeminent wakil in Basra. We knew it would not be an all-day affair and expected it to be the length of and in the style of a Friday sermon. And this was January, far from the unbearable summer heat. For most potential participants, this was a coordination issue: if they thought enough others would participate, they would also participate. One man was explicit about this to me beforehand, saying that this would be his first ever "march" and that he was only doing it because he knew many others were too. If he did not see crowds on the day of the event, though, he said he would return home. Other potential participants were more concerned about the time commitment and the risks of being in a crowd. But since many groups were organized at the neighborhood level, some might have felt pressure to participate. Ridha, mentioned earlier in this chapter, attended as a part of a group organized from his Friday mosque instead of going with me; perhaps he wanted to be seen by them as having participated.

At the designated time on 15 January, small groups converged—as instructed—at the two locations and marched to al-Abila. Along the way, each group carried its own distinct signs and banners, coordinated its own chants, and had its own people (often from a mosque) monitoring their section. The messages were diverse and unfocused: "Yes, yes to marja'iyya"; "Yes, yes to Islam"; "Colonialism is not freedom." Many demanded elections. Pictures of Sistani and other clerics (and a few of the martyr Bint al-Hooda [al-Sadr]) were everywhere. During the march, the Iraqi police—as expected—were out in force. I saw no guns in the crowd, and the only nonpolice armed men I saw were a few guards on top of al-Abila Mosque. During the entire march and subsequent speech, I heard only a single gunshot.

At al-Abila's grand mosque, the crowd spread out surrounding the mosque and quietly sat down and listened to what felt like a sermon from Sistani's wakil, who issued a rousing condemnation of the caucus plan and demanded direct elections. He explained that the November Fifteenth Agreement was hasty and unjust and did not reflect the wishes of most Iraqis. He urged Iraqis to not allow Blair and Bush to select their leaders for them. He demanded open elections and argued that they were feasible.

The crowd was by far the largest Basra had seen since the invasion: the British military—which monitored the event via a helicopter circling nearby—estimated that thirty thousand people attended. That number is large, but about 80 percent of Basra's 1.2 million residents at the time were Shi'a, and the vast majority of them follow Sistani. It was a demonstration of Sistani's authority, but despite the relatively low expected costs of participating, many times more followers stayed home than attended.

The same message with the same specific points was repeated in Friday mosques throughout Iraq the following day, Friday, 16 January. Afterward, this message was repeated ad nauseam to GC members and CPA officials in town hall meetings and forums that had been intended to stimulate public participation and discussion. But Sistani did not call for additional or costlier public mobilizations. Only a few hundred people, organized by the Sadr network, protested in downtown Baghdad the following week. After mid-January's demonstration, all Shi'a in Iraq recognized Sistani's (new, I argue) ability to coordinate public opinion on key issues and induce some followers to engage in peaceful, low-cost demonstrations.[29] This precedent established, they would increasingly look to and act on Friday sermons to coordinate on national initiatives because they expected other Iraqis (but, in reality, only other Shi'a) to look to and act on those sermons.[30]

Larry Diamond, a CPA official at the time, writes, "We understood that Sistani could reach the Iraqi people more rapidly and effectively than could the CPA, with its cumbersome communications machine."[31] He continues by quoting a top CPA governance official, "Our ability to communicate with the Iraqi people is much less than his [Sistani's], and he has the simpler message: 'We want elections.'" Sistani's message was simple, but it is unclear why Iraqis should have preferred that option over others. It was not just the simplicity of Sistani's message and the *who* of the deliverer; it was also the *way* that message was delivered—in a way that rendered it common knowledge among millions. Sistani's preexisting religious authority was expanding in a way that was self-reinforcing.

The TAL and Minority Rights

Sistani also shaped Shi'i opinion of the Transitional Administrative Law (TAL), Iraq's provisional or "crypto" constitution.[32] Kurdish leaders at the last moment insisted on the insertion of clause 61(c), which provided for a veto of a final constitution if two-thirds of voters in at least three governates rejected it in a planned national referendum. Immediately after the GC members unanimously agreed on the text of the TAL, Sistani's office privately rejected the principle behind 61(c) when they learned of it. Sistani critiqued (via proxy) a number of TAL provisions in a meeting between Sistani's son, Mohammad Rida, and GC member Mowaffak al-Rubaie on 3 March 2004.[33] Dramatically, the TAL signing ceremony scheduled for the following day was postponed when five prominent Shi'a on the GC did not show up. These Shi'i leaders, including the leaders of Da'wa and SCIRI, knew that their credibility among the Shi'i public would be damaged if they openly endorsed the TAL and then Sistani's mosques subsequently condemned it and thereby coordinated opinion against it. So they demanded the revisions that Sistani requested, despite having agreed to the text two days earlier. After meeting with Sistani in Najaf on 6 March and promising to fight this clause, the five holdouts agreed to sign. Immediately after the 8 March signing ceremony, Ibrahim Jaafari, speaking for twelve of the thirteen Shi'a GC members, stated Sistani's reservations about the TAL, and 61(c) in particular, pledging they would seek to modify the TAL in the future. Hours later, Sistani's office disseminated a message warning that the TAL hinders the production of a constitution that could "preserve the unity of the country and rights of all the sons of all ethnic groups and sects."[34]

The CPA planned an impressive, professionally managed public relations campaign to "sell" the TAL to the Iraqi public, including via radio and television shows and public service announcements, town hall meetings, thousands of public dialogues led by Iraqi facilitators working for the USAID-funded Research Triangle Institute (RTI International), and billboards. Sistani-affiliated preachers, however, vigorously critiqued the TAL in mosque sermons for several Fridays. They delivered a coordinated message that 61(c) imposed a "tyranny of the minorities" on the Iraqi public and that the TAL was written by an unelected and unrepresentative group of Iraqis. Sistani portrayed the TAL as usurping the right of Iraqis to choose their own constitution. His public statement on 8 March claims that the clause gives a minority the right to block the will of the majority of Iraqis.

Iraqi Shiʻa could easily have adopted a different interpretation of the TAL. For example, many Shiʻa I spoke with at the time strongly supported codifying minority rights; in interviews, several mentioned Baʻthist persecutions of Kurds and Christians (a prominent church in Basra had been closed for years after the regime allegedly killed several members and ordered it shut). Most Shiʻa would have accepted the veto in clause 61(c)—or not even noticed it—if Sistani's mosques had characterized it as an issue of minority rights. Instead, when the topic of the TAL came up, most repeated the message delivered through mosques. One pious Shiʻi I interviewed told me they would publicly oppose the TAL if Sistani said to but revealed that they privately liked it and thought the idea of a veto for the Kurdish governates was a positive development to unify the country. Sistani almost single-handedly shaped Shiʻa public opinion on the most important postwar CPA initiative before Iraqis had even read it. Larry Diamond, a CPA official at the center of drafting and selling the TAL to the Iraqi public, admits that they "lost the initiative to a less technically sophisticated but shrewder, more nimble set of Iraqi opponents, who understood their society and culture to a degree that we never even approached."[35] But what difference did it make? Despite holding such strong opinions on the TAL and seeming to (correctly) believe it would shape the permanent constitution, Sistani did not escalate what he asked of his followers. He undermined the TAL's legitimacy, but ultimately he conceded and accepted that this provisional constitution would not be ratified by an elected assembly.[36] A year after the invasion, Sistani's restraint suggests he understood the limits of how his authority had expanded.

Electoral Coordination in 2005

In January 2005, Iraqis were asked to vote in the country's first free election and decide between hundreds of unknown parties and candidates. Two elections occurred at the same time.[37] The first, to elect the 275 members of the transitional National Assembly, treated the entire country as a single district. The second, to elect a forty-one-member governate council in each governate (fifty-one members for Baghdad), treated each of Iraq's eighteen governates as a single district. In both contests, seats were allocated by party-list proportional representation with no electoral threshold.

Iraqis faced up to three dilemmas: whether to vote and, if so, for whom to vote on each of the two ballots. Academics often describe voting as a costly endeavor, especially if there are security concerns associated with turning out to vote or if it is time consuming to gather information about candidates. For Iraqis who decided to vote, they had to figure out what would be a plausible strategy for making their vote count. Iraqis' previous experience with elections provided little help in resolving these dilemmas. The first direct presidential "election" under the Baʻth was held in 1995 and consisted of a single question: "Do you approve of President Saddam Hussein being the President of the Republic?" At the time, the regime claimed that 99.96 percent of the 8.4 million valid votes cast were marked yes; only 3,052 people were reported to have marked no.[38] Allegedly, 99.47 percent of registered voters voted.

Sistani's mosque network helped Iraqis solve these dilemmas by increasing the expected costs to Shiʻa for *not* voting and provided a way for them to coordinate their votes on one of the two ballots but not the other. Mosques sermons repeatedly told congregations that voting was a religious requirement: one of Sistani's closest aides, Sayyid Ahmad al-Safi, said in an October sermon that anyone who did not vote would be thrown into hellfire.[39] When the Iraqi electoral high commission announced in October that it would open registration centers throughout Iraq on 1 November 2004, Sistani issued a ruling that said, "All citizens, male and female, who are eligible to vote must make sure that their names are properly registered on the electoral register. Whoever has not registered his name or has done so incorrectly must refer to the electoral committee in their area and provide the required documents for registration and/or amendments."[40] Such messages created incentives for Iraqis to register to vote and increased the expected costs of not voting. The risk of hellfire was sufficient motivation for some to vote. And since people knew that voters would be marked in ways such that others would know who had and who had not voted, the messages likely made some Shiʻa decide to vote to avoid possible social disapproval. And this incentive to vote likely increased the more one thought others would vote; it would be embarrassing to be the only one in the neighborhood without a voting mark. Because sermons described voting as a religious duty, many Shiʻa may have voted in order to publicly mark themselves as voters—literally, with purple ink on their fingers.

But for whom to vote in each of the two ballots? Voters in January faced a bewildering set of political entities from which to choose. Ultimately, on the national ballot there were over seven thousand candidates arranged under 111 options: nine multiparty coalitions; seventy-five political parties; and twenty-seven individuals running as independents.[41] The number of options in the governate elections varied, but there were over nine thousand total candidates across those various slates. The vast majority of these options were new and unfamiliar to voters; most of the older and recognizable parties were headed by individuals who had been outside of Iraq for years or decades. This posed a coordination dilemma for Iraqi voters: With so many unknown options, what is a plausible strategy to make your vote "count"? People do not need to have identical preferences to seek to coordinate. Even if people prefer different candidates, they might believe that they have enough in common with others that they would want to agree with them on some electorally viable candidate or slate that they all considered acceptable. Proportional representation systems might exacerbate such coordination problems among voters, particularly in the absence of any electoral history.[42]

Sermons helped Iraqi Shi'a strategically coordinate on one of their two votes. Sistani either formed or encouraged the major Shi'i parties to form a de facto unified Shi'i electoral list—which became known as the United Iraqi Alliance (UIA)—to contest the National Assembly election.[43] Parties and organizations and individuals who needed votes from Shi'a knew that Sistani's mosques would tacitly endorse the UIA list and, therefore, that remaining outside of it would be electoral suicide if voters indeed coordinated their votes on it. Until it became evident that Sistani would intervene in the election in this way, several Shi'i Islamist parties were exploring alternative nonsectarian electoral coalitions. Ali Allawi claims that Adel Abd al-Mahdi of SCIRI preferred a coalition with the secular INA and Kurdish parties, effectively recreating the "grand coalition" of the GC. He writes, "Sistani's decision to back the UIA essentially put paid to any alternative political proposal, and the main Shi'a parties scurried to join the deliberations for the new alliance."[44] The expectation that Sistani would coordinate voters drove Shi'i politicians to be politically Shi'i. In total, 228 candidates joined the UIA, including many Kurdish Shi'a outside of the Kurdistan Region.[45]

Although Sistani never issued an official written endorsement of the UIA, his mosque preachers clearly campaigned for the list and gave Iraqis the impression he had endorsed it. Sistani's visage appeared on UIA campaign posters, and three of his clerical deputies were candidates on the slate.[46] On the Friday before the election, Muhammad al-Basri, the preacher in Basra's al-Hakimiyya Mosque, told his congregation, "The marjayia composed and support a list, the United Iraqi Alliance, which carries the number 169, which carries the candle symbol. Did anyone not hear me? I want this word to reach even to the outside loudspeakers, so no one will be able anymore to say it is a lie. And I don't want to hear that the marjayia didn't support this list."[47] He told the congregation what times the polls open and close, what the identification requirements were, and how to check the proper box. The preacher also tried to create social sanctions for voting for Ayad Allawi's nonsectarian and secular Iraqi List, which was considered the UIA's main challenger. He implied that Allawi was trying to bribe voters by raising salaries immediately before the election. Imam al-Basri said, "No one knows when he will die—he might die at any moment. What will he say to our God? 'I voted for a certain list because they gave me money'? How can he face God with this answer?"

After hearing such a message, and knowing that so many other Shi'a (both neighbors and distant others) heard the message, a Shi'i might be embarrassed to tell others that they voted for Allawi's list. They certainly would not justify their vote by their recent raise. If they had voted for Allawi or another list, then when talking to people whom they knew had heard Sistani's call (i.e., other Shi'a) they might lie and say that they had voted for the UIA. From such clerical messages, Iraqi Shi'a coordinated on the UIA, even though many of them may have preferred to coordinate with other Iraqis—both Shi'a and non-Shi'a—on a different candidate or party or coalition of parties. Sistani's coordination of Shi'i voters on the UIA contributed to sectarianism in post-2003 Iraqi politics.

Sistani's mosques, however, did not endorse candidates for the governate council elections held at the same time. Shi'a did not have common knowledge, therefore, about how others (Shi'a or non-Shi'a) would vote on the governate council ballot. If Shi'i voters were able to coordinate with other Shi'i voters on national but not governate elections, we would expect to see a more fractionalized vote in the latter elections in Shi'a-majority areas, despite their being held on the same day and containing many of the same parties. We also would expect the vote in both elections in Sunni Arab–majority governates to be more fractured than the national vote in Shi'a-majority areas, and there is no reason to expect Sunnis to coordinate better on either election, which suggests the vote fractionalization for both elections should be similar in Sunni-majority areas.[48]

Although reliable data on sectarian population by governate are not available, Iraq's southern nine governates are overwhelmingly Shi'a, the central five are predominantly Arab Sunni, and the northern three are overwhelmingly Kurdish. Baghdad is mixed. Figure 6.1 shows Iraq's eighteen governates.

A commonly used measure of vote fractionalization is the "effective number of parties" by vote share (ENPV).[49] ENPV captures how dispersed votes are across parties—essentially, the extent to which voters coordinated. A low ENPV indicates greater vote coordination. If everyone voted for the same party, the ENPV would be 1. A higher ENPV indicates greater vote fractionalization—a larger number of parties receiving more votes. Table 6.1 displays ENVPs for each of Iraq's eighteen governates for each of the elections held in January 2005.[50]

Shi'a-majority governates did, in fact, exhibit low vote fractionalization in the National Assembly election and a substantially higher vote fractionalization in governate council elections. The Shi'a-majority governates had an average ENPV of 1.71 in the National Assembly elections, and this varied little across governates. This implies that Iraqi Shi'a successfully coordinated, both across and within governates, on the UIA, which captured at least 69 percent of the vote in each of these governates. Yet, those same Shi'a-majority governates had an average ENPV of 7.38 in governate council elections, and the standard deviation of 3.17 indicates that

FIGURE 6.1. Governates of Iraq

these elections varied considerably across governates. That large difference in the ENPV across the two elections in Shi'a-majority governates is striking. Shi'a voted for all sorts of political entities at the governate level, and many people "wasted" their votes by casting them for options with little chance of winning. They failed to coordinate their votes, although this was far worse in some governates (e.g., al-Muthanna) than in others (al-Wasit). Nowhere, however, did Shi'a vote at the governate level with the uniformity that they did everywhere at the national level, despite the elections occurring on the same day with many of the same parties.

Voters in Sunni Arab–majority governates did not coordinate their votes well either between or within governates in either election.[51] Baghdad, with a mixed population of Sunni Arabs, Shi'i Arabs, and Kurds, falls between the two extremes. Shi'a voters in Baghdad, like those elsewhere, coordinated their votes at the national level on the UIA but voted for an array of entities for the Baghdad governate council. Baghdad's vote fractionalization in the National Assembly elections falls between that found in Shi'i-majority and Sunni Arab–majority governates, as expected.

Popular alternative explanations for rising sectarianism in Iraq cannot adequately account for this difference in vote fractionalization within Shi'a-majority governates in January's two elections. If earlier decisions to allocate seats on the

TABLE 6.1. Electoral coordination in January 2005 elections

REGION	GOVERNATE	ENPV GOVERNATE COUNCIL	ENPV NATIONAL ASSEMBLY	DIFFERENCE
South (Predominantly Arab Shi'i)	Basra	6.03	1.87	4.16
	Missan	7.03	1.93	5.1
	Thi-Qar	8.75	1.50	7.25
	Al-Muthanna	14.3	1.60	12.7
	Qadissiya	8.89	1.72	7.17
	Al-Najaf	5.35	1.56	3.79
	Kerbala	7.34	1.87	5.47
	Babil	5.75	1.55	4.2
	Wasit	2.94	1.75	1.19
	AVERAGE	7.38	1.71	5.67
	STANDARD DEV.	3.17	0.16	
Baghdad Center (Predominantly Arab Sunni)	Baghdad	5.18	2.33	2.85
	Al-Anbar	1.80	3.56	−1.76
	Salahuddin	11.2	8.08	3.12
	Nineveh	2.22	3.98	−1.76
	Diala	3.94	3.93	.01
	Al-Tameem	2.51	2.55	−.04
	AVERAGE	4.33	4.42	−.09
	STANDARD DEV.	3.92	2.12	
North (Predominantly Kurdish Sunni)	Dahouk	1.57	1.10	.47
	Erbil	2.31	1.11	1.2
	Sulaimaniya	2.11	1.91	.2
	AVERAGE	2.00	1.37	.63
	STANDARD DEV.	.383	.465	
Out of country voting		NA	4.20	NA
All voters		NA	3.14	NA

Source: Independent Electoral Commission in Iraq.

GC by ethnic affiliation institutionalized sectarianism, if sectarianism was primordial, or if people turned to religion for comfort in the face of instability, why did Shi'a vote together on one ballot but split their votes on the other? And why were Sunni Arabs unable to coordinate their votes at either level?

Perhaps different identities are salient at different levels of politics. A Shi'i voter, for example, might see him- or herself at the national level as a Shi'i but in the context of their governate as a member of a tribe or an advocate for a particular ideology. This might explain some of the difference between national- and governate-level results in Shi'a areas, but it cannot explain why votes were so dispersed at the governate level across otherwise similar political entities. Islamist parties who ran together on the UIA at the national level competed with one another at the governate level, and voters—even those who preferred an Islamist option—failed to coordinate their votes.

Political scientists have argued that electoral coordination can result from cooperation among party elites, even in the absence of common knowledge dissemination. Some Shi'i Islamist parties in Iraq worked together at both the national and governate levels. The various Da'wa factions, SCIRI, and Badr formed unified electoral lists in most southern governates, just as they did nationally. But coordination among party elites was insufficient for voter coordination in the governate council elections. Voters must be taken into account.

By coordinating Shi'a for national elections, Sistani limited internecine fighting among Shi'i parties at the national level and encouraged previously secular politicians, such as Ahmad Chalabi, to portray themselves as culturally Shi'i—and even pious—in order to join the UIA. His coordination of parties and voters on the UIA list dealt a debilitating blow to secular movements in Shi'i areas and hindered attempts to form nonsectarian or cross-sectarian blocs and parties. The UIA list garnered 48 percent of the Iraqi vote, winning 140 of the 275 seats in the National Assembly. Intra-Shi'a politics throughout the south, however, remained highly fractured throughout 2005, in no small part because of the inability of voters to coordinate in governate council elections in January. Partly because of this, governate council elections were not held again until 2009.

Electoral Coordination in December 2005

Sistani initially announced that his network would not formally endorse any electoral list for parliamentary elections in December 2005. Believing that Shi'a voters therefore would be less incentivized to vote uniformly, several prominent Shi'i politicians left the UIA and formed their own lists, including Ahmad Chalabi and Ali al-Dabbah. Afterward, the UIA was composed almost exclusively of Shi'i Islamist movements, parties, and individuals. But as campaigning intensified and Ayad Allawi's secular Iraqi List launched a media blitz, Sistani's clerical network publicly supported the UIA electoral alliance, and Sistani himself issued a fatwa a few days before the election encouraging voters to coordinate. Sistani's fatwa instructs Shi'a that "one must not scatter [or 'disperse', or 'split' (tashtit)] the vote and let it be spent uselessly (ta'riduha li-al-daya')."[52] Elections for new governate councils were not held in December; only the election for the Council of Representatives occurred.[53] ENPV calculations for these elections are displayed in table 6.2.

In December's election, voters in Shi'i-majority governates again coordinated their votes extremely well. Voters largely ignored the parties that had left the UIA to run on different or their own slates and instead voted for the now almost ex-

TABLE 6.2. Electoral coordination in December 2005 elections

REGION	GOVERNATE	ENPV COUNCIL OF REPRESENTATIVES
South (Predominantly Arab Shi'i)	Basra	1.63
	Missan	1.32
	Thi-Qar	1.32
	Al-Muthanna	1.33
	Qadissiya	1.49
	Al-Najaf	1.47
	Kerbala	1.68
	Babil	1.69
	Wasit	1.51
	AVERAGE	1.49
	STANDARD DEV.	0.15
Baghdad Center (Predominantly Arab Sunni)	Baghdad	2.61
	Al-Anbar	1.73
	Salahuddin	5.69
	Nineveh	4.93
	Diala	4.37
	Al-Tameem/Kirkuk	3.08
	AVERAGE	3.96
	STANDARD DEV.	1.57
North (Predominantly Kurdish Sunni)	Dahouk	1.22
	Erbil	1.11
	Sulaimaniya	1.30
	AVERAGE	1.21
	STANDARD DEV.	0.095
All voters		4.03

Source: Independent Electoral Commission in Iraq.

clusively Shi'i Islamist UIA. Turnout was much higher in Sunni-majority governates in December than it had been in those areas in January, but voters in Sunni Arab–majority governates (average ENPV 3.96) again did not coordinate as well as voters in Shi'i-majority governates (average ENPV 1.49). Shi'a voted together, for one list. Sunni Arabs voted this time, but they did not vote together. Sunni votes were split across several electoral lists, including the Iraqi Accord Front, the National Dialogue Front, and the Liberation and Reconciliation list. Interestingly, it appears as though many Kurdish Shi'a living in Baghdad supported the UIA instead of the unified Kurdish list in December.[54]

But perhaps Shi'a knew that they could seize the state if they all voted as Shi'a.[55] At the national level, maybe they care about Shi'i parties winning. This could account for the observed variation in ENPV between governates. This is a less compelling explanation, however, for high ENPV scores in Shiʿa-majority governate council elections in January. In many Shiʿi-majority governates, votes were split between Islamist, regional, class, and tribal lists and candidates. It is unclear why an identity other than Shiʿi did not emerge at this level and lead to a less fractured vote there too. This "strategic identity choice" argument, though, is compatible with the analysis linking mosques and the production of common knowledge and coordination. The difference between the arguments, though, is whether the saliency of Shiʿi identity came first and drove voter coordination, or if it was a by-product of how Iraqis coordinated their vote. Did Shiʿa want to vote only with other Shiʿa to win the state, or did Iraqis want to vote with other Iraqis to make their vote count but did so in ways that reinforced sectarianism?

Sistani's statements and his network's sermons were fiercely antisectarian and consistently emphasized Iraqi national unity.[56] His representatives repeatedly stated that Sistani is a leader for all Iraqis and all Muslims, not just Shiʿa. Yet, his intervention into electoral politics had consequences for the entrenchment of Shiʿa-centric political actors in government and the weakness of nonsectarian and cross-sectarian groupings.[57] One way to interpret this is to see Sistani as acting deliberately to ensure Shiʿi politicians were unified and unified *as Shiʿa* to guarantee that they would win the election. An alternative interpretation is that many of the sectarian consequences of his actions were unintended.

Sectarian Violence and the Limits of Clerical Authority

Sistani and his network of mosques long helped to prevent violence in Iraq from escalating into a large-scale sectarian civil war. Examining these efforts elucidates the limits of what he could get his followers to do. Some insurgent groups, especially foreign and Iraqi jihadists and remnants of the Baʿth Party, tried to provoke retaliation by Shiʿa on Sunni Arabs.[58] This was the explicit strategy of Abu Musab al-Zarqawi, the transnational jihadist who by late 2004 had pledged allegiance to Osama bin Laden and renamed his already-existing organization al-Qaeda in the Land of the Two Rivers. A strategy letter widely attributed to Zarqawi states, "Targeting and hitting them [Shiʿa] in [their] religious, political, and military depth will provoke them to show the Sunnis their rabies ... and bare the teeth of the hidden rancor working in their breasts."[59] In an audio clip released on the Internet, he openly declared a "war on Shiʿa" in September 2005. Groups backed up these statements with action: suicide attacks targeted different Shiʿi towns, tribes, parties, and religious organizations. Numerous Shiʿi institutions and parties were targeted at some point in an attempt to provoke retaliation from Shi'i militias or mobs.

After every prominent attack, mosques in Sistani's network delivered a sermon that emphasized national unity (frequently referring to Sunnis as "brothers"), demanded officials provide security, and condemned any vigilante justice.[60] They publicly forbade militias and mobs moving against Sunnis and told congregations that this played into the hands of Zarqawi and other "strangers." Sistani couched his messages in religious language, calling on Iraqis to follow the Prophet and Imams, challenging the discourse of those using religion to justify violence.[61] Sistani's clerics occasionally marched alongside Sunni clerics in public displays of inter-sect solidarity.

Sistani's messages aimed to create a public consciousness that would decrease the likelihood of Shi'i retaliation. One component of this was to deter existing Shi'i militias from attacking Sunnis by ensuring public opinion would turn against them if they did. Another, albeit related component was to make it unacceptable for ordinary Shi'a to participate in or acquiesce to mob violence against Sunnis, such as what might occur after an attack in a market or during a fat-ha.

The bombing of al-'Askari Shrine in Samarra in February 2006 was either a turning point that triggered Iraq's sectarian civil war or an event that significantly accelerated a civil war that was already underway. The 'Askari Shrine complex contains the graves of the tenth and eleventh Imams; the graves of several of their relatives; and a mosque built over the spot where the twelfth and final Imam, Muhammad al-Mahdi, went into (minor) occultation in 874. The twelfth Imam, Twelver Shi'a believe, remains in (major) occultation—hidden by God from mankind—until the day he returns to reestablish justice on earth. For centuries al-'Askari had been one of the most important Shi'i shrines in the world, a place of pilgrimage, and a center of Shi'i scholarly study and training.[62] Its targeting in February 2006 was a deliberate strike against a central symbol of Shi'i faith, belief, and practice. Several thousand protesters reportedly gathered outside Sistani's office in Najaf and chanted, "God is great! . . . Take revenge, Shi'a, and shed blood in retribution for Imam Ali al-Hadi!"[63]

Within hours of the bombing (early on a Wednesday morning), Sistani's representatives distributed a message urging calm, calling for seven days of mourning, and explicitly forbidding attacks on Sunni mosques. Sistani made a rare appearance on Iraqi television: he was shown meeting with Najaf's other three most senior grand ayatollahs. Despite his repeated calls for restraint and warnings that retaliation played into the schemes of "foreigners," within hours of the bombing dozens of Sunni mosques were attacked—sometimes by militias, sometimes by "police," sometimes by mobs—and dozens to a few hundred

Sunnis were murdered throughout Iraq. In Basra, the offices of the Iraqi Islamic Party were attacked and several members were injured, five Sunni mosques were looted or firebombed, and gunmen bearing Ministry of the Interior intelligence badges entered the al-Mina prison, abducted twelve prisoners accused of being Sunni militants, and executed eleven of them (four Iraqis, seven foreigners).

Why was Sistani unable to prevent the violence from spiraling? He clearly tried. But after the February 2006 attack, the cost of obeying injunctions regarding sectarian violence increased. Militias, previously held in check by public opinion and the expectation of social disapproval, were no longer deterred from engaging in tit-for-tat killings or, in some cases, from seizing the homes and property of Sunnis. By mid-2006, over one hundred Iraqi civilians were reportedly being killed each day in bombings and by death squads. On 20 July 2006, Sistani issued a passionate statement that circulated widely. In it, he said,

> There are no words to describe the gruesomeness and horror of these events and the extent to which they violate all human, religious, and national values. I call on all sincere persons who are zealous for the unity of this country and future of its children, including intellectuals, religious and political leaders, tribal chiefs, and others to put forth the utmost effort in order to stop this serial bloodshed which, if it continues... as the enemies desire, will inflict the most grievous harm on the unity of this people and will stand as a long-term obstacle to the realization of its hopes for liberation, stability, and progress.[64]

Despite messages such as this, the violence continued and worsened.

Even if people believed in Sistani's message, standing up to or openly condemning the militias was dangerous. In response to his call, Shi'a did not, to any notable extent, stand guard at Sunni mosques or in their neighborhoods to protect Sunnis. Congregations did not confront militia members in their midst. Many Shi'a acquiesced to or supported the violence against Sunnis, either explicitly or tacitly. In June 2011, I visited one of the Sunni mosques in Basra that had been damaged in February 2006. Five years later, the al-'Ashira al-Mubashara Mosque was still filled with rubble and unusable; no one had bothered to clear it out. The mosque's name refers to ten companions of the Prophet whom some Sunnis believe were promised paradise during their lifetime. Shi'a reject this tradition and hold several of the ten in contempt. On the lintel and inside the mosque, the names of the first three caliphs—Abu Bakr, Omar, and Othman—had been marked over, and faded pro-Shi'i graffiti remained on the walls from 2006. I asked people in the area about the mosque's desecration. They said militia dressed as police did it and although "it was not right," the events were "part of the mourning process for al-Askariyya [al-'Askari]." When asked why residents had not cleared the rubble or covered the sectarian graffiti, they said it was not their responsibility and that the Sunni diwan should do it.

Some people took violence into their own hands. The 2006 al-'Askari attack triggered demonstrations throughout the country that occasionally turned violent. The day after the bombing, two guards from the Sunni diwan in Basra were killed, allegedly while distributing leaflets during a demonstration expressing Sunni condolences for the attack.[65] For the first time since the invasion, Iraqi authorities issued a daytime curfew, for the Friday after the al-'Askari bombing, preventing attendance at mosque sermons. The clerical establishment did not protest. If Friday prayers had been held, the situation would have required that they deliver sermons urging calm—sermons they knew would be ignored.

Assassinations and retaliatory attacks continued throughout 2006, and Iraq slid into sectarian civil war. In Basra, many Sunnis found written threats slid under their doors, warning them to leave or be killed. Some used the violence to settle old scores; one Sunni in Basra who received such a note told me that he suspected it was from a neighbor who held a grudge against his family. Several Sunni imams were murdered, and in early April, the Basra Sunni Endowment ordered all Sunni mosques in the city to close for two days to protest the violence. The previous week, a Sunni professor in town had been kidnapped and killed; another imam was killed; and a family of six—including a four-year-old—was gunned down in a central marketplace.[66] Sistani repeatedly called for restraint, to little avail.

Regardless of whether February 2006 was a turning point in Iraq's civil war, it was a turning point for Sistani's involvement; Shi'a saw fellow Shi'a ignore an explicit command not to retaliate. Sistani issued a number of statements on violence throughout 2006, calling on all Iraqis to "discard hatred and violence in favor of love and peaceful dialogue."[67] But he could not get Iraqis to take the costly actions that would have been necessary to stop the perpetrators of violence. One of his spokesmen in Baghdad reported that Sistani was very angry that his followers were ignoring his calls. Writing in 2007, Juan Cole says that Sistani "overestimated his ability to keep Shi'ites from taking revenge" and "was unable to do much in subsequent months to stem the rising tide of violence in the country."[68]

Authority Retrenched

As violence continued in 2006, Sistani continued to issue statements about sectarianism, terror, and the link between government corruption and violence on the street. In early September 2006, he reportedly informed members of his clerical network that he was withdrawing from public affairs.[69] Preachers affiliated with him continued to deliver sermons in Friday mosques, but aside from addressing the above topics and a few others, they played a significantly diminished role in coordinating messages across congregations. At the bloodiest height of Iraq's civil war, when the country appeared on the verge of partition, Sistani entered a period of relative isolation that would last until 2008.

There are different ways to interpret Sistani's decision. With the benefit of hindsight—knowing that he would later reengage on a number of issues—it is tempting to say that Sistani shifted from his activist interference because he had achieved in the 2003 to 2006 period his main goals of protecting the hawza of Najaf, safeguarding the interests of Iraq's Shi'a, hastening the transfer of power to a democratically elected Iraqi government, and establishing the role of the marja'iyya as a guiding institution instead of one that seeks to directly govern.[70] The Iraqi parliament had approved Nuri al-Maliki as Iraq's new prime minister in May, and some link this event with Sistani stepping back to give al-Maliki a chance to govern. And it is true that Sistani later intervened in matters that he saw as defending constitutionalism or responding to existential threats to Iraq's state and integrity, but he largely avoided involving himself in party politics and day-to-day administration.

At the time and without knowledge of future events, however, Sistani's diminished profile was dramatic and seemed clearly linked to his inability to stop the violence. In 2007 Juan Cole wrote, "He clearly had concluded that his popularity and authority had declined to the point where he could no longer effectively intervene to shape society, and continuing to issue pitiful pleas for calm that were promptly ignored would have the effect of frittering away what credibility he had left."[71] The information argument developed here sees Sistani's retreat from the megaphone—at a moment when Iraqis clearly needed guidance—as a strategy to preserve what remained of his authority and the marja'iyya's more generally. Two months earlier, when Sistani called on "all sincere persons . . . including intellectuals, religious and political leaders, tribal chiefs, and others to put forth the utmost effort in order to stop this serial bloodshed," people ignored or disobeyed his and his preachers' messages. This raised doubts about whether others would act on those messages in the future, even if they were common knowledge. If people disobeyed him on this issue, might they also disobey him on future ones? Authority is self-fulfilling, and doubts about whether others would obey mosque messages intensified as more messages were ignored. If Sistani faced more credible rivals to his overall authority, he likely would have been even more inclined not to risk damaging his authority. But in 2006 the real risk was making preachers impotent. This threatened to undermine not only Sistani's authority to address national issues but also preachers' ability to coordinate and induce low-cost contributions from congregations to address local issues. Sistani's abrupt decision was a retrenchment.

Sistani's relative disengagement continued from 2006 to mid-2008, when he publicly rejected elements of a proposed status of forces agreement (SOFA) being negotiated at the time between the Iraqi and US governments. There is evidence that two years on, Sistani's messages did not carry the weight that they once did. In November 2008, for example, his preachers called for a referendum on the SOFA. But as Sajjad Rizvi notes, "Little opposition materialized when the referendum did not occur."[72] Sistani remained engaged through the governate council elections held in January 2009, but then he largely withdrew again, until the ISIS threat in 2014.[73] Throughout the period 2006 to 2014 sermons continued and directives were occasionally issued; much of their focus was on government accountability and attempts to stem corruption. In the run-up to 2010 parliamentary elections, Sistani made it clear that he opposed closed lists of candidates. In 2014 he fed anti-incumbent sentiments by recommending that voters "abandon old faces that did not bring anything good to Iraq and replace them with new people."[74]

Sistani's worldview mattered for the content of his interventions, but his willingness to intervene also depended on whether he thought an intervention would be successful—if he could shape events using coordinating or low-cost edicts that people would actually obey—and how any intervention might affect his future influence. Several scholars argue that Sistani was consistent in that he intervened only in matters that affected the structure of Iraqi society or were existential for the state.[75] But identifying such instances is often post hoc. After the March 2010 parliamentary elections, for example, the government-formation process was deadlocked for nine months as two lists struggled over who would be the next prime minister. At the time, the extended impasse seemed like it could bring down the entire postinvasion political system that Sistani had worked so hard to establish. Yet he remained distant. Perhaps Sistani had learned the limits of his influence in 2006, from both his failure to stop the violence and from his limited ability to use public pressure to induce parties to resolve an impasse over a second term for Prime Minister Jaafari. When he decided in July 2014 to involve himself in the debate over whether Maliki should serve a third term as prime minster, Sistani did so through a private letter to Daʿwa Party politicians instead of using sermons to try to mobilize public pressure. His intervention was an important factor in political elites' decision to replace Maliki, but the means he used had changed. Shiʿa clerics can coordinate followers effectively and foster contributions when the actions required impose relatively small costs, but as these costs escalate, the effectiveness of their edicts diminishes. Sistani had learned the limits of his augmented authority, and this realism—along with his ideology and worldview—determined when and how he intervened in Iraqi politics after 2006.

Sistani's "Jihad Fatwa"

Many Shi'a say that they will do "whatever Sistani commands," but for most followers that is only true for commands that entail relatively low costs. Knowing this, Sistani should be reluctant to issue commands that will be disobeyed (those that are sufficiently costly). And, indeed, Sistani was judicious after 2006 in his interventions into the public political sphere. This makes the so-called jihad fatwa of June 2014 a useful case to examine. The collapse of the Iraqi security forces in Mosul on 10 June and the rapid seizure of approximately a third of Iraq's territory by the Islamic State of Iraq and Syria (ISIS, which would rename itself The Islamic State that same month) triggered an unprecedented crisis to which Sistani responded with arguably his boldest fatwa. The following day, 11 June, what has been called Sistani's "jihad fatwa" was posted to his website, and it was read in every Friday mosque in his network on 13 June. Sistani's fatwa is often described as having given rise to the several dozen militia and paramilitary forces collectively known as the Popular Mobilization Forces (PMF), or al-Hashd al-Sha'bi. The fatwa's actual influence, however, is not so clear-cut. What looks like widespread obedience to a high-cost religious command—tens of thousands responding to a call to arms—reveals that the limits to Sistani's authority still hold and that his messages can have unintended consequences.

Sistani's fatwa called on Iraqis to join the Iraqi state security forces for the purpose of fighting ISIS, which obviously entailed significant personal cost and risk. In Friday prayers on 13 June in Karbala, Sheikh Abdul Mehdi al-Karbalai said, "Citizens who are able to bear arms and fight terrorists, defending their country and their people and their holy places, should volunteer and join the security forces to achieve this holy purpose." Karbalai, and the text of the statement that was read throughout Iraq, calls on Iraqis—all Iraqis—to reinforce the security forces and to protect all religious sites, including Sunni ones. The command in Sistani's fatwa was clear and repeatedly emphasized in sermons over the following weeks: it called on Iraqis to join the official security forces—explicitly, not militias outside of state control—and to do so only in numbers necessary to reinforce them. It read, "The number of volunteers does not need to exceed the sufficient force that can accomplish the objective of protecting Iraq, its people, and its sacred places."

In response to the fatwa, thousands—perhaps tens of thousands—of Shi'a were said to have flocked to join the fight. The first thing to note is that millions of fighting-age Shiʻa men ignored Sistani's call. In 2014, approximately 6,331,635 Iraqis were men between the ages of eighteen and forty, and more than half of them were Shiʻa.[76] A conservative estimate puts the number of Shiʻa men in this age bracket who were following Sistani at two million. At best, a small fraction of them joined the fight based on his call. Several Shiʻa from Basra had told me many times over the years that they "would do anything Sistani asked," but none of them joined the fight against ISIS or sent one of their sons to do so. But this is not inconsistent with Sistani's call, which said the obligation to join the formal security forces existed only until they had enough volunteers—a point that was reached rather quickly.

What actually occurred was the (re-)mobilization of several already-existing Shiʻi Islamist militias, including the Badr Organization, ʻAsaʼib Ahl al-Haq, Kataʼib Hezbollah, Harakat Hezbollah al-Nujaba, Kataʼib Sayyid al-Shuhada, and the latest incarnation of Moqtada's Mahdi Army, now called the Peace Brigades (Saraya al-Salam). These organizations—and others that were reinforced—had fought the occupation or in the civil war or both, and some had become largely dormant military wings of political parties over the previous five years. Most of these militias were deeply unpopular among Iraqis, both Sunnis and Shiʻa, because of their ties to Iran, their abuse of power, and their involvement in both sectarian and intra-Shiʻi violence. Dozens of new militias were also created; at one point during this period, the Hashd had at least forty-two fighting units. Prior to the fatwa, some of these old and new militias had already enlisted Iraqi Shiʻa to fight in Syria. The Quds Force of Iran's Islamic Revolutionary Guard Corps organized the Abu Fadhl al-Abbas Brigade in 2012, and Sheikh Qasim al-Tai had issued a fatwa authorizing Iraqis to travel to Syria to defend the shrine of Sayyida Zainab. Members of ʻAsaiʼb Ahl al-Haq, Kataʼib Hezbollah, Saraya al-Salam, and other militias were also involved in those efforts before the fall of Mosul. There was little doubt that the groups Iran had organized to defend the regime in Damascus would be transferred and used in Iraq, and Nuri al-Maliki already on 10 June had called for popular militias to be established.[77] When Sistani issued his fatwa, the expression "popular mobilization" was already in use; its origins lie in Maliki's earlier attempts to create irregular forces tied to him directly, such as the Sons of Iraq.[78] One of Sistani's goals was to prevent already motivated volunteers from joining militias; he sought to strengthen the Iraqi state, not militias, and especially not militias connected to the Iranian government. His fatwa did not create the PMF or most of its component militias; instead, it strengthened and legitimated them.

For three weeks in a row, Sistani's preachers reiterated and clarified his core nationalist message: join the Iraqi Armed Forces to fight foreign *takfiris* in ISIS.[79] Abbas Kadhim and Luay al-Khatteeb say that Sistani's representatives went so far as to "issue an explanatory addendum to clarify the meaning of the fatwa so as not to leave any chance for misunderstanding."[80] On 20 June congregants at Sistani's mosques heard criticisms of the security forces' recruitment centers and a reinforcement of the message that this was not meant to be a defensive jihad against Sunnis. His preachers called on foreign Shi'a *not* to come to Iraq.

Kadhim and al-Khatteeb see Sistani's fatwa as deliberately giving "a green light to form a truly committed second army."[81] They argue that the formation of the Hashd was a strategy to avoid direct military intervention by either the United States or Iran. But what transpired was contrary to Sistani's repeated instructions: militias flourished. Even the shrines set up two fighting units, supposedly loyal to Sistani. It is estimated that the forty-plus "Hashd" militias had sixty thousand to ninety thousand members soon after the call. Much smaller numbers joined the Iraqi security forces; the Iraqi military consistently failed to meet its recruiting targets, largely because Shi'a preferred to join the militias over the army.[82] Sistani's office calls the militias "volunteers," but they did not volunteer in the way he instructed. Several of the militias proudly boasted of sending units to fight in Syria, internationalizing the conflict. This runs counter to Sistani's nationalistic calls, as do the direct involvement of Iranian officers in support of some Hashd units. Much evidence suggests that the militias at the time operated independently of the military.[83] Millions of Iraqis ignored Sistani's call to join the security forces. Those that did join the fight did so in ways that Sistani's representative specifically said they should not do.

An unintended consequence of Sistani's "jihad fatwa" was to contribute to the creation of a social environment among Shi'a where militias and their members were socially rewarded by a population that had heard sermons praising their efforts. Sistani ended up legitimizing Iran-leaning Shi'i militias, and he did so in a way that portrayed them as nationalist and nonsectarian.[84] There was a social mobilization around the call that encouraged people to make visible contributions of money or material or logistical support. Low-cost ways of "obeying" the edict later contributed to the problem of demobilizing the militias after the risk from ISIS had been checked and pushed back, when armed men returned home and communities acquiesced to their use of violence locally. Some of the militias affiliated with the Hashd were reviled as sectarian and predatory before their rebranding as saviors of the nation. In the 2018 parliamentary elections, the political wings of the core militias of the Hashd formed the Fatah Alliance and won the second-largest number of seats. Sistani's fatwa and the sermons of his preachers contributed to the rapid emergence of a social environment that legitimated and accepted these Iran-leaning militias and associated parties as central actors in Iraq's elected political institutions for the foreseeable future.

In October 2019, the largest and most sustained protests in Iraq's post-Ba'th era began. What were initially calls for the reinstatement of a widely respected general quickly came to focus on the country's ethnosectarian system of power sharing as being responsible for endemic corruption, high unemployment, and inadequate public services. Some of the militias that Sistani had unintentionally legitimized and empowered attempted to crush what some were calling Iraq's "October Revolution." In November, Sistani issued two statements on his website demanding that security forces cease their violence against civilians and voicing support for some of the demonstrators' demands, such as improving services, fighting corruption, reforming the electoral system, and reducing foreign involvement in Iraqi politics.

While some claim that Sistani has aligned himself with antigovernment demonstrators, his interventions via statements and his mosque network have focused consistently on condemning state security forces for not adequately protecting protesters and on calling for reform of the political system (instead of revolution). The timing and nature of his interventions also suggest he continues to watch how rival clerics align themselves. For example, Mohammad al-Yaqoubi issued a statement in October 2019, before Sistani's interjection, praising the uprising. And Sistani's preachers were particularly careful in how they discussed violence against protesters after Moqtada al-Sadr's supporters attacked sit-ins in February 2020. Sistani called for reforms but did not publicly involve himself in the protracted fight over who should be the interim prime minister to guide Iraq to expected early elections. Sistani was cautious, and his calls for action did not demand too much from anyone. One activist in Najaf at the time lamented, "There have been countless Friday sermons on the issue now, but unfortunately nothing has happened, it's like no one is listening. . . . When there was an edict to fight extremists, it was obeyed. But there's been no clear edict here, nothing that actually binds those in power to act."[85] A protester in Baghdad echoed that concern: "Al-Sistani's condemnation of the security forces was good, but he did not mention [prime minister–designate Muhammad] Allawi or say that he rejects him."[86]

Sistani as a Sphinx

Like protesters seventeen years later, coalition officials in Baghdad in the early years of the occupation spent considerable time trying to decipher Sistani's exact preferences. On 13 January 2004, for example, Jerry Bremer met with CPA officials from the southern governates in Saddam's old cabinet room in Baghdad's presidential palace. According to one participant, "The regional and provincial coordinators debated among themselves and with the governance staff what Sistani's agenda really was."[87] Similarly, a number of scholars since 2004 have examined Sistani's worldview and social-political philosophy.[88] Some see him as an enlightened and progressive figure, championing democracy and nonsectarian national unity. Others place him squarely in a tradition of constitutionalist Shiʻi clerics that dates back more than a century.[89] Yet others emphasize his pragmatism, describing him as a deft and wily political activist focused on preserving the independence and influence of the Najaf hierocracy in a period of rapid change. But there is a broad consensus on his worldview, even if there is disagreement about priorities.

Mosque sermons are most effective at creating common knowledge with short, simple messages that individuals can reasonably expect others to absorb, such as, "Any constitution adopted by a nonelected council will be rejected!" They are less effective at generating new common knowledge that is complex; individuals have less certainty that other members understood or interpreted nuanced messages in the same way. Sistani's network, therefore, often seems to be more reactive than proactive. It has never been used to articulate a clear vision of Sistani's preferences about Iraq's future. His strategy remained vague, and messages are often tactical, either for or against particular plans for one or two specific reasons. This worked to Sistani's benefit as he informally bargained with the United States, Iraqi officials, and rival clerics over various outcomes. But it also limited what he could reasonably expect to be able to get people to do at the national level. The way his authority could be effectively utilized made him less a scheming political activist and more a reactive quasi–veto player over others' proposals.

Alternative Explanations for Changes in Authority

Sistani's influence is almost always explained in terms of Shiʻi doctrine, specifically the relationship between a marjaʻ and a muqallid (follower). But this implies that there are few limits on the influence of a marjaʻ. If this was all that matters, Sistani should have had much more influence in the post-2003 period than he did and gotten a result close to his preferred outcome on more post-invasion issues (e.g., stopping the TAL, limiting violence). The conventional wisdom—which focuses on Shiʻi doctrine and Sistani's worldview—is not wrong, it is just incomplete. The limits of his authority and how those limits can change matter. Most scholars say little about the limits of his authority and power and instead focus on his ideological commitments and interests. But Sistani was highly judicious in the use of his authority. Calling Sistani a traditional authority is insufficient; he broke from decades-long precedent in how senior Shiʻa clerics should involve themselves. The context of a changing Iraq clearly created a possibility for this, but this traditional authority was not bound by precedents handed down from the past.

Sistani is not a charismatic authority in the Weberian sense. Although hundreds of books by Shiʻi religious scholars are now available in Iraq, the only widely found work by Sistani remains his guide to basic worship and transactions, required of all marajiʻ.[90] Sistani rarely leaves his (rented) home or his office, on a side street off al-Rasool Street in Najaf's old quarter, near the Shrine of Imam Ali. He almost never speaks in public and rarely allows photographs to be taken of him.[91] He purportedly still speaks Arabic with a thick Iranian accent; his clerical representatives insist that he be called "al-Sistani" instead of just "Sistani" because the definite article prefix *al-* helps to Arabize his name (Sistan is a geographical area in southeastern Iran, bordering Afghanistan). Before his portrait proliferated after the January 2004 demonstrations, most Shiʻa in Iraq—even those technically emulating him—likely had never seen his picture. But charismatic authority rests in a belief that an individual is extraordinary and endowed with supernatural, superhuman, or some other exceptional powers or qualities.[92] Such people typically have charming personalities and are skilled speakers. Sistani does not possess charismatic appeal himself, although there is certainly what Weber calls a "charisma of office" associated with the marjaʻiyya.[93]

Piety matters for obedience, but it alone cannot explain why some edicts are followed and others are not. While in Iraq, I occasionally played chess with two devout Shiʻa who told me they would do whatever Sistani asked. When I reminded them that Sistani religiously forbids chess, they said that this is different because it is private and does not hurt the community as a whole. This idea that, in practice, public spheres are different than private ones came up in several interviews when the power of clerical edicts was discussed. Public disobedience of norms and religious rulings (i.e., failing to coordinate with others) hurts the community as a whole and causes divisions, something for which no one wants to be responsible. Although adherence to religious guidelines in private is obviously considered beneficial for the individual, people do not think such violations hurt the community in the same way that public violations do. This was poignantly demonstrated by people clandestinely smoking in private during Ramadan or drinking alcohol only behind closed doors. Much of what we consider public expressions of piety can be understood as conventions, driven by a sense of "this is how we do things here." They are coordinated behavior, often with value as signals.[94]

If Shiʿa see other Shiʿa disobeying rules, it might affect their expectations that others would act on future messages. Common knowledge alone is insufficient for coordination. Individuals must also believe that other individuals will act on that knowledge. Disobedience reduces others' expectations that others will follow future messages, limiting coordination. My interviewees were correct: public disobedience divides the community in ways that private disobedience would not. Piety arguments alone fail to account for variation in individuals' willingness to comply with different types of behaviors, such as public versus private and coordination versus collective action subject to free riding. The credibility of sanctions is less important if people follow norms out of piety.

Other Potential Sources of Common Knowledge

Newspapers, radio, and television have the potential to generate common knowledge, but they did not do so in the first few years after the invasion of Iraq.[95] This was not for lack of news media; at least eighty-five new newspapers had appeared in Iraq by June 2003.[96] Every major party ran their own paper, several independent papers emerged, and pan-Arab dailies and weeklies quickly established Baghdad editions. Yet, despite this proliferation of print media, newspaper circulation and readership remained astonishingly low in Iraq. A CNN/USA Today/Gallup nationwide poll in March and April 2004 found that only 6 percent of Iraqis read a daily newspaper seven days a week, irrespective of time spent reading.[97] Occasional readership was also low: only 14 percent reported they read *any* paper at least four days per week. And 57 percent of respondents reported not reading a newspaper at all. These figures are consistent with my field research. Only one of my dozens of Iraqi contacts admitted to regularly reading a newspaper (and it was part of his job), and none of them thought many other Iraqis read papers regularly.[98] Although 72 percent of respondents in the CNN/USA Today/Gallup poll said they have a radio at home, only 24 percent listened daily, irrespective of station. When this is divided among the multitude of stations available, the confidence of any Iraqi that he heard what another Iraqi heard is low. Forty percent of respondents did not listen to a radio at all. This figure reflects the popularity of radio stations that broadcast recitations of the Quran and apolitical religious lessons; old recordings of the recently deceased cleric and poet Ahmad al-Waʾeli were extremely popular among Iraqi Shiʿa in 2003 to 2005. He had spent twenty-four years in exile before returning to Iraq and dying in July 2003.

Television can be a powerful medium to generate common knowledge if individuals watch and know others watch the same programs. In the previously mentioned 2004 poll, 95 percent of respondents reported owning a working TV set at home, and 76 percent watched daily, irrespective of channel. By far, the state-run al-Iraqiya was the most watched station in the first year after the invasion; 84 percent of respondents reported receiving it at home without difficulties, and 74 percent said they had watched it in the past seven days (no other station surpassed 28 percent).[99] Al-Iraqiya was the most watched station because it was free-to-air and, unlike all other stations, could be received without a satellite dish. The quality of al-Iraqiya was low immediately after the war, when Science Applications International Corporation (SAIC), a major US defense contractor, oversaw the Iraqi Media Network (IMN), which ran the station. I found that most Iraqis considered al-Iraqiya and IMN to be the mouthpiece of the CPA and occupation authorities; (correct) rumors circulated that IMN money purchased a teleprompter for Paul Bremer when Iraqi news anchors did not have them. In January 2004, the US Department of Defense gave Harris Corporation, another US-based firm, a $96 million contract to reinvent the station. Harris turned training and programming of al-Iraqiya over to the Lebanese Broadcasting Corporation International, and quality improved rapidly. By March 2004, however, Iraqis still gave al-Iraqiya low scores for its boldness and news-breaking ability.[100] When I asked Iraqis about the ability of al-Iraqiya to shape how people interpreted important events, I was reminded by more than one person that al-Iraqiya did not report the news of the deaths of Saddam's sons, Uday and Qusay, in July 2003 or the capture of Saddam Hussein in December 2003 until hours after other stations broke the news.

The ability of media in Iraq to generate common knowledge was limited by the reach of stations and Iraqis' beliefs about how many other Iraqis watched stations. Additionally, Iraqis may have considered or believed that other Iraqis considered al-Iraqiya to be a propaganda tool for the coalition and transition governments. Iraqis therefore would not have expected other Iraqis to act on messages from al-Iraqiya, even if they were common knowledge. Iraqis had to find other sources of common knowledge generation; they certainly did not expect other Iraqis to condition their behavior on television messages. Satellite dishes were banned under the Ba'th; although they were widely available after May 2003, their cost of about $170 (including installation) placed them out of reach for most Iraqis.

Political parties, both secular and religious, expected to quickly develop grassroots support in Iraq and shape public opinion. Elites faced tremendous incentives to coordinate and otherwise mobilize Iraqis on their preferred outcomes. Many Shi'i Islamist parties, such as Da'wa, SCIRI, and the Islamic Action Organization (Amal), have tens of thousands of supporters throughout Iraq.[101] The Iraqi Islamic Party, effectively the Iraqi branch of the Muslim Brothers, has significant support among the Sunni Arab community.[102] Secular parties, such as the Iraqi Communist Party, Ahmed Chalabi's Iraqi National Congress, and Ayad Allawi's Iraqi National Accord, also expected to capture followers. Based solely on graffiti in Basra in late 2003, one might have expected the National Democratic Party to be one of Iraq's dominant political forces.

Despite impressive organizations and financial advantages, Iraq's established political parties failed to significantly shape public opinion and mobilize impressive numbers in the first year after invasion. Parties tried many tactics to gain support, including publishing newspapers and holding press conferences and rallies. Although these endeavors created knowledge about parties' positions, they did not generate sufficient *common* knowledge. Iraqis did not know what other Iraqis knew or thought about particular parties. By late 2003, many prominent leaders and political parties had high name recognition and favorable ratings. Among Arab leaders on the Governing Council, Abdul Aziz al-Hakim (SCIRI), Sayyed Muhammed Bahr al-Uloom, Ibrahim Jaafari (Daʿwa), Adnan Pachachi, and Ahmad Chalabi were particularly well known. Surveys showed all of them except Chalabi commanding significantly higher favorable than unfavorable ratings from the public.[103] The ratings, however, never translated into an ability to influence public opinion and mobilization. My interviews showed that most Iraqis simply did not know what others thought. They had their own opinions but no idea how many others shared them. Parties and individual leaders could create knowledge but were not effective at creating common knowledge during the particular time period examined here. Of course, context matters. Some of these constraints may have existed during a particular period and then the later spread of the Internet and cell phone messaging apps changed parties' and groups' ability to reach people, sometimes in ways such that others knew who else was being reached. The media landscape also changed over time as privately owned stations began transmission—such as al-Sharqiya (in May 2004) and al-Baghdadiya (in 2005)—and developed news programs, dramas, and comedies that spoke to contemporary issues. In 2009, the *New York Times* estimated that more than 40 percent of Iraqis had access to satellite media and "that more than 47 channels, more than 150 newspapers and scores of radio stations have been launched since the fall of Saddam."[104]

Religious Rivals

It is difficult to exaggerate the variety of Shiʿi religious experience and claimants to religious authority that existed in Basra and throughout Iraq after the overthrow of the Baʿth. Shiʿi millenarian ideas were spreading like wildfire: "women dressing like men" and the US-led occupation (fulfilling a prophecy of

Rumis [Romans] in Kut and Basra) were commonly mentioned as evidence that the return of the Mahdi was imminent. I was asked on several occasions if the United States had fully occupied Iraq this time—unlike in 1991—because the CIA knew that the Mahdi had returned and they wanted to find and kill him. Pamphlets and magazines from Iran and Lebanon were for sale on street corners, and Mohammad Baqir al-Sadr's previously banned books seemed to be everywhere. A "lost" book by Mohammad Baqir al-Sadr on politics was rumored to have been found in a presidential palace, and it promised to chart a glorious path for Iraq's future. VCDs of lectures by the recently deceased cleric al-Wa'eli were as common as those of sermons by Grand Ayatollah Mohammad Mohammad Sadiq al-Sadr. New hussainiyas were popping up and hosting stories of the martyrdom of Husayn. Passion plays and processions including groups of people flagellating or cutting themselves were held in the street during the first ten days of Muharram.

Claimants to religious authority were ubiquitous. Rumors swirled that Grand Ayatollahs Kazem al-Haeri or Muhammad Hussein Fadlallah or both were about to return to Iraq. The Sadrists had split into rival factions, with the followers in Basra of newly proclaimed Grand Ayatollah Mohammad al-Yaqoobi appearing to be particularly well organized and richly endowed financially. Dozens of Islamist parties were occupying government buildings. Ominously, rumors circulated that a "committee for commanding right and forbidding wrong" had appointed itself for the city. Faleh Jabar correctly notes that the term *hawza* is "politically amorphous or ambiguous," and there were perhaps a dozen people or groups claiming to represent it, from the Office of the Martyred Sadr II to SCIRI.[105] Some claimants to religious authority were existential challenges to the maraji' and the clerical establishment; Sayyid Ahmad al-Hassan claimed to be the messenger of the Mahdi, which would make the hawza and all the Shi'i clergy suddenly redundant. Western scholars and analysts have paid almost no attention to neo-Akhbari movements in postinvasion Iraq, but the spread of these ideas is deeply threatening to the Shi'a hierocracy and many sermons directly or indirectly addressed these threats.

The initiation of Friday sermons and Sistani's interventions must be understood in this context. Iraq after the Ba'th was a cacophony of competing voices and messages being delivered in different ways to different audiences. Parts of the religious establishment had connections to many of these groups and rituals, and most were based to some extent on religious networks that dated to the sanctions era or earlier. Even Ahmad al-Hassan's claim to speak for the Mahdi predated the invasion, to 2002 at the latest. Friday sermons had a unique ability to allow a single voice to rise above the din and to do so on a regular schedule and to a regular audience. Once Sistani began to disseminate his statements via his network of preachers, a single voice figuratively (never literally) was heard through that medium, again and again. Other facets of religious experience and other claimants to religious authority mattered, including those that emphasized muscle and service provision instead of the loudspeaker. But they mattered for certain things or periods of time or for limited and fluid audiences. Sermons were different because of their infrastructure, the initial power of clerics' preexisting authority, and the hierarchical networks that render them effective at disseminating a similar message in different locales.

It is useful to compare Sistani's and Sadr's influence and ability to mobilize Iraqi Shi'a after 2003 with the relative failure of the Shiraziyyin to do so. The three actors share some similarities but vary in important ways. The Shiraziyyin are a Shi'i religious and political movement that initially developed around the marja'iyya of the ambitious and charismatic Grand Ayatollah Mohammad al-Shirazi (died 2001), and it remains closely associated with his extended clerical family and network. The Shirazis are an illustrious clerical family, having produced a number of maraji' who were Karbala-based rivals to Najaf's senior scholars and played prominent roles in leading or endorsing both the 1891 revolt in Iran against a tobacco concession to Great Britain and the 1920 Iraqi revolt. Mohammad al-Shirazi moved to Iran after the 1979 revolution, and from there his network spawned a large array of interlinked political movements, religious institutions, business endeavors, and media platforms in Shi'i communities throughout the Gulf.[106] After Mohammad al-Shirazi's death in 2001, his brother Grand Ayatollah Sadeq al-Shirazi became the principal religious reference for the movement.

Immediately after the invasion, the Iraqi Shiraziyyin movement enjoyed many organizational advantages that Sistani and Sadr did not. First, they had a long experience with political organization and adaptation. Sayyid Mohammed Taqi al-Modarresi, nephew of Mohammad al-Shirazi, led the Islamic Action Organization—one of the most prominent exiled Iraqi political and paramilitary organizations—for decades. The Shiraziyyin had experience relocating transnationally, having moved from Iraq to Iran and from there to Kuwait and Syria and elsewhere. They had repeatedly proven themselves to be flexible organizationally and ideologically. They successfully adapted after a falling-out between Shirazi and Khomeini in the mid-1980s and the loss of Iranian support. Shiraziyyin leaders have shifted over time from supporting guardianship of the jurist to espousing democratic principles and from Iraqi nativism to Shi'i transnationalism. Relative to other Iraqi groups in 2003, the Shiraziyyin were organizationally "modern" and extremely experienced in political and religious communication. The movement's activists have decades of experience (since the 1960s) distributing religious, political, and cultural material via publications (e.g., books, monthlies, weeklies, dailies) and radio, cassette tapes, and satellite television channels. Mohammad al-Shirazi had encouraged this innovation and outreach, and over one thousand books are attributed to him. Shirazi's marja'iyya probably was the first to make wide use of the Internet to disseminate his rulings and opinions. Finally, the Karbala-based Shiraziyyin have a long history of popular mobilization through controversial rituals that the Najaf clergy shun but the masses see as part of Shi'i heritage, especially processions and pilgrimages that feature self-flagellation (using a chain with blades to beat one's back; *zanjeel*) and head cutting (striking one's head with a sword; *tatbir*). They had tools other parties and clerical networks lacked.

The Shiraziyyin utilized all of these seeming advantages after the invasion. Mohammed Taqi al-Modarresi, now a grand ayatollah, returned to Karbala, and the Islamic Action Organization set up offices throughout Shi'i areas and touted their long history of resistance to the Ba'th. Since Grand Ayatollah Sadeq al-Shirazi remained in Qom and was a more "traditional" and relatively apolitical marja', members and potential members of the movement could decide whether they preferred a more distant and scholarly source of emulation (in al-Shirazi) or a more active and political one (in al-Modarresi). Shiraziyyin books, pamphlets, and newspapers flooded into Iraq immediately after the invasion, and new media outlets sprouted up inside the country. In addition to its existing radio and satellite stations, the movement launched al-Anwar TV in 2004 to broaden its outreach, particularly to nonmembers, by featuring religious lectures and videos of pilgrimages and mourning sessions with controversial ritual practices. The thing the Shiraziyyin lacked in April 2003 was a network of Friday mosques within Iraq. Having been forced into exile in the 1980s, the Shiraziyyin had affiliated mosques only in Karbala and some surrounding villages. Elsewhere, they operated out of hussainiyas, not Friday mosques. They got their message out, but not in ways that generated common knowledge. Shiraziyyin leaders, including al-Modarresi, are savvy and ambitious; they have religious credentials, political experience, and a wide array of media outlets. But they lack Sistani's or even Sadr's more limited ability to generate common knowledge in widely dispersed locales. Instead, the Shiraziyyin's influence has been limited to Karbala and its surrounds.

In the first year after the occupation, many supporters of Sistani chafed when the brash twenty-nine-year-old Moqtada al-Sadr was mentioned alongside the esteemed and accomplished grand ayatollah. There are some important differences between them, most notably Moqtada's low clerical standing and his youth. Another difference is the status that comes from being a member of the Sadr clerical family, especially the oldest surviving son of the late charismatic Grand Ayatollah Mohammad Mohammad Sadiq al-Sadr and a blood relative and son-in-law of the venerated Mohammad Baqir al-Sadr. But Sistani and Sadr shared a key source of influence in postinvasion Iraq that no other individual or organization did: they each controlled a sizable clerical network and access to Friday mosques throughout the country.

As mentioned earlier, Grand Ayatollah Sadr had resumed Friday sermons in a number of mosques in the late 1990s, most of which ceased after his assassination in 1999. After the invasion, many—perhaps most—of Sadr's clerical deputies restarted Friday sermons and sought to reestablish the moribund network of the late marja'. Moqtada, as the eldest surviving son, came to head the Office of the Martyred Sadr II. But not all of Sadr's wakils turned to Moqtada. At least two of Sadr's former students declared themselves to be maraji', and some of Sadr's older wakils turned to an established grand ayatollah, Kazem al-Haeri in Qom. By late 2003, three distinct "Sadrist" sermons were being held in Basra: Sheikh Adnan Silawi had attached himself to Haeri's marja'iyya and delivered messages from him in a mosque near the center of the city; followers of the newly christened Grand Ayatollah Mohammad al-Yaqoubi held Friday prayers in a prayer area they fashioned in an open area near Hayyaniah; and clerics affiliated with Moqtada and the OMS preached a coordinated sermon to up to four congregations spread around the city. While preachers affiliated with Haeri and Yaqoubi delivered their own sermons (and they each controlled only a few Friday mosques throughout the entire country), the OMS could coordinate sermons in several mosques in the largest cities and towns and perhaps one to three in smaller towns. And, although the OMS said it officially looked to Haeri on new issues, the sermons delivered in OMS mosques were always separate and distinct from Haeri's messages and what his official wakils said in sermons. After Sistani's clerical network, the OMS's was by far the largest.

Although Sadr was a low-ranking cleric, his challenge to Sistani came from within the established hierocracy. Sadr was not trying to eradicate the hawza, like some neo-Akhbari movements might have hoped to do; he wanted (and tried) to speak for it. His method of outreach was orthodox and traditional in that it was based on a marja'iyya, albeit that of a deceased marja'. It also relied heavily on the tradition of Friday sermons that his father had rejuvenated for Shi'a and which Sistani and his marja'iyya were now mimicking.

Sadr and his preachers, however, consistently overreached in what they asked followers to do. Speaking from his father's former pulpit in the highly symbolic mosque in Kufa where Imam Ali governed, Sadr in July 2003 rejected the Governing Council as "puppets" and in October announced his plan to establish a shadow government. He repeatedly asked followers to engage in costly and often dangerous actions, and when his messages were ignored, it undermined listeners' confidence that any messages—even ones aimed at coordination or low-cost endeavors—would be followed. While fiery, most OMS sermons therefore motivated few followers to act on them. In October 2003, rumors swirled around Basra that graffiti in Arabic saying "We came to fuck all Iraqis" had been seen on a wall at a field hospital run by the Czech military in the middle of the city. The Sadrists organized a protest to begin outside the hospital and then move to the CPA building; some hoped to exploit the moment to trigger an uprising against the occupation. They told potential participants that fifteen thousand protesters would join, but fewer than five hundred showed up for the 10:00 a.m. event. (I later learned that the graffiti was in English and read "We came and did fuck all.") As the OMS increasingly clashed with other Shi'a groups and the coalition, its preachers issued ever more outrageous—and costly to follow—messages. In May 2004, Abdul Satar al-Bahadali, OMS head in Basra, gave a sermon while holding an assault rifle and offered rewards of $18 for the capture of any of the twenty-five members of the GC; $71 for the capture of a male US or British soldier; and $178 for the capture of a female British soldier, who would be "treated as a concubine" after being handed over to Sadr.[107]

Ironically, Moqtada and his preachers had undermined the effectiveness for their followers of the ritual that their venerated Sayyid al-Shahid had revitalized and for which he was best known. At the same time, his rival, Sistani, was cautiously and gradually augmenting his authority through its use. Over time, the OMS came to rely increasingly on coercion and the Mahdi Army, many of whose members were paid or found ways to extract compensation for their participation in costly endeavors, such as via providing protection.

Unintended Sectarianism

After the invasion, and facing new issues and previously unknown dilemmas, Iraqis could improve their lot if they collectively acted with other Iraqis. The Ba'th regime, however, destroyed or limited most means of generating the common knowledge necessary for coordination and the emergence of self-enforcing social rules. Friday mosque sermons quickly emerged after the war as an important way that Iraqis could know what their neighbors knew about a particular event or topic and what their neighbors would think and do in various circumstances.

For Shi'a, mosque sermons became the basis for knowing what Shi'a in far-distant areas thought about complex new topics like federalism, elections, and attacks meant to provoke retaliation. Shi'a know with which marja' their local mosque is affiliated, and they know that Shi'a attending other mosques affiliated with that marja'iyya will receive similar messages. Sistani and Sadr, by controlling the largest networks of mosques in Iraq, could disseminate the same message to millions of Iraqis each week in a way that listeners will know that these millions of other Iraqis received it. Other political entrepreneurs, lacking effective ways of generating common knowledge, largely failed to shape opinion and mobilize large numbers of Iraqis.

By late 2003, sermons in Shiʿi Friday mosques could generate common knowledge across congregations within an ayatollah's network. I experienced this phenomenon during fieldwork. After I attended a Friday sermon in a Shiʿi mosque affiliated with Sistani, I sometimes could correctly anticipate what Shiʿa who attend other Sistani-affiliated mosques would say if I asked them national political questions addressed in that week's sermon. Shiʿa public opinion often converged on the mosque message, despite having varied prior to the sermon.[108] After a sermon, Shiʿa knew what other Shiʿa had heard. If they expected others to act on what was heard, they might do likewise.

My Sunni and Christian contacts, however, often did not know what Shiʿa thought. Ironically, several times Sunni and Christian interviewees asked *me* what their Shiʿi compatriots thought about issues. They thought I "understood" Shiʿi society in ways they did not. In reality, I simply heard on Fridays what most Shiʿa heard, and I could tell which messages would resonate with other listeners and which, if given, would not. One Sunni in Basra whom I knew well complained to me that he increasingly felt like all other Iraqis instantaneously reached consensuses without him. Before he had even heard of transition initiatives or breaking news, he said Shiʿa had been "brainwashed" by their clerics on how to think about it. Over time, he felt increasingly threatened by what he saw as a monolith of Shiʿi public opinion that emerged quickly and in ways mysterious to him.[109] He eventually fled Iraq, a country he said he no longer understood.

Sectarian identity is not a natural or historically dominant cleavage in Iraq, and the extent to which it increased in salience in the sanctions era is an open question. Other cleavages often have been more salient in modern Iraqi history, such as language, class, tribe, or region or city of origin. Sistani's moral authority grew when he was seen as defending Iraq's national identity and independence; many non-Shiʿa came to see him a trusted representative for the nation and someone who checked, as much as he could, the excesses of sect-centric Shiʿi Islamist parties.[110] Yet, one consequence of the ability of Sistani and other religious leaders to coordinate followers through mosques was an inadvertent and unintended increase in the saliency of sectarian identity in Iraqi politics.

Thomas Schelling wrote, "The participants at a square dance may all be thoroughly dissatisfied with the particular dances being called, but as long as the caller has the microphone, nobody can dance anything else."[111] Religious authorities held the microphones in Iraq. Millions of Shiʿa heard Sistani's and Sadr's calls and danced together. Many may not like the positions and strategies they heard, but their preference to join a group action if a sufficient number of others participate led them to accept these options. Secularism in Iraq seemed to disappear in postinvasion Iraq not because there was no support for it among Shiʻa, but because there is little support for it in Sistani's and Sadr's offices.

7
THE LIMITS OF SUNNI RELIGIOUS AUTHORITY

In the run-up to the 2003 Iraq war, journalists, scholars, and US government analysts drew up lists of Iraqis whom they thought might be influential and potential leaders after the removal of the Baʿth regime.[1] The Sunni Arabs who appeared on these "who's who" lists were diverse and typically included secular Arab and Iraqi nationalists who had served in government before the Baʿth came to power (e.g., Adnan Pachachi); monarchical figures (Sharif Ali bin al-Husayn); tribal leaders (Ghazi al-Yawer); Baʿth Party defectors (Salah Omar al-Ali); exiled military officers (General Nizar al-Khazraji); and leaders of political parties and émigré opposition groups (Iraqi Islamic Party). Some had participated in coup attempts against the Baʿth as far back as the 1960s and as recently as 1997. Some were widely known and respected in Iraq for their previous government or military service. Some were thought to potentially have wide and cross-sectarian appeal; most of them did not see themselves as Sunnis first and foremost. Unlike the Shiʿa and Kurds on those prewar lists, almost all of the Sunni Arabs who appeared on them quickly found themselves irrelevant after the invasion.

One of the enduring puzzles about post-2003 Iraq is why no unifying Sunni Arab leaders emerged. Sunni Arabs consistently failed to reach a consensus on key issues and remained disunified; their leaders' influence has tended to be local or transitory or both. Yet, in the first years after the invasion, two new political associations—both led by and largely composed of Sunni Arab clerics—became prominent actors. The first was a new organization, the Association of Muslim Scholars (AMS), which quickly became arguably the most influential mobilizer of Sunni Arabs at the national level. Nationalist and antisectarian, the

AMS broadly encouraged nonparticipation in the transition process but avoided overt support of armed resistance. Separately, a religious scholar who had been appointed to head the new Iraqi government agency responsible for overseeing religious institutions brought together disparate Sunni parties and personalities to participate in the December 2005 elections, where their coalition won forty-four seats. What explains this surprising influence of Sunni clerics and clerical associations after the invasion? And if their influence was based on a mechanism of information dissemination similar to Shi'i clerics', why were Sunni Arabs unable to achieve similar within-group consensuses?

The production of local social order through mosque sermons, described in chapters 4 and 5, occurred in both Shi'i- and Sunni-majority areas. Many Sunni Arabs came to rely on messages from their local Friday mosques to coordinate together and solve low-cost contribution dilemmas. It remains unclear how the preinvasion standing of Sunni preachers compares to their Shi'i counterparts'. In general, we might have expected Shi'i clerics to have greater traditional authority than Sunni clerics because of the doctrines of Usuli Shi'ism. But Sunni clerics gave Friday sermons before 2003, while Shi'i ones did not and had largely remained distant from mundane affairs. Sunni clerics by the 1990s had been Ba'thified and to be authorized to preach, must have passed security clearances.[2] It is unclear if that would have helped or hurt their standing in their communities postinvasion.

Regardless of relative preinvasion standing, Sunni preachers saw their authority augmented locally in ways similar to how Shi'i preachers' authority increased: through their ability to disseminate messages in ways that made those messages common knowledge within congregations. But Sunni clerics differ from their Shi'i counterparts in a critical respect: they had no equivalent to Sistani and his marja'iyya. They lack an organizational structure that could consistently induce preachers to deliver the same message in different localities. The preexisting religious authority of grand ayatollahs and the hierarchical nature of the clerical networks they controlled allowed them to broadcast messages to adherents sitting in geographically dispersed congregations every Friday afternoon. Shi'a could coordinate together nationally, and Shi'i political parties fell in line with Sistani's preferences because they knew he could coordinate the opinions of millions of Shi'a to reach consensus positions related to the transition process. The clerical structure of Sunni Islam explains why their clerics could generate common knowledge and coordination *within* congregations but could not consistently disseminate similar messages *across* congregations, which hindered the ability of Sunni to similarly coordinate across localities. This partially accounts for the failure of a cohesive Sunni Arab leadership and shared positions on the transition process to emerge postinvasion, leaving the community both politically and socially marginalized in postinvasion Iraq.

Sunni Clerics after the Invasion

The Baʻth regime tightly controlled the licensing, employment, and oversight of Sunni clerics, even after it had created a cadre of loyal "Baʻthized" religious leaders.[3] A document in the Baʻth Party archives states that "absolutely no permission is to be given to sermon-givers who are not officially licensed to give sermons in the mosques."[4] The extensive system of formal regulation over Sunni clerics vanished overnight when the regime collapsed, and Sunni clerics found themselves free to speak on whatever topics they liked. The Baʻth-era Ministry of Religious Endowments was abolished, and the Governing Council, with the CPA, established three separate bureaus to oversee religious endowments (*awqaf*) for Sunnis, Shiʻa, and religious minorities (Christians and others).

Because of their experience giving and hearing mosque sermons, Sunnis might have been more predisposed than Shiʻa to turn to them for mobilization postinvasion. Since the early 1980s, Friday preachers were required to give the same regime-dictated sermon but could also, if approved by the local committee for religious awareness, discuss local issues.[5] There is little evidence that communities used sermons for mobilization under the Baʻth, but it is possible that some congregations had experience developing common knowledge about local issues from sermons. Just as Shiʻi clerics did, Sunni clerics emerged as important generators of common knowledge and facilitators of coordination and low-cost collective action in the immediate areas around their mosques. One of the most striking features of postinvasion Iraq is the rapid and unexpected influence of Sunni Arab clerics. Coalition troops often found clerics to be the most influential Sunni Arab representatives in towns and urban neighborhoods. Individuals in many Sunni Arab areas expressed as much support for religious leaders as individuals did in Shiʻi areas. By late 2003, for example, polls of Fallujah and Ramadi show 82 percent and 76 percent of respondents, respectively, supported the inclusion of Iraqi clerics in future Iraqi governments.[6] It is unclear how much of that standing dates to the sanctions era and how much was generated through postinvasion activities.

The number of Sunni Friday mosques per capita in Iraq is much higher than the number of Shiʻi Friday mosques per capita.[7] Dozens of new mosques were built in Sunni-majority areas after 1994 during the Faith Campaign; in some Sunni Arab towns, each neighborhood has its own mosque. Shiʻi jurisprudence states that Friday mosques should be at least 4.8 to 5.5 kilometers from one another, and, although the rule is often ignored in practice, this creates a strong inclination to keep some distance between sermons. In contrast, in some areas Sunni mosques hold Friday sermons within sight of one another. The proximity of Sunni mosques in Iraq is evident during the call to prayer and on Fridays, when loudspeakers compete to have their sermons reach as many listeners as possible. This large number of Sunni Friday mosques and sermons implies that Sunni mosques have smaller exclusive catchment areas and greater areas where mosques' catchment areas overlap. Sermon-generated common knowledge among Sunnis, when it occurred, was highly localized—even more so than Shi'a's. Sunnis attending a Friday sermon did not know what messages were being delivered in mosques in adjacent streets, much less what was being said in other neighborhoods or towns or governates. This compartmentalization of common knowledge hindered the emergence of a unifying sense of "we-ness" for Sunni Arabs above the hyperlocal level. It also implies that, other things being constant, there would be less community-created order in Sunni-majority areas than in Shi'i areas. Sunnis were more disordered spatially, as well as organizationally.

The fractured landscape of Sunni religious infrastructure may partially explain the strength and diverse nature of the insurgency that took hold in Sunni Arab areas. A greater sense of disorder—exacerbated by too many mosques in close proximity—contributed to a grievance-based sense of Sunni identity, one based on a belief that they, as a group, were disadvantaged and ignored in Iraq's new political system. Disorder that mosques cannot address also leaves opportunities for militias and outside groups to enter and coercively create order. Finally, the absence of a coherent political leadership limited the ability of and incentives for the US and Iraqi governments to negotiate with Sunni Arabs.

Attempts to Organize Sunni Clerics

Unlike in Usuli Shi'i Islam, there is no institutional or clear clerical hierarchy in Sunni Islam. Clerics are relative status equals, and following the invasion, Sunni clerics were largely independent from one another and free to shape their own messages on both local and national issues. Even under the Ba'th, Iraq lacked a hierarchy among Sunni clerics and there was no "head" Sunni religious official or grand mufti of Iraq after the early 1970s.

Yet Sunni preachers might have been predisposed to coordinate sermons. There were several local- and governate-level organizations from the Ba'th era that accredited, supervised, and coordinated clerics: committees for religious awareness and "leagues of Islamic scholars." Presumably, these interpersonal connections between Baʿthized religious leaders endured. Despite having no chief mufti or hierarchy analogous to Shiʿi Islam, two religious figures emerged as prominent Sunni political entrepreneurs: Harith al-Dhari and Adnan al-Dulaimi. Although al-Dhari and al-Dulaimi are not equivalents to Sistani or even al-Sadr, their prominence rests partly on a similar foundation: a modest ability to coordinate sermon messages across congregations, albeit without an equivalent religious standing that Shiʿi clerics enjoy.

Five days after the fall of Baghdad, on 14 April 2003, the Association of Muslim Scholars (AMS) was formed as a loose coalition of Sunni Arab clerics. There are different versions of the founding of the AMS; some accounts attribute the founding to Abdul Salam al-Kubaisi, others to Harith al-Dhari.[8] In any case, al-Dhari, an al-Azhar–trained scholar who had trained clerics in Iraq before leaving the country in 1999, emerged as the figurehead and chief spokesperson of the organization soon after it was established. The AMS was based in Baghdad's massive Mother of All Battles Mosque (built from 1993 to 2001 as one of Saddam's President Leader Friday Mosques), which was renamed the Mother of All Villages (Umm al-Qura) Mosque after the invasion. Samuel Helfont sees the AMS's membership as the clearest remnants of the former regime's Baʿthification of religion.[9] Although the AMS was a new organization in 2003, it traces its roots to religious networks from the sanctions period, particularly interpersonal ties between graduates of the Institute for the Preparation of Imams and Sermon-Givers and Saddam University for Islamic Studies. Members may also have served together on governate and local committees before 2003, such as the committees for religious awareness. The AMS was nominally organized into eighteen branches, one in each governate, which might have reflected Baʿth-era governate-level committees that oversaw preachers.[10]

The AMS portrayed itself as the higher coordinating authority for the country's Sunni clerical establishment. Al-Dhari claimed at one point that the organization controlled five thousand to eight thousand Sunnis mosques throughout Iraq, but it never demonstrated a significant capacity to coordinate sermons across more than a small fraction of that number of mosques. Sheikh Yosuf al-Hasan, the director of the AMS for Basra Governate until his assassination in 2006, told me in December 2003 that the explicit goal of the group is to serve as a "Sunni marjaʿ, like Sistani."[11] He emphasized the importance of Friday sermons in educating the people and crafting a common national message, but he acknowledged that Sunni clerics often ignored the AMS and selected their own positions. Al-Hasan shared with me some of the materials the AMS offers preachers to improve their effectiveness as speakers, but it was clear that the organization had limited financial or material resources to offer preachers (and thereby induce compliance).

There was no official "membership" in the AMS. Some Sunni clerics I interviewed in Iraq admitted that they have a relationship with the AMS; others would not say. What relationships do exist often appear to be ad hoc and informal. Several told me that they hoped the AMS eventually would provide stipends, training, and support, but no one I spoke with wanted oversight and regulation of the content of their sermons. Most Sunni preachers, at least in the south, did not support a return to state oversight of sermons and mosques, perhaps fearing that the Ministry of Endowments and Religious Affairs would once again require them to adopt religious positions with which many disagreed. What unified AMS-affiliated preachers was a general opposition to the foreign occupation of Iraq.

But the AMS faced a rival Sunni clerical association. After the Ministry of Religious Endowments was abolished, a bureau (*diwan*) was established to oversee Sunni endowments, including most Friday mosques. The Iraqi Islamic Party (IIP) influenced the Iraqi Governing Council to appoint Adnan al-Dulaimi as head of the Sunni diwan, and he quickly became one of the most—arguably, *the* most—prominent Sunni Arab political figure in the first few years of occupation.[12] Some sources say that Dulaimi was a professor of Islamic studies at the University of Baghdad prior to the invasion, but Nathanial Rabkin (citing his autobiography) claims that Dulaimi was an Arabic teacher—not an Islamic scholar—with a decades-long history of Muslim Brotherhood activism who had fled Iraq for Jordan in the 1990s and traveled the Arab world raising money for charitable networks. As head of the diwan, Dulaimi had access to financial resources that the AMS lacked, and his influence was partly due to paying salaries. He also leveraged interpersonal connections from his time at the College of Sharia and Fiqh at the University of Baghdad (the third major Sunni seminary in Iraq and the one that predates the Baʿth) and, if his autobiographical account is correct, from his years in exile. Dulaimi did not participate in the January 2005 elections, but as discussed below, he organized an electoral list for the December elections that year. During that time, in July 2005, he was removed as head of the diwan and replaced by his deputy, Ahmad Abd al-Ghafur al-Samarrai, who engaged in less direct electioneering.[13]

Neither Harith al-Dhari nor Adnan Dulaimi were on anyone's radar before the invasion as potentially influential figures for the Sunni Arab community. Both are members of influential tribes, and al-Dhari's grandfather is famous for his role in helping spark the 1920 revolt against the British (he shot a lieutenant colonel in the back). But other aspiring Sunni Arab politicians had similar—or even more prestigious—tribal and religious backgrounds. Why did these two emerge as arguably the most influential Sunni Arab politicians in the first few years after invasion? The key factor is that they controlled the two postinvasion organizations that specifically sought to coordinate Sunni Arab preachers.

Although their influence, both pre- and postinvasion, pales in comparison to Sistani's, it comes from the same information mechanism that helped augment Sistani's traditional religious authority. But their ability to induce compliance among Sunni preachers was limited, and neither demonstrated an ability to consistently coordinate messages across mosques for sustained periods of time.[14] Harith al-Dhari was openly criticized by AMS members at times, and it was not uncommon to find different statements posted in AMS-affiliated mosques and delivered in Friday sermons. For example, in April 2005, sixty-four prominent AMS and IIP clerics issued a religious ruling calling on Sunni Arabs to join Iraq's fledgling military and police forces. Although this was widely hailed as a breakthrough in Sunni Arab political participation, it quickly became evident that Sunni Arab clerics were not united on that position. The signers coordinated sermons in their mosques the following Friday, reading the statement.[15] Hundreds of other Sunni Arab mosques, many also nominally affiliated with the AMS, ignored or openly condemned the call. In other words, not only were Sunni Arab preachers divided across different organizations, but those organizations—despite being partly based on preexisting religious networks—lacked the resources or leadership needed for intranetwork compliance. The AMS's network structure may or may not have resembled the centralized network structure of a marja'iyya network, but it certainly lacked a leader at the center with preexisting religious authority. Ahmad Khaleel, an academic and NGO activist in Iraq after the invasion, argues that Sunni Arabs might have found such a leader in Abdul Karim Zaidan, the prolific scholar and former dean of Islamic studies at the University of Baghdad who mentored Dhari, Dulaimi, and many other Iraqi clerics.[16] But Zaidan was living and teaching in Yemen before the invasion and did return to Iraq before his death in 2014. Even if he had, however, the octogenarian scholar would have faced the same challenges of inducing compliance among clerics, and other Sunni clerical organizations would have emerged to challenge his authority. Zaidan's religious credentials were arguably on par with Sistani's, but he—and Sunni Arabs more generally—lacked an analogous organization.

Other examples demonstrate that having a preexisting religious network and authority from before 2003 was insufficient for widespread political mobilization of Sunnis. The three main Sufi orders in Iraq—the Qadiriyya, Rifa'iyya, and Naqshbandiyya—were not particularly influential, even with members, in the years immediately after the invasion. And the orders disagreed, both internally and with other orders, about what political stances to take. Baram says that the Qadiris and Rifa'is initially were not opposed to the post-Ba'th political order.[17] During my fieldwork, the Rifa'is in Basra were widely considered to be apolitical, which meant that their members' only unified position on political issues was not to openly discuss them. The local Rifaʻi leaders in Basra were unwilling to be interviewed by me, perhaps out of concern that a foreign researcher would emphasize some of their more sensational ritual practices. It is only when the civil war escalated in 2006 and 2007 that the Sufi orders became institutionally involved in insurgency.

Sunnis' Failure to Coordinate

Khaleel, himself a Sunni Arab in postinvasion Iraq, writes that "the Sunnis' choices were hard to make too: to resist or not to resist, to participate in the elections or not to participate, to accept the new situation or not, and so on and so forth."[18] The failure of Sunni Arabs to coordinate nationally was poignantly demonstrated in the national referendum on the proposed Iraqi permanent constitution in mid-October 2005. Sunni Arabs would have been better off if they had coordinated on either all voting no, and thereby vetoing the permanent constitution, or all boycotting the vote, thereby allowing the constitution to pass but denying it the legitimacy of Sunni Arab participation in the referendum. The worst-case scenario for the Sunni Arabs, however, is what transpired: they failed to make a group choice, they failed to coordinate. Tens of thousands of Sunni Arabs voted (significantly more than in January's elections), but the constitution still passed. Just days before the referendum, the Iraqi Islamic Party and a few other groups endorsed the constitution and encouraged a yes vote, claiming it had secured a clause allowing the new parliament to revise the document. IIP mosques told Sunni Arabs to vote and to vote in the affirmative. Some AMS preachers encouraged Sunni Arabs to vote no; others advocated a boycott. Predictably, some Sunni Arabs voted yes, some voted no, others boycotted. In the end, Sunni Arabs eclipsed the two-thirds rejection rate in only two governates but failed to turn out to vote no in sufficient numbers in either Diyala or Nineveh to defeat the constitution in a third governate, which was necessary for a veto. Throughout the constitution-writing process, many Shiʻi and Kurdish leaders complained that the Sunni Arab negotiators did not have a unified position and seemed to be against everything. An inability to coordinate significantly reduced their collective bargaining power, contributing to the perception that Sunni Arabs as a community were being shut out of the political process or deliberately marginalized.

Sunnis also failed to coordinate in elections in 2005. The AMS encouraged Sunni Arabs to boycott the elections in both January and December, often warning that the United States would dictate the results. The IIP planned to participate in the January elections, but it pulled out of the transitional National Assembly elections the week prior, although some of its slates did compete in the governate elections held on the same day. For the December vote, Adnan al-Dulaimi—by this time removed from his position as head of the Sunni diwan—organized the Iraqi Accord Front, which garnered 1.8 million votes and thereby won 16 percent of the seats in the Council of Representatives, surprising most observers.

Dulaimi called on hundreds of Sunni preachers to tell their congregations to vote for the Accord Front.[19] But the Sunni Arab vote was highly fractured, split across the Accord Front (forty-four seats, spread over three groupings); Saleh al-Mutlaq's neo-Ba'thist National Dialogue Front (eleven seats); Mishan al-Jibouri's Liberation and Reconciliation Bloc (three); Mithal al-Aloosi's list for the Iraqi Nation (one); and the Ayad Allawi–headed Iraqi National List (twenty-five). In contrast, Shi'i parties—just as fractured across ideological, class, and regional lines as Sunni groups—ran on a unified list backed by Sistani's network. The Shi'i vote was not split, and the United Iraqi Alliance won 128 seats and de facto power in the Iraqi parliament.

Over time, the political influence of both Sunni clerical associations waned. As sectarian violence increased following the February 2006 bombing of the al-'Askari Shrine in Samarra, the AMS's tacit support for armed resistance to the occupation sounded to many like an endorsement of Salafi jihadi militants. Facing an arrest warrant, al-Dhari fled to Jordan in 2006 and died there in 2015; the AMS's headquarters in the Mother of All Villages Mosque was taken over by the Sunni diwan in 2007.[20] The Sunni diwan—a government bureau, subject to pressure from Iraqi cabinets—reduced its direct involvement in politics after the removal of Dulaimi in July 2005. For his part, Dulaimi led the fractious Accord Front until he resigned in July 2007 (reportedly from exile) and faded from the political scene. He died in Iraqi Kurdistan in 2017. Sunni clerics remained divided into different factions, including during the 2012 to 2014 protest movement in al-Anbar. Rabkin notes that religious leaders "jumped to the forefront of the protest movement" and used large Friday prayer services for protests, but he blames those religious leaders "for the movement's inability to agree on a common set of demands."[21] Some demanded an autonomous Sunni Arab region; others rejected that demand. Clerics and the official Fiqh Council (formed in 2012) issued competing and contradictory fatwas. The council, formed as yet another attempt to coordinate Sunni preachers, "soon proved unable to fulfill the leadership role it claimed and for which it had won state recognition."[22]

The Ongoing Challenge of Sunni Inclusion

There are two conventional wisdoms about the central challenge of Sunni Arab participation in post-Saddam Iraqi governments. The first is that Iraq's main Shi'i political groups are supremacists; the second is that Iraq's Sunni Arab politicians are chauvinists.[23] According to the Shi'i supremacism perspective, Iraq's Shi'a believe that a Sunni minority monopolized power and discriminated against them since the founding of the modern state of Iraq. Now, however, Shi'a can use their numerical majority to win elections, ensconce themselves in state institutions, and seek vengeance on the Ba'th Party's Sunni supporters. From this perspective, the challenge of Sunni inclusion is to pressure Shi'i political parties to give Sunni Arabs a representative and meaningful share of power.[24] The second perspective, that of Sunni chauvinism, is based on the idea that Sunnis fundamentally reject Iraq's post-Saddam political order because they do not dominate it; an Iraqi government headed by Shi'a is illegitimate. Some Sunnis Arabs are described as delusional, believing that they are the true numerical majority in Iraq. From this perspective, the core challenge of Sunni inclusion is for Sunni irredentists to be defeated and the Sunni minority to reconcile itself with no longer holding privileged access to state resources and power.

Both of these perspectives, however, make the same fundamental error: They conflate a category (Sunni and Arab) with groupness. Fanar Haddad writes that prior to 2003, "there was little in the way of a differentiated sense of unique 'we-ness' among Sunni Arabs in Iraq and little need to express a Sunni Iraqi identity."[25] Haddad explains this by focusing on their underdeveloped myth-symbol complex. Compared to Shi'a, he says, Sunnis "lack the symbolic heritage and iconography with which to develop coherent instruments of identity-assertion," and Haddad traces efforts by Sunni Islamic organizations to produce symbols of group definition.[26] Although the *idea* of a "Sunni community" exists—as became particularly clear with the Sunni protest movement of 2012 to 2014—that community has been divided relative to the repeated consensuses that Shi'a demonstrated. Haddad would attribute this to the stronger sense of "we-ness" that Shi'a possessed for a variety of historical reasons. Others would emphasize that the Ba'th Party prevented any alternative forms of organization to exist among Sunni Arabs; Khaleel says they lacked leaders with vision.[27] This chapter shows, however, that Sunni Arabs did possess several forms of religious networks that were sufficiently robust to survive the fall of the regime and reemerge to play new roles postinvasion. But the structure of those networks and the lack of a central leader with standing who could enforce internal discipline limited the ability of Sunni

Arabs to create and act on a sense of "we-ness" similar to that displayed by Shiʻa in the early years after the invasion.

This book offers a different explanation for Sunnis' lack of "we-ness": it is not that they lack symbols and iconography or potential leaders; what Sunnis lack is a mechanism to consistently and reliably generate common knowledge and an expectation that others will act on that knowledge across a geographically dispersed population. Sunnis in Iraq lack a mechanism to reach consensuses on new issues and create an imagined community. The extent to which they aspire to be a group is debatable—Haddad sees a sense of Sunni victimhood as "necessitating the creation of Sunni symbols"—but the analysis here implies the shared symbols will be insufficient for joint actions in the absence of a coordinated way to use those symbols.[28]

The challenge of "Sunni inclusion" is a misnomer. The United States and neighboring Arab states invested considerable time and resources to nurture Sunni leaders in Iraq. And a wide variety of Sunni Arabs have been included in Iraqi governments since 2003: former Baʻthists; opponents of the Baʻth; pre-Baʻth Iraqi nationalists; exiles; technocrats; secularists; Muslim Brothers; Sufis; Salafis; tribal leaders; regional leaders. At times, Sunni Arabs have been overrepresented in post-2003 Iraqi governments. After the 2014 parliamentary election, a 20 percent vote share for Sunni Arab and nationalist parties gave them 32 percent of ministerial slots (eight of twenty-five), including defense, agriculture, education, electricity, and trade, plus the speaker of the parliament, a vice president, and a deputy prime minister. The problem in Iraq is not a lack of Sunni leaders; it is a plethora of them.

Iraq's Shiʻa are as diverse as its Sunnis—and diverse in similar ways—but Grand Ayatollah Sistani had a standing capable of being augmented and an institutional capacity to coordinate Shiʻa to reach consensus on a variety of issues, while Sunni leaders lacked both, but particularly the latter. The Sunnis lack an analogous mechanism, and consequently, no coherent imagined community of Sunni Arabs has emerged. The discrepancy between relative Shiʻi coherence and Sunni fragmentation is why many still see the challenge of "Sunni inclusion" as a central issue determining stability in Iraq. The problem is not political; it is structural. Finally, Sunni fragmentation, the lack of a cohesive imagined community—a sense of "we-ness"—and frustration help explain why the Islamic State rose from and spread among Iraq's Sunni Arabs after December 2013.

8

BEYOND BASRA AND BEYOND SERMONS

This final chapter does several things. First, it goes beyond Basra—and Iraq—by looking at the coordinating role and coordination of Friday sermons in other places and times. It also discusses the book's further contributions to the third problem of enduring significance discussed in the introduction and touched on throughout the book: the rise of political community and collective identity. Finally, it goes beyond sermons by explaining how the general argument speaks to broader issues of culture and social order.

Sermons beyond Basra

It has long been customary in Muslim communities to mention the ruler's name in the Friday sermon, often asking God to bless his (seemingly always "his") reign, and this practice is said to have originated in (the original city of) Basra in the late 650s. According to Ibn Khaldun, it was there that a caliph was prayed for in a sermon for the first time, when the governor, Ibn Abbas, said from the pulpit, "O God, help Ali (who represents) the truth." Ibn Khaldun writes, "This practice was continued afterwards," partly "because a prayer at such an hour was thought likely to be heard."[1]

The argument developed in this book helps explain why failing to mention the ruler's name is often understood as an act of rebellion. Because each listener knows that everyone else in attendance also heard the omission, the preacher's challenge becomes common knowledge, even if it alone is insufficient to stimulate a revolt.

In this instance, what is not said can be as consequential as what is said. Recognizing this, Muslim rulers have long attempted to strictly control who preaches in the main mosques of the largest cities, particularly the capital. There was nothing unique about the Baʿth Party's desire to regulate Islamic preaching.

The historian Richard Bulliet calls coinage and the Friday sermon "the emblems of sovereignty in medieval Islam."[2] When a city was conquered or a ruler overthrown, reciting the *khutbah* in the name of the new ruler was a signal that power was being consolidated. The first Friday sermon in Ayasofya, Istanbul's grand imperial mosque, after Mustafa Kemal (not yet Atatürk) and the new Turkish Grand National Assembly abolished the Ottoman caliphate in February 1924 did not mention the incumbent caliph, Abdulmejid II. With this omission, the city's residents immediately knew (and knew that others knew) that the age of the caliphate was over, which helped the nascent republic consolidate its authority as it transitioned from a religiously based understanding of society to a nation-state. Almost a millennium earlier, in 969, when the Fatimid army—led by the general Jawhar the Sicilian—entered Fustat, the capital of Egypt, they bypassed the Mosque of Ibn Tulun, despite it being the administrative seat of Fustat, and continued on to the smaller Mosque of ʿAmr, known as the old congregational mosque and the site of the Friday prayer and sermon.[3] On the following Friday, the preacher there, dressed in Fatimid white, delivered the Friday sermon in the name of the Ismaili Fatimid caliph, al-Muʿizz, cementing the leadership of the Shiʿi dynasty over Egypt. Sometimes when a city surrendered to an army, the public would learn about it on Friday when the new sovereign's name was invoked in the sermon. In 1037 (or 1038), although the elites of Nishapur in northeastern Iran had surrendered the city to the Seljuk Turks days earlier, "the populace did not really believe it" until they heard the Friday preacher invoke the name of the Seljuk leader, Tughril Beg, instead of the Ghaznavid ruler.[4]

In those examples, it was sufficient for legitimation and wide coordination for the sermon to take place in one Friday mosque because it was central. But what happens when there are multiple mosques? This book explored cases where the Sadrists coordinated sermons in a handful of mosques; Sistani consistently did in dozens; and the AMS and Sunni diwan inconsistently did in some unknown number. In July 2016, the government of Egypt moved to standardize Friday sermons at more than sixty thousand mosques nationwide, having all prayer leaders read the same unified sermon (*khutbah muwahhadah*).[5] The first such coordinated sermon focused on corruption. Sadr, Sistani, and the Sunni Arab organizations in Iraq coordinated sermons through clerical networks of preachers who had studied together and were more and less reliant on the network for their jobs, standing, and salaries. It is conceivable that a nonstate network could coordinate over thousands of mosques, but it would likely require a sufficient unity of purpose. Aside from that, it takes a state—like Egypt. Since 2016, tens of millions of Egyptians are supposed to have heard a message each week and know that tens of millions of their countrymen heard the exact same message, word for word. Whether people will come to expect others to act on those messages is another question. They will have common knowledge; the question is if they—the Egyptian government and the public—will use that knowledge to collectively act. In May 2017, as the Iraqi government was retaking western Mosul from ISIS's control, the Sunni diwan in Iraq instituted a "unified sermon" policy in eastern Mosul's Sunni Friday mosques, appointing all preachers (most of them new, since ISIS had killed many and installed its own preachers) and requiring them to deliver (and record themselves delivering) a single, preapproved message in their sermons.[6] The directive presumably offered the Sunni diwan an opportunity to coordinate residents of Mosul on how to treat those who had collaborated with ISIS and on other messages related to rebuilding the central government's administration of the city.

Identity Out of Order

A core insight of this book is that an ability to induce coordination and low-cost contributions defines and constrains clerical authority, both locally and nationally. Networks controlled by Iraq's most senior grand ayatollahs allowed them to disseminate similar messages reliably and consistently in different mosques, generating common knowledge and shared behavioral beliefs across geographically dispersed congregations. Sistani used his network to coordinate "followers" on a diverse set of issues, such as electoral strategies and positions on constitutional issues. Iraqis knew that other Iraqis living far away, people whom they would never meet but who attended sermons within the same ayatollah's network, would know what they know on particular topics; this is a key feature of sharing an identity and imagining being part of a community. For Benedict Anderson, an imagined community of national consciousness was spread by printers aggressively and competitively expanding markets for vernacular books.[7] In Iraq, a different technology of communication—sermons—helped make communities imaginable. The potential stretch of the imagined community activated by networked Friday sermons did not reach everyone. It only reached Shi'a who attended Friday mosques in the network, and it did not reach—it could not reach—Sunnis and non-Muslims. The reach of the technology defined the boundaries of the imagined community.

Being part of Iraq's imagined community of Shi'a became more salient for members, even though messages driving that change were not explicitly Shi'i. Sistani's messages were consistently inclusive and spoke in national, not sectarian, terms.[8] Sistani tried to reach out to Sunnis and non-Muslims, frequently meeting with representatives of those communities. But his messages were most consistently and reliably and usefully delivered via a medium that was exclusive to Shiʿa. This is consistent with Fanar Haddad's idea of "antagonistic notions of unity" and his argument that sectarianism in Iraq centers on different notions of Iraqi nationalism. The sense of Iraqi-ness or national interest that developed through sharing sermons could not reach non-Shiʿa. It was not intended to be a boundary between "us" and "them"—between Shiʿa and non-Shiʿa—but it became one. Iraqis frequently say, "There is no difference between us; we are all Iraqis" (*Maku farq baynana; kullna Iraqiyyin*); for the most part, such sentiments are sincere. But the process by which order was created amid state collapse unintentionally contributed to a widespread sense of community and nation that left out Iraq's non-Shiʿa.

Beyond Sermons

Because Friday sermons had not been held in Shiʿa areas before the invasion, attending this ritual, listening to the message, and then acting on it because others would too is an example of a "new" institution. This book offers a rare account of such an occurrence, particularly in a stateless context. It traces how such beliefs, and the institutions they support, came about under anarchy. It explains why some actors, but not others, became authorities or saw their traditional authority expand beyond those traditional boundaries. The argument elucidates the extent of the authority of those authorities. The creation, sustenance, and limits of legitimacy are accounted for as part of the argument. The authority that emerged was self-fulfilling, but it was also fragile. Finally, the book contrasts the institutional development (and nondevelopment) of imagined communities. The three central puzzles of the book—how societies produce and maintain social order, the sources and limits of authority and leadership, and the saliency of political community—have spawned large but disconnected literatures. This book shows the interconnectedness of these topics and treats them as sequential problems.

Although focused on Islam and Iraq, the approach taken has broad applications for how we think about culture, authority, and community. It is a truism that culture matters. The questions for researchers are whether we can identify the conditions under which it matters, which behaviors it will guide and which it will not. Although couched here in terms of an Islamic ritual, the approach is relevant for investigating the effects—and limits—of a wide variety of cultural institutions.

What is specific and what is generalizable about Basra in the first few years after the invasion? What I see as general are the interactions between people:

the "games" people were playing, the means by which they acquired information, the conditions under which they obeyed "authorities," and the unintended effects of relying on particular technologies of strategic communication. These patterns are what travel. This book suggests that some (religious/ethnic/social) cleavages, and even particular groups within those cleavages, have advantages in mobilizing individuals because of their institutional ability to create common knowledge. The controllers of those "ethnic" institutions determine what information is disseminated and when common knowledge is generated. By controlling which interpretations and behaviors individuals will coordinate on, such political entrepreneurs can determine which of the possible Pareto-improving group actions individuals will engage in. Scholars have identified the potential importance of common knowledge but have yet to link it theoretically and empirically to significant macro outcomes. This book contributes to this literature by arguing that common knowledge and the institutions that generate it are key components of identity formation, maintenance, and political entrepreneurship.

Finally, the book also has implications for the literature on failed states. William McCants argues that ISIS's strategy of seizing and governing territory was influenced by a 2004 book titled *The Management of Savagery: The Most Critical Stage through which the Islamic Nation Will Pass*.[9] Writing under the nom de guerre Abu Bakr Naji, the author argues that violence directed against strategic state assets will lead the government to withdraw from territory in the periphery of the state, leaving disorder and "areas of savagery." Jihadists can then fill that vacuum by providing order—basic security, public goods, God's law—where it no longer exists. An Islamic state and, eventually, a new caliphate can be built across these spaces of disorder through the effective "administration of savagery." The collapse of the Iraqi state in 2003 shows that under certain conditions, people can mitigate savagery without a top-down imposition of order by foreign forces or intrepid state builders backed by militias. After the outbreak of the so-called Arab Spring in 2011, the Iraqi, Libyan, Yemeni, and Syrian states withdrew or were forced out of large swathes of their sovereign territories, at least temporarily. People in those areas were forced to find alternative ways of providing order, and the dilemmas and mechanisms of resolving those dilemmas described in this book are highly relevant to those places.

The historian Thabit Abdullah noted that the city of Basra was at its greatest during periods of tremendous instability.[10] From the seventh to the tenth centuries, Basra was the scene of Islam's Golden Age civil war (the Battle of the Camel in 656); uprisings against imperial authority (such as that led by Ibn al-Ash'ath in 701); "slave" rebellions (Zott in 820–835, Zanj in 869–879); and repeated pillaging and massacres by religious fanatics from the Gulf, some of whom are remembered as "greengrocers" for their purported vegetarianism (Qarmatians in 923 and after). Despite this disorder, Basra was a commercial, financial, industrial, agricultural, religious, and intellectual metropolis throughout these centuries.[11] The poetry, literature, and rules of grammar produced in the city shaped the wider Muslim and Arabic-speaking worlds. Order can be produced in the absence of a Leviathan, and life without one is not always solitary, poor, nasty, brutish, or short. But forms of order have their limits. A durable and scalable order that could provide costly public goods did not emerge from local mosque sermons. Finding a balance between the self-enforcing production of order and the need for a Leviathan is a dilemma all societies face.

Notes

PREFACE

1. The rumors were true. Nicholas Berg, for example, was abducted in Baghdad on 9 April 2004, and beheaded by Abu Musab al-Zarqawi in a video released on the Internet the following month. I also was in Baghdad, staying not far from Berg's hotel, when he was abducted. At least seven other foreign hostages were executed in 2004.

2. According to media reports and my contacts in Basra, several dozen masked militiamen burst into a hotel located several blocks from the house where I had lived, demanded that the staff show them the guest registry, and then pulled the journalist, who was in town on an assignment for the *Sunday Telegraph*, from his room. They released a video demanding US forces end their siege of Sadrist militiamen in Najaf. BBC 2004b.

3. Al-Mohammed 2012, 598.

4. Wong 2005a.

5. Vincent 2005.

6. Worth 2005.

7. It is fortunate that I did not return. In September 2005, violence erupted in Basra after the British military arrested an aide to Sadr. Two British military or intelligence personnel disguised as "Arabs" engaged Iraqi police in a firefight and were detained by policemen affiliated with the Mahdi Army. British armored vehicles arrived and broke through a wall of the police station (either an exterior security wall or a wall of the main building) where either the two operatives or a British military team sent to retrieve them were being held. A mob (or organized gathering) of several hundred to two thousand Iraqis quickly massed near the police station and attacked the British vehicles. If I had been in Basra as planned, there is a high probability that I would have been abducted and possibly killed in response to this British operation.

8. Carroll 2005. See also Oppel 2005. Basra city had 2,500 to 3,000 police officers at the time; Sade's figures refer to his governate-wide force. Sade, a former special forces officer in Saddam's army, was appointed by Ayad Allawi. His statements reflect the Iraqi central government's weakness in Basra at the time.

9. Frances 2010, 17–18.

10. The fifteenth day of Shaʿban, the eighth month in the Islamic calendar, is a holy day for all Muslims, known as the Night of Salvation. But Shiʿa also commemorate the birth of the Twelfth Imam, Muhammad al-Mahdi, on the date, and Iraqis associate the date with the beginning of the 1991 uprisings against Saddam. The Fifteenth Shaʿban militia in Basra claimed to have been part of the wider insurgent group Movement of the Fifteenth of Shaʿban, which sought refuge in the southern Iraqi marshes in the early 1990s and attempted to assassinate Uday Hussein in 1996. The Sadrists claimed that TharAllah and Fifteenth Shaʿban were affiliated with the Badr Organization; Badr leaders suggested the death squads were connected to the Sadrists.

11. Many in Basra believe that Yusuf al-Mosawi ordered the execution of Steven Vincent. For years after 2008, it was rumored in Basra that Mosawi was captured by Iraqi security forces during Operation Charge of the Knights, brought before Prime Minister Nuri al-Maliki, and executed immediately afterward. But "Sayyed Yusuf" resurfaced a

decade later, and in 2020, another Iraqi prime minister again sent security forces to raid TharAllah's headquarters, this time for firing at protesters. *Asharq al-Awsat* 2020.

1. ORDER, AUTHORITY, AND IDENTITY

1. Sayej 2018.
2. On more or less contentious forms of sectarianism, see Haddad 2011, 25–28.
3. See Visser 2012 on the "sectarian master narrative" in reports and stories on post-2003 Iraq. Few academics make explicitly primordialist arguments (Osman 2015 is a notable exception), although such assumptions underlie many analyses.
4. Allawi 2007, 132.
5. Ripley 2014, loc. 3480.
6. Ucko 2013, 137.
7. Hardin 2013.
8. This distinction is a common one made in the literature on social order.
9. Chwe 2001.
10. Calvert 1992.
11. The late grand ayatollah's (1943–1999) given name is Mohammad; his father's (1906–1986) given name is Mohammad Sadiq; and their family name is al-Sadr. His correct name, therefore, is Mohammad Mohammad Sadiq al-Sadr. He is often incorrectly referred to as Mohammad Sadiq al-Sadr, which is his father's name.
12. Bates et al. 1998; Levi 2004; Greif 2006.
13. *Istikan* is the Iraqi term for the small glass in which tea is served. The word has the same meaning in Farsi, and some say it is related to the Russian word *stakan*, meaning glass or bowl.
14. Scholars of Arabic have largely ignored the spoken Arabic of the city of Basra and the surrounding area, perhaps assuming it can be subsumed under either "Iraqi" (i.e., Baghdadi) colloquial or the dialect of Kuwait. See Mahdi (1985) for a descriptive study of Basrawi Arabic. It is sufficiently different that Basrawis easily can be identified when in Baghdad or Kuwait.
15. Rotberg 2004, 14.
16. Gordon 2010, 131.
17. Gordon 2010, 131–132.
18. On the rewards system, see Sassoon 2012, Khoury 2013, Faust 2015, and Blaydes 2018.
19. Posner 2004, 248.
20. Al-Samara'i 2006.

2. THE SANCTIONS-ERA ROOTS OF POSTINVASION DEVELOPMENTS

1. Harling (2012, 65) sees the trajectories as "distorted," but he emphasizes a continuity from before the invasion to after.
2. Haddad 2011, 87.
3. Makiya 1989, 1993.
4. See, for example, Sassoon 2012; Khoury 2013; Faust 2015; Blaydes 2018; Helfont 2018.
5. Barakat 2005, 574.
6. Technically, this was the second Oil-for-Food program, passed in April 1995 as UN Security Council Resolution 986. Iraq had rejected an earlier UN-approved Oil-for-Food program in 1991.
7. The remainder went to a compensation fund for Kuwait, costs of the UN weapons inspectors, UN administrative costs, and a portion for the Kurdish area. Gordon 2010, 25–29.

8. Gordon 2010, 25.
9. Simons 1996; Halliday 1999; Gordon 2010; Mazaheri 2010; Gunter 2013; Blaydes 2018; Woertz 2019.
10. Woertz 2019.
11. Woertz 2019, 102.
12. Woertz 2019, 102–105; Mazaheri 2010.
13. Sassoon 2012, 248.
14. Gordon 2010, 131.
15. Gordon 2010, 131.
16. Sassoon 2012, 281.
17. The Baʻth had long used sheikhs to provide security in border areas and track down deserters, but state engagement with tribes expanded in the 1990s. Jabar 2003b; Baram 1997; Faust 2015, 141–146.
18. Rohde 2010, 56.
19. Rotberg (2004, 5) places Saddam's Iraq in a special category of weak states: "The seemingly strong one, always an autocracy, which rigidly controls dissent and is secure, but at the same time provides very few political goods."
20. Posner 2004.
21. Haddad 2010, 103–106.
22. Jabar 2003a, 272.
23. Baram 2014, xiii, xvi.
24. Baram 2014, 9–10.
25. Helfont 2018.
26. Rohde 2010, 60–61.
27. Baram 2014, 311–314.
28. Haddad 2011, 2015.
29. "Declaration of the Shia of Iraq," Al-Bab, July 2002, http://al-bab.com/albab-orig/albab/arab/docs/iraq/shia02a.htm; e.g., al-Shahristani 1994.
30. Haddad 2011.
31. Al-Salihi 1998, 51.
32. Baram 2014, 233–239.
33. E.g., Sassoon 2012, 2–3.
34. Helfont 2018, 146.
35. Faust 2015, 133.
36. Blaydes 2018.
37. Baram 2015; Helfont 2018.
38. Kadhem 2012.
39. Haddad 2011, 52–54.
40. When I had to broach the subject, I sometimes indirectly referenced it by asking, for example, whether "Abd al-Qadir" or "Abd al-Husayn" prays in a particular mosque, which I knew would be understood as asking if it was for Sunnis or Shiʻa.
41. Haddad 2015; also see Harling and Nasser 2010.
42. Litvak 1998. This contrasts with the institutional structure of the Sunni ulama in the Ottoman Empire and the Shiʻi clergy in Qajar Iran, both of which benefited from access to state patronage and revenue from landed endowments.
43. On the financial role of *khums* for Shiʻi ulama, see Jabar 2003a, 146–151. On monies from the holy cities, see Nakash 1994.
44. Some marajiʻ recognize a third category—*muhtat* (literally, cautious)—where the believer follows the strictest ruling among the rulings of different marajiʻ. Sistani, for example, says, "If he [a Muslim] is neither a Mujtahid nor a follower (Muqallid), he should act on such precaution which should assure him that he has fulfilled his religious obligation.

For example, if some Mujtahids consider an act to be haram, while others say that it is not, he should not perform that act. Similarly, if some Mujtahid consider an act to be obligatory (Wajib) while others consider it to be recommended (Mustahab), he should perform it." If someone is not a mujtahid and is unable to act on such precautionary measures, it is obligatory to follow a mujtahid. It is also assumed that a proper *muhtat* will make themselves aware of all the relevant rulings. See "Following a Jurist (Taqlid)," Official Website of His Eminence al-Sayyid Ali al-Husseini al-Sistani, accessed 15 August 2015, http://www.sistani.org/english/book/48/2116/.

45. This marks the transition from the Minor Occultation (*Ghaybat al-Sughra*) to the Major Occultation (*Ghaybat al-Kubra*), which continues today.

46. The title was applied retroactively to earlier clerics who never used it themselves. Calmard 2012.

47. Amanat 2009.

48. Akhbaris believe that people do not need to emulate scholars to live a moral life; they can interpret the reports (*akhbar*) of the lives of the Prophet and Imams on their own. Usulis (reasoners) believe that only trained scholars fully immersed in the study of those reports can judge their authenticity and deduce practical legal norms from them.

49. Walbridge 2014, 20, 76. The central such treatise is Ayatollah Muhammad Kazim Tabataba'i Yazdi's *Al-'Urwa al-Wuthqa*, which is typically studied closely during the final stage of study, *dars al-kharij*.

50. Walbridge 2014, 10–13.

51. Litvak 1998, 8.

52. Ayatollah Mohammad Baqir al-Sadr was among those who fiercely criticized this organizational feature of Iraqi Shi'ism. He advocated the replacement of what he called the "individualistic" marja'iyyah with an "institutional" one. His reforms sought to move the hawza away from what he saw as ad hoc, individual decision making and the inconsistent, inadequate training of students.

53. Litvak 1998, 28. Ayatollahs' networks resemble the "star" or "spoke" network controlled by the Medici in Florence. The Medici sat at the center of a spoke-like network structure while their network partners were segregated by social attributes and by neighborhood. Padgett and Ansell (1993) argue this structure facilitated collective action and coordination within the network if the actions were led by the Medici and hindered attempts to control the network by other actors within it. This book makes a similar argument but also provides an information-based microfoundation.

54. Litvak 1998, 28.

55. Weber 1978, 215–245.

56. Weber 1978, 215.

57. Al-Wardi 1969, 6.1:261.

58. Nakash 1994, 49–72.

59. See Kadhem 2012, 149 on the anticommunist fatwa, and Kadhim 2011, 72–73 and Nakash 1994, 121–125 on support for tribal uprisings.

60. Kadhem 2012, 175.

61. Kadhem 2012, 147.

62. There were successful coups in 1936, 1941, 1958, 1963 (two), and 1968, and many more unsuccessful ones. Interim constitutions were adopted in 1958, 1964, 1964, 1968, and 1970.

63. Kadhem 2012, 161.

64. Kadhem 2012, 149–150.

65. Kadhem 2012, 157, 168–174.

66. Kadhem 2012, 206–217.

67. Kadhem 2012, 286–287.

68. Corboz 2015, 131.
69. Khoei had a played a more overt political role in earlier decades, before Hakim's death. Kadhem 2012, 289–290.
70. Corboz 2015, 131n37.
71. Corboz 2015, 173. On relations with the Baʿth, see Kadhim 2013; Baram 2015; Helfont 2018.
72. Haddad 2010, 71. See also Makiya 1993, 74–76.
73. Haddad 2010, 71.
74. Visser 2005, 121–125. Haddad 2011, 69–73.
75. Ra'uf 2002. Abdul Satar al-Bahadali, Moqtada's representative and head of the Office of the Martyred Sadr II in Basra, gifted me a copy of this book in 2003, saying it was an important book for me to read to understand the current situation in Iraq.
76. By the late 1970s, Khoei seems to have favored Nasrullah Mustanbit as his successor, and Mustanbit appears seated to Khoei's right in some well-known pictures of Khoei with his students. But Mustanbit died in 1985 or 1986, before Khoei, and today is buried in the same chamber (number 31) in the Imam Ali Shrine with Khoei and his sons. Walbridge 2014, 78. Mohammad Sadeq Rouhani was considered by some to be Khoei's preferred successor in the 1980s. Corboz 2012, 105.
77. "Biography," Official Website of His Eminence al-Sayyid Ali al-Husseini al-Sistani, accessed 25 January 2022, https://www.sistani.org/english/data/2/.
78. Exceptions include Khalaji 2006; Walbridge 2014; Rizvi 2010, 1307–1308.
79. Corboz 2012, 102.
80. Although Golpaygani resided in the Islamic Republic of Iran and had prayed over Khomeini's body at his funeral, he was not considered a supporter of *wilyaet-al-faqih* and was not the Iranian regime's preferred marjaʿ (Muhammad Ali Araki was), so it was acceptable for Iraqis to follow him. Walbridge 2014, 56. The al-Khoei Foundation initially followed Golpaygani.
81. See list in Mauriello 2011, 19.
82. Although he has written many books, Walbridge (2014, 97) noted that "Sistani did not produce major religious writings, either in jurisprudence (fiqh and usul) or in theology, Quranic studies, or philosophy. His only intellectual work is limited to written lectures on al-ʿUrwa al-Wathiqa of Kazim Yazdi; others are merely booklets on jurisprudence or his legal opinions as part of the manual of law."
83. Walbridge 2014, 95–96.
84. Minister of Endowments and Religious Affairs to the Presidency of the Republic—Office of the Secretary of the National Security Council. "Issuing of a Fatwa," Baʿth Regional Command Collection (hereafter BRCC), 028-5-1 (583–585), 18 or 19 May 1997; Party Secretariat to Deputy Secretary General of the Party BRCC, 009-2-5 (0001–0007), 30 September 2002.
85. Corboz 2012, 107.
86. Corboz acknowledges this sensitive claim (2012, 107). See also Walbridge 2014, 239; Mauriello 2011, 106–107; Rizvi 2010, 1307; Rizvi 2018, 178.
87. Corboz 2012; Khalaji 2006.
88. The Sadrists were, of course, trying to contrast Sistani's behavior with the martyred Sadr's.
89. Walbridge 2001, 237.
90. Sassoon 2012, 261.
91. Sassoon 2012, 261–262.
92. Baram 2014, 314.
93. Baram 2014, 314–315; Helfont 2018, 38–40.
94. Helfont 2018, 41–42.

95. Helfont 2018, 93–98, 118–120, 139–140.
96. Helfont 2018, 131–132.
97. Helfont 2018, 165.
98. Sassoon 2012, 262.
99. Faust 2015, 141.
100. Baram 2014, 278.
101. Baram 2014, 92.
102. Haddad 2011.

3. COLLAPSE

1. Woods et al. 2006, 105–109.
2. Ripley 2014, loc. 3266.
3. Woods et al. 2006, 104.
4. For an account of the invasion, see Gordon and Trainor 2006.
5. The first quote is from Major General Robin Brims, the commander of the First (UK) Division; the second is from Brigadier Graham Binns of the Seventh Brigade. Ripley 2014, loc. 1450. See also Chilcot et al. 2016, vol. 8.
6. Ripley 2014, loc. 2151.
7. Chilcot et al. (2016), particularly vol. 6, makes clear that the United Kingdom was unprepared to take responsibility for a geographical sector of Iraq.
8. Chilcot et al. 2016, sec. 8.16.
9. Rossiter 2009, 263–264.
10. The first words in L. Paul "Jerry" Bremer's memoir of his time as head of the Coalition Provisional Authority, which would soon take over administration of the country, are "Baghdad was burning." Bremer 2006, 3.
11. Human Rights Watch 2003, 8–9.
12. Khoury 2016, 136–137.
13. Quote from a June 2010 private hearing of the the Iraq Inquiry, quoted in Chilcot et al. 2016, sec. 9.1, 154.
14. Barr 2002.
15. Inexplicably and wonderfully, one of the very few metal statues along Basra's waterfront that was spared by looters was of Basrawi poet Badr Shakr al-Sayyab. Or, perhaps, the statue was removed and returned after the looting had ceased.
16. This was compounded by the steady brain drain of the 1990s (Gordon 2010, 137–139) and Iraq's reliance on foreigners for technical assistance, especially maintenance and repairs, in many ministries and offices. Most of these foreign professionals left before the invasion.
17. Estimates of the number of Iraqis directly affected by de-Ba'thification vary tremendously—from sixty thousand to six hundred thousand, depending on if they count only civil servants "removed" or include those "excluded," if they count the four hundred thousand members of the Iraqi Army and one hundred thousand members of disbanded intelligence and security agencies, and if informal purges of Ba'thists and alleged-Ba'thists from government-affiliated trade unions and associations are considered. De-Ba'thification policies and processes evolved over time and, as early as September 2003, were almost entirely in Iraqi hands. See Lafourcade 2012 for an analysis of how de-Ba'thification changed over time.
18. The now declassified "Future of Iraq Project" predicted this state breakdown: "As the structure of the state disintegrates, senior officials . . . and others responsible for issuing orders and running the engine of state, can be expected not to report to work. The chain of command in the government departments and agencies will be broken, creating tempo-

rary but serious administrative paralysis. Cities and towns will be left without a civil administration, leading to disruption of law and order, the food distribution systems and emergency health care. Because of the high likelihood of a political vacuum and the possible administrative vacuum in the period immediately preceding and following the fall of the regime, other strategies must be devised to fill these needs quickly." Quoted in Synott 2008, 156. A declassified prewar UK Ministry of Defence intelligence report, "Basra: Post Saddam Governance," also anticipated widespread looting. Defence Intelligence Analysis Staff 2003.

19. Quoted in Packer 2005, 136.
20. Eberly 2009, 140.
21. Eberly 2009, 96.
22. Packer 2005, 139; Phillips 2005, 134–135.
23. Makiya 1989; Rohde 2010; Jabar 2003b, 89.
24. Sassoon 2012, 249, 252.
25. Kubba 2001, 38.
26. Davis 2005; Bashkin 2009; Hadid 2014.
27. Sassoon 2012, 122–128; Faust 2015, 155–157; Blaydes 2018.
28. Faust 2015, 248fn29; Blaydes 2018.
29. Kanan Makiya (1989, 38) estimated that "one-fifth of the economically active Iraqi labor force (about 3.4 million people) were institutionally charged during peacetime (1980) with one form or another of violence." On the regime's security agencies, see Makiya [al-Khalil] 1989, 1993; al-Marashi 2002; Woods et al. 2006.
30. Woods et al. 2006, 48.
31. Woods et al. 2006, 51–55.
32. They said they were forced to pay $200 in penalties and another 500,000 Iraqi dinars (about $400 at the time, they estimated) to avoid three months in jail.
33. See, for example, Oxford Research International 2003. In this October–November 2003 poll of 3,244 Iraqis, 89.4 percent of respondents chose this response.
34. Blaydes 2018, 174.
35. Khoury 2016, 134.
36. Sassoon 2012, 195.
37. Dodge, 2007, 27.
38. Al-Mohammad 2012, 603.
39. Eric Davis (2005), for example, examines the role of historical memory in shaping a collective understanding of Iraqi nationalism.
40. Haddad 2011, 65–86.
41. Davis 2005.
42. See Phillips 2005; Ricks 2006; Special Inspector General for Iraq Reconstruction 2009; Rudd 2011; Chilcot et al. 2016.
43. Phillips 2005, 131. See Rudd 2011 for a history of ORHA.
44. Sluglett 2006. For a sampling of this literature, see Fallows 2004; Anderson 2004; Diamond 2005; Etherington 2005; Shadid 2005; Packer 2005; Bremer 2006; Allawi 2007.
45. Chilcot et al. 2016, vols. 6.4 and 6.5.
46. Ripley 2014, loc. 3480.
47. Ripley 2014, loc. 3426 and note 41.
48. By the time I arrived in Basra in September 2003, the British military had two bases just outside the city and three inside: their headquarters in the outlying Basra International Airport; a logistic base at Shaibah, southeast of the city; the isolated Basra Palace, on the southern edge; the Shatt al-Arab Hotel near the closed city airport in the north of the city; and the Old State Building. The remainder of the British force, as well as other national forces in the British sector (e.g., Australians, Spanish, Japanese, Dutch, Danes,

New Zealanders), were spread through Iraq's four most southern governates: Basra, Muthana, Maysan, and Thi Qar.

49. Ucko 2013, 137.

50. Major General Brims said he was someone "with whom he could do business." Chilcot et al. 2016, sec. 9.1, 1453.

51. North 2009, 18.

52. Fairweather 2003a, 2003b.

53. Synnott 2008, 29.

54. Chilcot et al. 2016, sec. 15.1.

55. Human Rights Watch 2003.

56. Human Rights Watch 2003; North 2009, 21.

57. Human Rights Watch 2003, 20.

58. Kernaghan to Blunkett, 23 May 2003, "Iraq—Visit by Chief Constable PR Kernaghan," UK Government Web Archive, http://www.iraqinquiry.org.uk/media/236555/2003-05-23-report-kernaghan-to-blunkett-iraq-visit-by-chief-constable-p-r-kernaghan.pdf.

59. Prices fluctuated, but in late 2003 I found basic Chinese Type 56 assault rifles readily available for about $50. A wide range of AK-47s and variants (e.g., AKMs) could easily be purchased.

4. THE EMERGENCE OF LOCAL ORDERS

1. This distinction between coordination games and collective action problems is common in the literature. See, for example, Ullmann-Margalit 1977; Hechter 1990; Hardin 1982, 1991; Wrong 1994; Rawls 2001, 6; Hechter and Horne 2009; Cronk and Leech 2013.

2. Olson 1965.

3. Hardin 2013.

4. Hardin 2007, 85; on Hume and coordination, see also Sabl 2012.

5. This point is made by Sabl (2012, 42) and others.

6. Chwe 2003, 97–99.

7. Samuelson 1998. See Cronk and Leech (2013, 151–68) on coordination being emergent.

8. Schelling ([1960] 1980, 58–77) describes these and other qualities that tend to make something focal.

9. This role of common knowledge was developed by Lewis (1969), from work by Schelling ([1960] 1980), and mathematically represented by Aumann (1974, 1976). Chwe (2001) extends the concept to account for a wide range of existing empirical regularities and original data. He argues public rituals can be understood as social practices that generate common knowledge.

10. Chwe 2001.

11. Greif (2006, 148) calls this legitimacy. He writes, "One universal source of legitimacy is the observation that rules issued by the social unit in the past have been followed." See also Schelling [1960] 1980. Schelling (57) does not clearly distinguish between common knowledge (knowing what others know) and expectations that others would act on that knowledge. He writes, "Most situations—perhaps every situation for people who are practiced at this kind of game—provide some clue for coordinating behavior, some focal point for each person's expectation of what the other expects him to expect to be expected to do." Perhaps Iraqi Arabs were not sufficiently "practiced at this kind of game" in April 2003.

12. See Cronk and Leech (2013, 151–168) for a critique of this literature.

13. Hechter 1990.

14. Hechter 1990, 14.
15. See Weingast (2002) for a summary of the two strands of rational-choice institutionalism.
16. Greif 2006, particularly chap. 5, is the clearest outline of the approach.
17. Chwe 2001, 12.
18. Variants of such threshold or tipping models are examined in Granovetter 1978; Schelling 1978; Kuran 1997; and Laitin 1998.
19. By definition, a coordination problem is one in which each person wants to participate in a group action but only if others also participate. Even if an individual preferred an alternative group action (and even if everyone knew that everyone else preferred that alternative group action), individuals would not participate in that action unless they thought a sufficient number of others would also participate. The existence of cogent and widespread information about an alternative nonchosen strategy could be evidence that the situation is indeed a coordination dilemma, which is normally an assumption. When an individual's choice of behavior is independent of what others do, cogent and widespread information should be sufficient and common knowledge unnecessary for the aggregate behavior.
20. Ullman-Margalit (1977) uses the example of a fire alarm in a theater to show how similar situations could be either a coordination dilemma or a cooperation problem. If the fire is spreading rapidly and not everyone will make it out safely, the rush to the few exits might mean that fewer make it out than the maximum possible. But if the fire is spreading slowly, everyone can make it out if they coordinate and exit in a calm and orderly fashion.
21. A preference to coordinate together need not be a fundamental preference; it could be the product of circumstances, generated by the postinvasion environment, and time sensitive. Katznelson and Weingast 2005.
22. Abdullah 2001, 25.
23. Abdullah 2001, 23.
24. Alderson 2007, 14.
25. UNDP and Iraqi Ministry of Planning and Development Cooperation 2004.
26. This builds on Chwe's (2001) argument that public rituals should be studied as social processes that generate common knowledge.
27. Qutbuddin 2019, 275–277; Wensinck 1986.
28. Women join the men in some communities, but this was unusual in Iraq during the time of my field research.
29. The former is from the Arabic root *jama'*, implying gathering, assembling. The latter is from the Arabic root *sajada*, implying the religious prostration and bowing characteristic of Muslims' five daily prayers (*salat*). The English word *mosque* is derived from *masjid* and refers to both types. Friday mosques are sometimes called *masjid jami'* or *jami' masjid*; this is particularly common in non-Arab Muslim communities.
30. Some Islamic scholars say that distracting others from listening to a Friday sermon nullifies the disturber's prayer, requiring them to repeat it.
31. Chwe (2001) argues that the formalization and repetition of rituals increases individuals' confidence that others did not miss their messages.
32. Both sermons typically praise God, exhort the people to observe piety, invoke blessings on the Prophet (and the Imams, in Shi'i mosques), and include short chapters of the Quran. Messages on current events and dilemmas can appear in either or both sermons.
33. Messages about expected behavior can be embedded in stories about the Prophet, his Companions, or the Imams (in Shi'i mosques). While attending Friday prayers in Iraq, I sometimes heard but did not understand messages embedded in sermons because, as

a non-Muslim outsider, I did not have other attendees' shared understandings of Islamic history, especially details of Imam Husayn's martyrdom at Karbala and stories of his supporters that most pious Shiʻa in Iraq learn as children. In one discussion I organized with several men after we had all attended a sermon in the same mosque, I quickly realized that everyone except me had developed common knowledge of a contemporary issue that had been discussed with reference to the life of one of the Imams.

34. Putnam and Campbell 2010, 30. Alan Wolfe (2003, 228) also makes this observation: "Islam has not traditionally had churches in the way Christians understand that term. Rather than a congregation with a fixed membership, mosques in Muslim societies were—and continue to be—convenient places into which one steps in order to pray, depending on where one is in the course of the day.... But in the United States, mosques inevitably come to resemble churches."

35. Putnam and Campbell 2010, 29–30.

36. This lack of attention to Islamic ritual is common. Starrett's (1997, 293) review of anthropological work on Islam found that, "ironically, studies of Islamic ritual form by far the smallest subset of anthropological research on Islam."

37. Gaffney 1994 and Antoun 1989 are two influential anthropological accounts of contemporary Islamic preaching. Gaffney focuses on Minya, a city in Egypt, while Antoun analyzes sermons in a Jordanian peasant village, focusing on a single preacher. Qutbuddin (2019) discusses sermons in several Muslim-majority countries.

38. Borthwick 1965.

39. Ram 1991; Azodanloo 1992; Fathi 1980, 1981; Bakhash 1984. Kurzman (2004, 39–61) argues that the mosque network only became involved in the Iranian revolutionary movement long after it had begun. It helped sustain and grow the movement, but it was not involved at the outset.

40. On Shiʻa and Friday Prayers in modern times, see Sachedina 1988, 177–204.

41. Qutbuddin 2019, 279–280.

42. Machlis 2014, 145–146; Katz 2013, 135–138.

43. See Cole 1988, 127–137, on the controversy in their establishment in India.

44. Machlis 2014, 146–147.

45. Qutbuddin 2019, 284; Katz 2013, 131–134. The reason and legal justification for invoking the leader's name is debated by both Sunni and Shiʻi jurists, but since Umayyad times, it has been standard practice to include a prayer for the well-being of the caliph.

46. Amanat 2009, 167n48.

47. Machlis 2014, 145.

48. Dai 2009, 23fn15; Raʾuf 1999, 144; Raʾuf 2000, 48–51.

49. The nature of the relationship between the Baʻth regime and Sadr remains highly controversial and politicized. Sadr's critics allege he was a regime agent; his supporters say he merely took advantage of the regime's Faith Campaign. The Baʻth—and probably Saddam himself—must have approved of or decided to tolerate Sadr's resumption of Friday prayers. It is widely claimed that the regime preferred that an Arab marjaʻ would succeed Khoei and allowed the Arab Sadr latitude that it denied other marajiʻ, including Sistani. Or the regime simply may have preferred that Shiʻi clerical leadership remain unconsolidated and divided. There are claims that the regime encouraged Shiʻa to emulate Sadr, such as by granting his wakils access to governmental favors. Over time, though, it is clear that Sadr's sermons came to criticize the Baʻth, culminating in his assassination in February 1999. On the relationship, see Cockburn 2008; Kadhim 2013.

50. Adnan al-Silawi, interview with author, 4 March 2004, Basra. At the time of the interview, Silawi was Grand Ayatollah Kazim al-Haeri's wakil in Basra.

51. Cockburn 2008, 90, 100.

52. Cockburn 1998, 90–91.

53. Adnan al-Silawi, interview with author, 4 March 2004, Basra.
54. Kadhim 2013, 36.
55. Adnan al-Silawi, interview with author, 4 March 2004, Basra.
56. See al-Sadr n.d. for the text of his sermons. For a sympathetic description of his sermons and their impact, see al-Asadi 2002, 30–35.
57. Kadhim 2013, 36–37.
58. Kadhim 2013, 43.
59. Cockburn 1998, 90, 93.
60. Cockburn 1998, 93.
61. Kadhim 2013, 47.
62. Kadhim 2013, 48–49.
63. Kadhim 2013, 50.
64. Patel 2008. Most analysts and Iraqis blame the top echelons of the Ba'th regime for the assassination. Baram (2014, 275–276) insinuates that Iran may have killed Sadr.
65. Adnan al-Silawi, interview with author, 4 March 2004, Basra. His emphasis on these points was perhaps a response to accusations that Sadrist clerics were Saddam pawns.
66. Hamid al-Tayeb, interview with author, 4 October 2003.
67. Helfont 2018.
68. Rosen 2006, 19; Cockburn 2008, 127–132.
69. Cockburn 2008, 127.
70. Cockburn 2008, 128.
71. Rosen 2006.
72. For details of the fatwa, see Party Secretariat to Deputy Secretary General of the Party, BRCC, 009-2-5 (0001–0007), 30 September 2002. It does not appear in al-Khaffaf's (2007) de facto official collection of Sistani's statements.
73. Liaison Office of Grand Ayatullah Seestani—London 2003. Curiously, the statement does not appear to be included in al-Khaffaf's (2007) and others' compilations of Sistani's statements and communiqués in Arabic.
74. The quote is from the English text released by the London office, with a few grammatical corrections made by the author.
75. Al-Fardan 2013, 202.
76. See al-Fardan 2013, 202–206 for the necessary conditions, according to Sistani's rulings.
77. Fatwas dated 20 and 27 April 2003. See Khaffaf 2007 for others.
78. Fatwa dated 16 May 2003.
79. Al-Khaffaf 2007, 11–12.
80. Reider Visser (2006) argues that three distinct periods in Sistani's postinvasion career can be identified: a nonpolitical, quietist period prior to 26 June 2003, an "activist intermezzo" from 26 June 2003 until December 2004, and a return to relative seclusion and focus on matters of faith after December 2004.
81. Haddad 2011.
82. It could also be a subtle warning to do so because you could die at any moment; al-Jawad died in his mid-twenties, allegedly poisoned by his wife.
83. Dilley 2003. The account of the sermon content comes from Abdul Kathem Hussayn, the mosque's caretaker.
84. Al-Khaffaf 2006.
85. Cockburn 2008, 130.
86. Kadhim (2013) has a citation to 1999 ruling.
87. Liaison Office of Grand Ayatullah Seestani 2003. See Cook 2000 for a discussion of this principle in Islamic thought.

88. In contrast, no central "authority" disseminated norms among the Shasta Country ranchers studied by Robert Ellickson (1991). The ranchers' overarching substantive norm is that one should be a "good neighbor." It is unclear why some specific workaday norms, instead of other possible ones, emerge from this larger norm. Ellickson suggests that norms among whalers emerged to maximize objective welfare.

89. Cable from US Embassy, Baghdad, to Secretary of State, Washington, DC, dated June 2006 and obtained by the *Washington Post*, http://www.washingtonpost.com/wp-srv/opinions/graphics/iraqdocs_061606.pdf.

90. It need not be mud. Technically, it can be either earth or some product of the earth that cannot be eaten or worn.

91. Basra's principal Chaldean cathedral, the gothic Church of the Virgin Mary, had been closed since 1981, although it housed displaced poor during the Iran-Iraq War. The size of Basra's Christian population has shrunk dramatically since 2003.

92. It was widely believed among Basrawis that the British military or CPA South contracted with the Kuwaiti cell company to set up a cell tower or two in Basra so they could communicate with one another and with their operations in Kuwait. It also was widely believed that some phone numbers—those that began with certain digits—received priority on the network.

93. Chwe (2001, 65) suggests strong links are better at forming common knowledge (particularly in local clusters) than weak links which might be better for communicating widely.

94. Bash'ayan 2013, 3:1092–1093.

95. Khoury 2016, 139–140.

96. Sassoon 2012, 211.

97. Some neighborhoods in Iraqi cities were designated for certain professions, and the state gave land to or subsidized its purchase by teachers, engineers, and soldiers. Basra, for example, has neighborhoods named for engineers, teachers, naval officers, and noncommissioned officers. A greater sense of community may exist in these occupationally named areas, and some professional clubs coterminous with locality may have survived the war. But I found little evidence that these neighborhoods differed from other neighborhoods in Basra. Many grantees appear to have sold or leased their free or subsidized land to others. Under sanctions in the 1990s, the state may have given such plots to professionals expecting them to immediately sell them for hard currency. This may have been a way for the cash-strapped Iraqi state to induce skilled professionals to remain in Iraq instead of seeking higher salaries abroad.

98. Batatu [1978] 2004, 153–210.

99. Bash'ayan 2013, 3:1187–1188.

100. Sadruddin Aga Khan, "Report to the Secretary-General on Humanitarian Needs in Iraq by a mission led by Sadruddin Aga Khan, Executive Delegate of the Secretary-General," United Nations, New York, 1991.

101. Gordon 2010, 86–91.

102. Alderson 2007, 25, 39.

103. Jabar 2003b. For descriptions of tribal institutions in southern Iraq, see Fernea 1969 and Batatu [1978] 2004.

104. Jabar (2003b) calls this "etatist tribalism," as opposed to "social tribalism," which is detached from the state.

105. In southern Iraq, the *ra'is* of each *hamoula* controls such resources. A *hamoula* (plural *hama'il*) is a level of sub-sub-clan within Iraqi tribes, consisting of a large extended family of typically between seventy and one hundred adult men and their families.

106. This might be different in analogous areas of Baghdad, where the journalist Hazem al-Amin (2003) in summer 2003 found parts of Sadr City still organized by tribe and place or origin.

107. Barakat 1993, 15.

108. Tribal sheikhs in postinvasion Iraq often positioned themselves as manpower subcontractors to the coalition and contractors. A number of military and Western contractors, including representatives of prominent security firms and Kellogg, Brand & Root (Halliburton), told me that they gave contracts to sheikhs because Iraqis listen to sheikhs. In contrast, I argue that Iraqis listen to sheikhs when sheikhs get contracts.

109. Traditionally, the fakhath is the basic spatial unit of the tribe, since it organizes pasture and water access in a given territory.

110. Baridi 2012, 63–73.

111. Baridi 2012, 167–178.

112. Baridi 2012, 145.

113. The Iraqi expression *fat-ha* is a colloquial pronunciation of *Fatiha*.

114. Olsen's memoir (Olsen and Hoffmann 2004) is available in Danish.

115. Chilcot et al. 2016, vol. 15.1.

116. Synnott 2008, 21.

117. Dominic d'Angelo, interview with author, 24 January 2004.

118. One of the CPA "bike boys," interview with author, 26 January 2004.

119. Underhill 1999, 45–51.

120. Underhill 1999, 42–44.

5. THE GEOGRAPHY OF ORDER

1. The ability of Iraqi women to coordinate together and to cooperate together, both locally and nationally, during this time is important and unstudied. Since women are much less likely than men to attend Friday sermons, however, women had to find other ways to generate common knowledge and expectations that others would act on that common knowledge. As a foreign male researcher, I had much less access in Iraq to women than to men.

2. Al-Khattab 1972, 218–219.

3. Al-Khattab 1972, 219.

4. Al-Khattab 1972, 219–220.

5. Sheikh Muhammad Jawad al-Sahlani was not an ordinary mosque preacher. He initially came to Basra as Muhsin al-Hakim's wakil and continued as one of Khoei's before being forced to leave Iraq in 1982. Afterward he served as Khoei's wakil in Damascus. One of his sons, Fadil al-Sahlani, was head of the al-Khoei Foundation's New York branch, had a seat on its board since at least 1996, and served as its—and thereby Sistani's—de facto representative in North America. After returning to Basra in October 2003, the elder Sahlani sought to build a grand mosque in another part of the city and, despite his protestations, served as a sort of "local marjaʿ."

6. Abu Dhar al-Sahalani, interview with author, 9 June 2011, Basra.

7. This would not be a Hobbesian ceding of authority to (and the concurrent creation of) a Leviathan, however; we—the congregation—did not transfer any coercive capacity to the group. This would have been a Humean acquiescence of their "authority," and their authority would have been created by and conditional on our coordinated acceptance of them.

8. Al-Mohammad 2012, 604.

9. Al-Mohammad 2012, 609.

10. Shadid 2005, 156–157.

NOTES TO PAGES 95–102

11. Shadid 2005, 156–57.
12. Babism and Bahaism also later emerged at least partly from his teachings.
13. Matthiesen 2014, 393–396.
14. Built between 1982 and 1997, it is said to be able to accommodate twelve thousand prayer-goers.
15. Matthiesen 2014, 395.
16. Synnott 2008, 183–184.
17. Abdul Hafiz al-Ata, deputy governor for local government, interview with author, 5 October 2003
18. United Nations Development Programme and Iraqi Ministry of Planning and Development Cooperation 2005. In April and May, 21,668 households were surveyed. Much of this shooting, especially in the south, was related to celebrations, not crime or insurgent activity.
19. Basrawis abandoned the habit of sleeping on rooftops to cope with summer heat, especially on Thursday nights.
20. Quran 5:32. The translation is from Arberry (1955). The sign omits the first part of this Quranic quote, which is "That is why We decreed for the children of Israel that. . . ."
21. Because it did not specify sanctions, there was no information to expect others to condition their behavior on. Perhaps Save the Children's sign should have read, "Do not allow celebrators to kill your children. Immediately inform shooters that they are endangering children." However, residents would not have acted on that message if they thought doing so was dangerous.
22. This differentiates Iraq's Friday mosque congregations from Christian church congregations. Today in many places, Christians might select a church based on denomination, worship style, the preacher's charisma, or the characteristics of the congregation (e.g., language, racial composition, political orientation). Church sermons can generate common knowledge within their congregation, but this congregation might not live in a geographically defined area. This has implications for the type of behaviors and public goods it can affect.
23. At the time, the relationship between Moqtada al-Sadr, his late father's supporters, and Grand Ayatollah Kazem al-Haeri was complex and fraught. Sadrist preachers did not want to discuss intra-Sadrist disagreements. Instead, in interviews, they emphasized that all three sermons were in the traditions of Mohammad Mohammad Sadiq al-Sadr.
24. As mentioned earlier, Twelver Shi'i jurisprudence does provide an answer of sorts: the distance between places where Friday prayers are offered should be no less than one *farsakh* (and this antiquated unit of distance varies from 4.8 to more than 5.5 kilometers). This ruling was ignored in Basra.
25. Drawing a circle around a mosque is a simple—arguably, simplistic—way to think about catchment areas. For example, it assumes that people on one side of the boundary all attend the same mosque and that all those on the other side do not attend it. But this way to visualize and map catchment areas requires fewer assumptions than alternatives and, critically, is less likely to find a relationship between mosque location and order when none exists. Dividing the city into areas based on distance to each mosque would create what is known in mathematics as a Voronoi diagram, which is the partitioning of a continuous space into a set of regions by associating all locations in that space with the closest member of a set of distinct, isolated points (Okabe et al. 2000). (In GIS, these are often referred to as Thiessen polygons.) John Snow (1855) famously used such a technique to link water pumps with cholera clusters during an outbreak in London. But a Voronoi diagram created from locations of Basra's Friday mosques yields many oddly shaped catchment areas that, by definition, preclude overlapping areas. Another option is to think of Friday mosques as magnets that attract those living nearby most powerfully and those farther away less powerfully.

Although this is realistic, creating such a "heat map" requires more assumptions than the simpler idea of single circles centered on mosques. Finally, infrastructure might segregate, define, and constrain mosque catchment areas. Walls and roads can segregate populations and reinforce social divides. Basra's canal system might delineate boundaries that people would not cross to reach a Friday mosque, although all of the city's canals have several crossings. Again, though, such an approach requires additional assumptions, as well as data.

26. E.g., Fischer 2008; Berman, Shapiro, and Felter 2011; Condra and Shapiro 2011; Berman, Cullen, Felter, and Shapiro 2011; Biddle, Friedman, and Shapiro 2012; Weidmann and Salehyan 2013; Shapiro and Weidmann 2015.

27. The rational choice approach to crime has its roots in Becker 1968.

28. Wilson and Kelling 1982.

29. I define the boundaries of Basra City as the outer perimeter of the municipal councils that existed in early 2004, except for the east bank of the Shatt al-Arab (al-Tuwaysa and a few villages) and Sindbad Island. This includes the closest villages in what locals would call Abu Khasib but not the much larger rural area of Abu Khasib south of Basra that consists of villages.

30. See Berman, Shapiro, and Felter 2011 for a discussion of weaknesses in the SIGACT data.

31. See "Documented Civilian Deaths from Violence," Iraq Body Count (website), accessed 23 January 2022, https://www.iraqbodycount.org/database/.

32. See Fischer 2008 for a discussion on Iraqi civilian casualty estimates, including the SIGACT data.

33. This may not be true for Baghdad or central and northern Iraq. In Baghdad, data entered the SIGACT dataset based on where coalition troops were present. If coalition troops avoided areas near mosques (because they feared either being attacked or being drawn into a firefight that would damage mosques), then the risk of bias is severe. In Basra, however, the British relied on Iraqis to provide data, and there is no reason to suspect that events near or far from mosques were more or less likely to be recorded.

34. As a first-pass test of correlation, how likely would it be to get a distribution of murder events like this one if murders randomly occurred within the boundaries of Basra? I calculated the distance from each murder to the closest Friday mosque and then generated fifty thousand random points within Basra and calculated their distance from the closest mosque. A t-test reveals that the means of the two sets of distances are statistically different from one another. I take from this that the location of mosques and the location of murders are correlated, but the relationship is not necessarily causal (e.g., maybe mosques and murder both occur in densely populated areas).

35. Some of the area that is not within any mosque's catchment area (e.g., more than .75 kilometers away from any mosque) is unpopulated—parks, empty lots, or governmental or industrial areas. It is, therefore, not included in the spatial analysis because of a lack of underlying population data.

36. The murder rate (by area) is the number of murder events in each of those two areas (one mosque's catchment area versus two or more mosques' overlapping catchment areas) divided by the overall size of that area (in square kilometers). The analysis was rerun over fifteen buffer sizes, from 200 meters to 1,600 meters, iterated by 100 meters. I ran a binomial probability test for each pair of rates and found them all to be statistically significant.

37. Central Statistical Organization 1997.

38. There are several theories about the meaning of the name *Basra*. Some say it is "probably derived from the nature of the soil" (Pellat and Longrigg 2012); others trace the name to ancient Aramaic *Basriyatha* or *Basriyi*, meaning "the place of huts" or "settlement" (Thabit 2001, 9).

39. Cited in Pellat and Longrigg 2007, 51.

40. Interestingly, Ibn Battuta (1962, 276–277) found that the (then-Sunni) population trekked the two miles back to the Mosque of Ali for Friday prayers. He writes, "It is closed after that and they do not visit it except on Fridays." He attended Friday prayers and claims that the preacher committed many gross errors of grammar in his sermon. Ibn Battuta later added, "In this town there is not a man left who knows anything of the science of grammar," despite the fact that the Basra school had systematized the rules of Arabic grammar six centuries earlier.

41. Bashʿayan 2014, 15.

42. Sluglett 2003, 224; Pellat and Longrigg 2007, 2012; Barakat 1993, 9–10. It is unclear if these and other population figures include the tens of thousands of seasonal laborers in the date harvesting and packing industries.

43. Abdullah 2001, 22, 26.

44. Abdullah 2001, 22–23.

45. Sabians (Mandaeans) are a religious community who follow the teachings of John the Baptist. I heard of only a handful of Sabian families still living in Basra in 2003.

46. Al-Khattab 1972, 2.

47. On British tribal policies, see Dodge 2003 and Sluglett 2002, 228.

48. Sluglett 2002, 224, 230.

49. Barakat 1984, 517–520.

50. Khamsa Meel (Five Miles) is located five miles to the west of the Basra-Baghdad railway station. Curiously, Survey Department photos of Basra from 1962 show almost nothing in what is today's Hayyaniyah. See photos in al-Khattab 1972, 170.

51. Al-Khattab 1972, 161.

52. Barakat 1993, 46.

53. See al-Samarraʾi 2006 for a useful, albeit incomplete, list of mosques in Basra.

54. Abdullah 2001, 24.

55. Al-Samarraʾi 2006.

56. Barakat 1993, 19.

57. Barakat 1993, 38–39.

58. Helfont 2018, 176.

59. Helfont 2018, 178.

60. Awqaf officials in Basra in 2003 claimed that official records were destroyed in the 1991 bombing of the Ministry of Local Government and looting of ministries in 2003.

61. E.g., Easterly and Levine 1997; Alesina, Baqir, and Easterly 1999; Miguel and Gugerty 2005.

62. If a neighborhood is overwhelmingly Sunni or Shiʿi, the few religious others might have an incentive to learn what messages are delivered in the main mosque and go along.

63. Some Iraqis claim a lingering "ethnic" identity from previous generations, such as Turkish, Bahraini, Arabian, or even Yemeni.

64. Abdul Hafiz al-Ata, interview with author, 5 October 2003.

65. I created the dataset by georeferencing maps and information on local councils provided to me by Basra's deputy governor for local government and the Basra office of RTI International, a nonprofit that was working for the US Agency for International Development to train Iraqis in local governance systems.

66. Lefebvre [1974]1991.

67. Lynch 1960, 47.

6. AYATOLLAHS' NETWORKS AND NATIONAL AUTHORITY

1. See, for example, Litvak 1998; Amanat 2009, chap. 7.

2. For Greif (2006, chap. 5), this defines legitimacy.

3. Sistani's representatives say a complete list of his announcements is available on his website, which is administered by his office in Qom, Iran. But the office does not post every fatwa and announcement in every language. At one point, sixty-six were posted in Arabic while only twenty-four were posted in English. What is translated and posted appears to be deliberate and strategic. Visser (2006, 8) points out that the website, for example, did not translate into English Sistani's declaration (in the Arabic Q&A section) that Muslims living in non-Muslim states are permitted to evade paying taxes to those states, provided it does not hurt the general reputation of Muslims. Frustrated at people claiming to represent Sistani, Hamid al-Khaffaf, one of Sistani's chief deputies, published a book (2007) of his official statements, but even this volume leaves out several controversial or potentially embarrassing messages, such as his preinvasion fatwa regarding noncooperation with invading forces.

4. Not coincidentally, a popular Iranian card game of trumps is called *hokm*, where one player selects the trump suit for all players.

5. Kadhem 2012, 256–257.

6. The Western media often describes Sistani as the head of Najaf's four most prominent grand ayatollahs. Although the other three agree with Sistani on many issues, they still compete with him on some level for followers and influence. He is the first among (relative) equals. There are rival grand ayatollahs, such as Mohammad al-Yaqoubi in Iraq and others outside Iraq, who would benefit from a decline in Sistani's authority.

7. Kadhem 2012, 216–217.

8. Al-Sadr 2002.

9. For a discussion of clerical opposition to Muharram self-flagellation and how the competition between ayatollahs can manifest itself along these lines, see Ende 1978.

10. Sistani, Q&A on A Code of Practice for Muslims Living in the West. See https://www.sistani.org/english/book/46/.

11. Dziadosz and Salman 2014.

12. Diamond 2005, 35, 54.

13. Jabar 2003a, 24, 26, 273.

14. Walbridge 2001, 237–240.

15. International Crisis Group 2003.

16. McCarthy 2003. On the 2002 fatwa, see Party Secretariat to Deputy Secretary General of the Party, BRCC, 009-2-5 (0001–0007), 30 September 2002.

17. Khalaji 2006, 8.

18. Walbridge 2001, 239. Khalaji (2006, 9) reported in 2006 that the most accurate estimate of Sistani's annual income is $500–700 million and his worldwide assets exceed $3 billion, but those figures are misleading because the vast majority of this money is donated and spent locally, with minimal input from Sistani's main offices in either Najaf or Qom.

19. Visser 2006, 11.

20. Visser 2006, 11.

21. Sayaj's (2018) is the most focused on Sistani.

22. For details, see Arato 2009, 110–113.

23. According to the November Fifteenth Agreement, a fifteen-member organizing committee would be established in each governate. For each, the national Governing Council would appoint five members, the governate council would select five members, and the local councils of the governate's five largest cities would each select one. CPA Baghdad appointed the GC, and many of the governate and local councils were appointed by regional and governate CPA officials and coalition military commanders. Most members, therefore, would be appointed by US appointees. Each governate organizing committee would then select between one hundred and two hundred governate notables for

a selection caucus (with at least eleven of the fifteen members approving an individual) after soliciting nominations from political parties, councils, associations, university faculties, tribes, and religious groups. This selection caucus in each governate would then elect governate representatives to the transitional National Assembly, proportional to the governate's share of the national population. With regard to this plan, the November Fifteenth Agreement was vague on a number of details. According to Larry Diamond (2005, 81), a CPA insider at the time, "The procedures were so complicated that even many within the CPA had trouble understanding how they were going to work."

24. Allawi 2007, 215.

25. Statement (Arabic) from the Office of Sayyid Sistani, Najaf, dated 3 Shawwal 1424 (28 November 2003).

26. Al-Khaffaf 2007, 222. Translation by Kadhim 2011.

27. Allawi 2007, 216; Chandrasekaran 2006, 201–207.

28. This fits well with Fanar Haddad's (2011) work on the multiplicity of Iraqi national identity.

29. Ironically, Bremer returned to Washington on the same day to consult with Bush administration officials. According to Diamond (2005, 103), "His departure gave the governance staff an opportunity for a breather.... People had been working at their usual impossible pace and had vowed to take the morning off." While CPA took the day off, Iraqis saw firsthand just how influential Sistani's network could be if fully mobilized. The mid-January demonstration created common knowledge among all Iraqis that Sistani was willing to intervene in politics. Western journalists and analysts quickly discarded the adjective *quietist*, which had been commonly used to describe Sistani and Najafi mujtahids in general.

30. Sistani eventually backed down from his demand for direct elections by 30 June 2004, but only after he forced the UN to send an assessment team. Kofi Annan initially sent a letter to Sistani via Adnan Pachachi, then chair of the GC, informing him that for technical reasons, elections were not practical before 30 June. Rejecting the conclusion in Annan's letter, Sistani said the UN needed to send an investigatory team before making such an assessment. A month later, Sistani accepted a similar conclusion from a UN team led by Lakhdar Brahimi after meeting with him for hours in Najaf. In effect, Sistani agreed to a delay in elections until December 2004 in exchange for a guarantee that the transitional National Assembly would be directly elected, not selected through caucuses.

31. Diamond 2005, 84.

32. The TAL's formal name was the Law of Administration for the State of Iraq for the Transitional Period.

33. Allawi (2007, 223) says, "The Shi'a caucus had not done their homework."

34. Quoted in Visser 2006, 12.

35. Diamond 2005, 191.

36. Arato 2009, 307n24.

37. In additional to federal and governate legislative elections, voters in the Kurdish Autonomous Region also voted for the 111-member Kurdistan National Assembly.

38. "No Surprise in Iraqi Vote," Reuters, October 17 1995.

39. On Safi's sermons, see Allawi 2007, 342.

40. Statement (Arabic) from the Office of Sayyid Sistani, Najaf, dated 26 Sha'ban 1425 (Friday, 1 October 2004).

41. Katzman 2005, 2.

42. Blais, Erisen, and Rheault 2014.

43. There are diverging accounts of whether Sistani (or his office) created the list, encouraged it to formed, or approved of it after Jaafari or someone else drew it up. Allawi

(2007, 343) says the genesis of the UIA came from inside Sistani's inner circle and he directed its creation.

44. Allawi 2007, 342–343.

45. The 228-candidate list included several independent candidates, SCIRI, Daʿwa Islamic Party, Daʿwa Islamic Party/Iraq's Organization, Iraqi National Congress, Badr Organization, Hizbollah Movement, Hizbollah al-Iraq, al-Fadhila Islamic Party, Center Assembly Party, Shaheed al-Mihrab Organization, Islamic Action Organization, Sayyid al-Shuhada Organization, Future Iraq Assembly, Justice and Equality Assembly, Fayli Kurd Islamic Union, Islamic Fayli Assembly, Turkomen Loyalty Movement, and the Islamic Turkomen Union.

46. Visser (2006, 25) claims Sistani's London office spoke of UIA candidate Husayn al-Shahristani as a member of the "board authorized by Grand Ayatollah Sistani to form the United Iraqi Alliance."

47. Packer 2005, 433–434.

48. De facto independence from Baghdad for a decade allowed Kurdish society to develop other ways of creating common knowledge and coordinating. The two major Kurdish political parties, especially when working together, controlled impressive apparatuses to coordinate Kurdish voters.

49. ENPV is calculated as:

$$\text{ENPV} = \frac{1}{\sum_{i=1}^{n} p_i^2}$$

where n entities receive votes and p_i denotes the proportion of votes received by entity i. See Laakso and Taagepera 1979. This measure is standard in the literature; see Cox 1997 and Chhibber and Kollman 2004.

50. Turnout in al-Anbar was extremely low in January 2005. Only 2 percent (13,753) of registered voters voted in the National Assembly elections and only 0.56 percent (3,803) voted in the governate council elections (in which only three parties registered). Turnout for the National Assembly and governate council elections was approximately 17 percent (201,477 votes) and 14 percent (166,798 votes), respectively, in Nineveh and 29 percent (144,598) and 28 percent (139,310) in Salahuddin.

51. In Nineveh's governate council election, a Kurdish electoral list received 109,295 of the 166,798 votes cast, suggesting it was Kurdish voters, not Sunni Arabs, who coordinated.

52. Fatwa dated 10 December 2005. Translated in Visser 2006, 19.

53. There was a change in the electoral system between January's transitional National Assembly election and December's election for the Council of Representatives. Although the general system of proportional representation was retained, December's election allocated seats according to a two-tiered system. January's election had a single nationwide district, while December's allocated 230 of the 275 seats to governates as multimember districts, with a share of seats proportional to its share of national registered voters. The remaining forty-five seats were compensatory seats, filled to match electoral lists' national proportionality. For details on electoral design and selection for both January's and December's elections, see Dawisha and Diamond 2006.

54. The Kurdistani Gathering list garnered only 26,542 votes (1 percent) in Baghdad in December, versus 45,525 votes (2.1 percent) in January.

55. Posner (2005) argues that actors select an identity that puts them in a minimum winning coalition, making relative demographics key.

56. Sayej 2018, 138–147.

57. See Haddad 2015 on these Shiʿa-centric actors and their role in state-building.

NOTES TO PAGES 140–151

58. This strategy fits David Lake's (2002) argument that extremists use terrorism in order to provoke retaliation against their own group in order to radicalize moderates.

59. Coalition Provisional Authority's English translation of a letter purportedly written by Abu Musab al-Zarqawi and obtained by the US government, February 2004, https://2001-2009.state.gov/p/nea/rls/31694.htm.

60. Al-Khaffaf 2007, 242–249.

61. Sayej 2018, 144.

62. See Panjwani 2012 for several studies on the importance of Samarra for Shiʿa.

63. Quoted in Cole 2007, 76. Imam Ali al-Hadi is one of the two buried at al-ʿAskari Shrine.

64. Quoted in Cole 2007, 82.

65. Cable from REO Basrah to US Department of State, "Situation in Basrah Calmer, But Still Volatile," 23 February 2006, https://wikileaks.org/plusd/cables/06BASRAH27_a.html.

66. Cable from REO Basrah to US Department of State, "Following Violence, Sunni Mosques in Basrah Close," 5 April 2006, https://wikileaks.org/plusd/cables/06BASRAH46_a.html.

67. Quoted in Sayej 2018, 143.

68. Cole 2007, 74.

69. Cole 2007, 82.

70. Rizvi 2018, 185–186; Sayej 2018.

71. Cole 2007, 78.

72. Rizvi 2010, 1310–1311.

73. Rizvi 2018, 185.

74. On the official website of the office of His Eminence Al-Sayyid Ali Al-Husseini Al-Sistani, it says in Arabic, "The text of the Friday sermon delivered by his eminence Sheikh Abd al-Mahdi al-Karbalai, representative of the marjaʿiyya, in Karbala on 4 April 2014 (about the National Assembly elections)." https://www.sistani.org/arabic/archive/24730/.

75. See, for example, Sayej 2018.

76. Calculated using the US Census International Database, https://www.census.gov/data-tools/demo/idb/.

77. Smyth 2014.

78. Day 2020, 37.

79. *Takfiris* are Muslims who declare other Muslims to be non-Muslims.

80. Kadhim and al-Khatteeb 2014.

81. Kadhim and al-Khatteeb 2014.

82. Parker 2015.

83. Habib 2015.

84. Day 2020, 38.

85. Al-Jazeera 2020.

86. Ibrahim 2020.

87. Diamond 2005, 85. This account resembles Padgett and Ansell's (1993, 1262) description of Cosimo de' Medici as "an indecipherable sphinx." Like Sistani, Cosimo never assumed lasting public office and hardly ever gave public speeches. The structure of his network was sufficient to coordinate his supporters and get what he wanted on many issues.

88. Cole 2006, 2007; Khalaji 2006; Visser 2006; Rahimi 2007; Allawi 2007; Riggs 2012; Sayej 2018; al-Qarawee 2019.

89. Rizvi 2010, 1309–1310.

90. A small bookstore near his office in al-Najaf sells copies of his numerous books, but they are rarely found elsewhere in Iraq, and demand seems low.

91. Cassette and VCD speeches of other ayatollahs are widely available and distributed in Iraq. The only recording of a Sistani speech I found in Iraq was a VCD that included his oration at Khoei's funeral. Guiders14, "Funeral of Ayatollah Khoei Recited by Ayatollah Sistani," YouTube, 26 April 2112, https://www.youtube.com/watch?v=zxm1fF-N3SA.
92. Weber 1978, 241.
93. Weber 1978, 248.
94. Patel 2012.
95. See, for example, the role of print language in the emergence of national consciousness in Anderson 1991.
96. Allawi 2007, 153.
97. CNN/USA Today/Gallup Poll 2004. In March to April 2004 the Pan Arab Research Center of Dubai supervised face-to-face interviews with 3,444 adults in all parts of Iraq, representing about 93 percent of the total Iraqi population.
98. Unprofitable newspapers remained in business because funding from parties, donors, and aid organizations was readily available. Several party figures and civil society organizers told me they fund low-quality papers with poor circulation because they believed it might facilitate registration and certification with future Iraqi governments or bring money from Western aid agencies who support "civil society." Iraqis might have expected future governments to re-create many of the bureaucratic controls that existed under previous Iraqi or other Arab regimes. Publishing a newspaper for a few years might have helped parties prove themselves as a preexisting entity not subject to any potential new regulations for initial registration.
99. In comparison, only 33 percent and 32 percent of respondents received the pan-Arab satellite stations al-Jazeera and al-Arabiya, the next two most received stations. Twenty-eight percent of respondents said they had watched al-Arabiya in the past seven days when channels were read out to them; 27 percent had watched al-Jazeera in that period. These were the second- and third-most watched stations.
100. Ten percent of respondents in the 2004 poll said al-Iraqiya was the first to break the news, compared to 58 percent and 55 for al-Arabiya and al-Jazeera, respectively. Abu Dhabi Satellite TV came higher, at 17 percent, than al-Iraqiya.
101. For histories of Da'wa, SCIRI, and Amal, see Wiley 1992; Baram 1994; Jabar 2003a; al-Khayyun 2011b.
102. Compared to other Islamic movements in Iraq or Muslim Brother groups in other countries, relatively little research exists, in English or Arabic, on the Muslim Brothers in Iraq. See al-Khayyun 2011a, 17–107; al-'Azami in Abdul-Jabar 2002.
103. See, for example, US Department of State 2003, based on 1,444 interviews between 20 August and 5 September 2003 and additional findings from a Gallup poll. Aside from the two prominent Kurdish leaders, Jalal Talabani and Masoud Barzani, these were the only five members of the Governing Council with greater than 50 percent name recognition at the time. Of respondents expressing an opinion on each individual, al-Hakim had 58 percent favorable, 12 percent unfavorable; Bahr al-Uloom 57 percent favorable, 12 percent unfavorable; Jaafari 54 percent favorable, 10 percent unfavorable; Pachachi 41 percent favorable, 13 percent unfavorable; and Chalabi 26 percent favorable, 35 percent unfavorable. Even the relatively unknown GC members received an unfavorable rating of at least 8 percent, suggesting that a significant percentage of respondents expressed an unfavorable rating for anyone participating on the Governing Council.
104. Mellor 2009.
105. Jabar 2003a, 26.
106. See Louër 2008 on the Shiraziyyin over the years in Iraq and the Gulf.
107. BBC 2004a.

108. This was especially noticeable when a major initiative, such as the November Fifteenth Agreement or draft interim constitution, allowed me to anticipate the topic of the week's sermon and therefore gauge variance in opinion before and after the sermon message.

109. The smaller the Sunni community in an area, the more threatening this may have seemed to Sunnis.

110. Sayyej 2018.

111. Schelling [1960] 1980, 144.

7. THE LIMITS OF SUNNI RELIGIOUS AUTHORITY

1. One such list is "The Iraqi Opposition," al-bab.com, accesssed 26 January 2022, http://al-bab.com/iraqi-opposition.

2. Helfont 2018.

3. The decades-long creation of this cadre is examined by Helfont 2018.

4. "Important and Special Suggestions on the Position of Men of Religion and Those Who Have Been Endorsed by the Meeting of the Comrades of the Secretariat of the Leadership of the Branches Included under the Tanzims of Governates of the Central Region," BRCC, 3559_0001 (0163-4). Undated but probably from 1992.

5. Helfont 2018, 38–39.

6. This was as high as nonmajority Sunni Arab areas; Baghdad polled 78 percent, Basra 72 percent, and Najaf 95 percent. US Department of State 2003.

7. According to Jabar, the ratio of mosques to Iraqis was 1:3,500 in the 1990s (cited in Haddad 2011, 108). This presumably includes many non-Friday mosques used by Sunnis.

8. See Zeidel (2009, 23) for the AMS's official account of their founding. See also Meijer 2005 and al-Khayyun 2011, 177–207.

9. Helfont 2018, 226–227.

10. Zeidel 2009, 23.

11. Sheikh Yosuf al-Hasan, interviews with author, December 2003, Basra's Grand Mosque.

12. Rabkin 2018.

13. Rabkin 2018.

14. In Basra, I periodically asked Sunnis I met whether they attended Friday prayers and about the sermon topics from the previous week. Their responses suggest that there was no relationship between messages in different Sunni mosques on any given week. When I asked what they thought other Sunnis heard in other mosques, most Sunnis would not venture a guess. In contrast, Shiʿa attending Sistani mosques assumed other Shiʿa had heard a similar message if national-level political or social topics were addressed. When asked, they usually would tell me what they thought other Shiʿa had heard.

15. Some of the sixty-four signers were prominent Sunni Arab clerics from the AMS or IIP, including Ahmad Abd al-Ghafur al-Samarrai (from Baghdad's Umm al-Qura Mosque), Sheikh Ahmad Hasan al-Taha (Abu Hanifa Mosque), and Sheikh Ziyad Mahmud al-Ani (Islamic College in Baghdad).

16. Khaleel 2019, 45.

17. Baram 2014, 311–314.

18. Khaleel 2019, 44.

19. Wong 2005b.

20. Rabkin 2018.

21. Rabkin 2018.

22. Rabkin 2018.

23. Rayburn (2014, 73–131) develops these perspectives.

24. The Obama administration decided that Prime Minister Nuri al-Maliki's policies had worsened sectarian relations and that he needed to be replaced with someone more willing and able to reach out to Sunni Arab politicians.

25. Haddad 2014, 94.

26. Haddad 2014, 102, 108–109.

27. Khaleel 2019, 45.

28. Haddad 2014, 110.

8. BEYOND BASRA AND BEYOND SERMONS

1. Ibn Khaldun 1958, 71.
2. Bulliet 1972, 65.
3. Sanders 1994, 43–44. Within a year, Jawhar would found the new city of Cairo and the institution of al-Azhar as a Shi'i seminary.
4. Bulliet 1972, 18n35; Berkey 2001, 13.
5. Michael 2016; Middle East Eye 2016.
6. Rabkin 2018.
7. Anderson 1991.
8. Sayej 2018.
9. McCants 2015, 83–84.
10. Abdullah 2001, 9–10.
11. Pellat and Longrigg 2007.

References

Abdullah, Thabit A. J. 2001. *Merchants, Mamluks and Murder: The Political Economy of Trade in Eighteenth-Century Basra*. Albany: State University of New York Press.

Abhath, Fariq. 2010. *Sira' al-markaziyah wa-al-lamarkaziyah fi al-Basra*. Beirut: Dirasat Iraqiyah.

Alderson, Andrew. 2007. *Bankrolling Basra*. London: Constable & Robinson.

Alesina, Alberto, Reza Baqir, and William Easterly. 1999. "Public Goods and Ethnic Divisions." *Quarterly Journal of Economics* 114, no. 4: 1243–1284.

Allawi, Ali A. 2007. *The Occupation of Iraq: Winning the War, Losing the Peace*. New Haven, CT: Yale University Press.

Amanat, Abbas. 2009. *Apocalyptic Islam and Iranian Shi'ism*. New York: I. B. Tauris.

Al-Amin, Hazem. 2003. "Baghdad allati lam taf'al bi 'asha'iriha ma taf'aluhu al-mudun bi'l-'asha'ir." *Al-Hayat*, 10 July 2003.

Anderson, Benedict. 1991. *Imagined Communities: Reflections on the Origin and Spread of Nationalism*. New York: Verso.

Anderson, Jon Lee. 2004. *The Fall of Baghdad*. New York: Penguin.

Antoun, Richard T. 1989. *Muslim Preacher in the Modern World*. Princeton, NJ: Princeton University Press.

Arato, Andrew. 2009. *Constitution Making under Occupation: The Politics of Imposed Revolution in Iraq*. New York: Columbia University Press.

Arberry, A. J. 1955. *The Koran Interpreted*. New York: Simon & Schuster.

Al-Asadi, Mukhtar. 1999. *Al-Sadr al-Thani: Al-Shahid wa al-Shahid, al-Zahira wa Rudud al-Fi'l*. Beirut: Mu'assasat al-A'raf.

Asharq al-Awsat. 2020. "Iraq PM Makes First Move against Iran's Militias." 12 May. https://english.aawsat.com/home/article/2279681/iraq-pm-makes-first-move-against-irans-militias.

Aumann, Robert. 1974. "Subjectivity and Correlation in Randomized Strategies." *Journal of Mathematical Economics* 1, no. 1: 67–96.

———. 1976. "Agreeing to Disagree." *Annals of Statistics* 4, no. 6: 1236–1239.

Al-'Azami, Basim. 2002. "The Muslim Brotherhood: Genesis and Development." In *Ayatollahs, Sufis, and Ideologues: State, Religion, and Social Movements in Iraq*, edited by Faleh Abdul-Jabar, 149–176. London: Saqi Books.

Azodanloo, Heidar G. 1992. "Formalization of Friday Sermons and Consolidation of the Islamic Republic of Iran." *Critique: Critical Middle Eastern Studies* 1, no. 1: 12–24.

Bakhash, Shaul. 1984. "Sermons, Revolutionary Pamphleteering and Mobilization: Iran, 1978." In *From Nationalism to Revolutionary Islam*, edited by Said Amir Arjomand, 177–194. Albany: State University of New York Press.

Barakat, Rajab. 1984. *Baladiyyat Al-Basra 1869–1981*. Basra, Iraq: Markaz Dirasat al-Khalij al-'Arabi.

Barakat, Sultan. 1993. *Post-War Reconstruction in Iraq: The Case Study of Basrah and Fao*. York, UK: Institute of Advanced Architectural Studies, University of York.

———. 2005. "Post-Saddam Iraq: Deconstructing a Regime, Reconstructing a Nation." *Third World Quarterly* 26, no. 4/5: 571–591.

Baram, Amatzia. 1994. "Two Roads to Revolutionary Shi'ite Fundamentalism in Iraq." In *Accounting for Fundamentalisms: The Dynamic Character of Movements*, edited by Martin E. Marty and Scott Appleby, 531–588. Chicago: University of Chicago Press and the American Academy of Arts and Sciences.

———. 1997. "Neo-Tribalism in Iraq: Saddam Hussein's Tribal Policies 1991–96." *International Journal of Middle East Studies* 29, no. 1: 1–31.

———. 2014. *Saddam Husayn and Islam, 1968–2003*. Baltimore: Johns Hopkins University Press.

Baridi, Husayn Hajim. 2012. *Al-'Asha'ir alBasriyah: Tarikhuhum, nasabuhum, furu'uhum, musakinhuhum*. Beirut: Dar al-Rafidayn lil-Tiba'ah wa al-Nashr wa al-Tawzi'.

Barr, Cameron W. 2002. "Jailbirds Fly Free in Iraq." *Christian Science Monitor*, 22 October 2002. https://www.csmonitor.com/2002/1022/p07s01-wome.html.

Bash'ayan, Ahmed. 2013. *Mawsu'at Tarikh al-Basra*. 4 vols. London: Dar al-Hikma.

———. 2014. "A Guide to al-Basra." Studylib. June 2014. https://studylib.net/doc/9072656/-al-basra-directory-.-dr-ahmed-bash-ayan.

Bashkin, Orit. 2009. *The Other Iraq: Pluralism and Culture in Hashemite Iraq*. Stanford, CA: Stanford University Press.

Batatu, Hanna. (1978) 2004. *The Old Social Classes and the Revolutionary Movement in Iraq*. London: Saqi Books.

Bates, Robert H., Avner Greif, Margaret Levi, and Jean-Laurent Rosenthal. 1998. *Analytic Narratives*. Princeton, NJ: Princeton University Press.

BBC. 2004a. "Iraq Reward Offer for UK Soldier." 7 May 2003. http://news.bbc.co.uk/2/hi/middle_east/3694735.stm.

———. 2004b. "UK Journalist Kidnapped in Basra." 13 August. http://news.bbc.co.uk/2/hi/middle_east/3560892.stm.

Becker, Gary. 1968. "Crime and Punishment: An Economic Approach." *Journal of Political Economy* 76, no. 2: 169–217.

Berkey, Jonathan Porter. 2001. *Popular Preaching and Religious Authority in the Medieval Islamic Near East*. Seattle: University of Washington Press.

Berman, Eli, Michael Callen, Joseph H. Felter, and Jacob N. Shapiro. 2011. "Do Working Men Rebel? Insurgency and Unemployment in Afghanistan, Iraq, and the Philippines." *Journal of Conflict Resolution* 55, no. 4: 496–528.

Berman, Eli, Jacob N. Shapiro, and Joseph H. Felter. 2011. "Can Hearts and Minds Be Bought? The Economics of Counterinsurgency in Iraq." *Journal of Political Economy* 119, no. 4: 768–819.

Biddle, Stephen, Jeffrey A. Friedman, and Jacob N. Shapiro. 2012. "Testing the Surge: Why Did Violence Decline in Iraq in 2007?" *International Security* 37, no. 1: 7–40.

Blais, André, Cengiz Erisen, and Ludovic Rheault. 2014. "Strategic Voting and Coordination Problems in Proportional Systems: An Experimental Study." *Political Science Quarterly* 67, no. 2: 386–397.

Blaydes, Lisa. 2018. *State of Repression: Iraq under Saddam Hussein*. Princeton, NJ: Princeton University Press.

Borthwick, Bruce. 1965. "The Islamic Sermon as a Channel of Political Communication in Syria, Jordan, and Egypt." PhD diss., University of Michigan.

Bremer, L. Paul. 2006. *My Year in Iraq: The Struggle to Build a Future of Hope*. New York: Simon & Schuster.

Bulliet, Richard W. 1972. *The Patricians of Nishapur: A Study in Medieval Islamic Social History*. Cambridge, MA: Harvard University Press.

Calmard, J. 2012. "Mardja'-i Taklid." In *Encyclopaedia of Islam*, 2nd ed., edited by P. Bearman, Th. Bianquis, C. E. Bosworth, E. van Donzel, and W. P. Heinrichs. Brill online ed., 2012.

Calvert, Randall L. 1992. "Leadership and Its Basis in Problems of Social Coordination." *International Political Science Review* 13, no. 1: 7-24.
Carroll, Rory. 2005. "Basra Police Out of Control, Chief Says." *Guardian*, 31 May.
Central Statistical Organization. 1997. "1997 Population Census Questionnaire: Instructions for Filling the Census Questionnaire" (in Arabic). Baghdad: Board of Ministers, Planning Commission.
Chandrasekaran, Rajiv. 2006. *Imperial Life in the Emerald City*. New York: Alfred A. Knopf.
Chhibber, Pradeep, and Ken Kollman. 2004. *The Formation of National Party Systems: Federalism and Party Competition in Canada, Great Britain, India, and the United States*. Princeton, NJ: Princeton University Press.
Chilcot, John, Lawrence Freedman, Martin Gilbert, Roderic Lyne, and Usha Prashar. 2016. *The Report of the Iraq Inquiry*. London: House of Commons. http://www.iraqinquiry.org.uk/.
Chwe, Michael Suk-Young. 2001. *Rational Ritual: Culture, Coordination, and Common Knowledge*. Princeton, NJ: Princeton University Press.
Cockburn, Patrick. 2008. *Muqtada: Muqtada al-Sadr, the Shia Revival, and the Struggle for Iraq*. New York: Simon & Schuster.
Cole, Juan R. I. 1988. *Roots of North Indian Shiʻism in Iran and Iraq: Religion and State in Awadh, 1722-1859*. Berkeley: University of California Press.
——. 2006. *The Ayatollahs and Democracy in Iraq*. ISIM Paper 7. Amsterdam: Amsterdam University Press.
——. 2007. "The Decline of Grand Ayatollah Sistani's Influence in 2006-2007." *Die Fridens-Warte* 82, no. 2/3: 67-83.
Condra, Luke N., and Jacob N. Shapiro. 2011. "Who Takes the Blame? The Strategic Effects of Collateral Damage." *American Journal of Political Science* 56, no. 1: 167-187.
Cook, Michael. 2000. *Commanding Right and Forbidding Wrong in Islamic Thought*. New York: Cambridge University Press.
Corboz, Elvire. 2012. "The Al-Khoei Foundation and the Transnational Institutionalization of Ayatollah al-Khuʼi's Marjaʻiyya." In *Shiʻi Islam and Identity: Religion, Politics, and Change in the Global Muslim Community*, edited by Lloyd Ridgeon, 93-112. London: I. B. Tauris.
——. 2015. *Guardians of Shiʻism: Sacred Authority and Transnational Family Networks*. Edinburgh: Edinburgh University Press.
Cox, Gary W. 1997. *Making Votes Count: Strategic Coordination in the World's Electoral Systems*. New York: Cambridge University Press.
CNN/USA Today/Gallup Poll. 2004. CNN/USA Today/Gallup Poll—Nationwide Poll of Iraq. 22 March-9 April 2004. http://www.cnn.com/2004/WORLD/meast/04/28/iraq.poll/iraq.poll.4.28.pdf.
Cronk, Lee, and Beth L. Leech. 2013. *Meeting at Grand Central: Understanding the Social and Evolutionary Roots of Cooperation*. Princeton, NJ: Princeton University Press.
Dai, Yamao. 2009. "An Islamist Social Movement under the Authoritarian Regime in Iraq during 1990s: A Study on the Shiʻite Leadership of Sadiq al-Sadr and Its Sociopolitical Base." *Annals of Japan Association for Middle East Studies* 25, no. 1: 1-29.
Dar al-Islam Foundation. 2002. *Al-Sadr al-Thani: Darasat fi fikrahu wa jihadahu*. London: Dar al-Islam Foundation.
Davis, Eric. 2005. *Memories of State: Politics, History, and Collective Identity in Modern Iraq*. Berkeley: University of California Press.
Dawisha, Adeed, and Larry Diamond. 2006. "Iraq's Year of Voting Dangerously." *Journal of Democracy* 17, no. 2: 89-103.

Day, Adam. 2020. *Hybrid Conflict, Hybrid Peace: How Militias and Paramilitary Groups Shape Post-Conflict Transitions*. New York: United Nations University.

Defence Intelligence Analysis Staff. 2003. "Basra: Post Saddam Governance" (declassified). UK Ministry of Defence, London, 11 March. https://webarchive.nationalarchives.gov.uk/ukgwa/20171123123237/http://www.iraqinquiry.org.uk//media/52027/2003-03-11-DIS-report-Basra-post-Saddam-governance.pdf.

Diamond, Larry. 2005. *Squandered Victory: The American Occupation and the Bungled Effort to Bring Democracy to Iraq*. New York: Times Books.

Dilley, Ryan. 2003. "Basra's Looters Repent." BBC News Online, 15 April 2003. http://news.bbc.co.uk/2/hi/middle_east/2946769.stm.

Dodge, Toby. 2003. *Inventing Iraq: The Failure of Nation Building and a History Denied*. New York: Columbia University Press.

———. 2007. "State Collapse and the Rise of Identity Politics." In *Iraq: Preventing a New Generation of Conflict*, edited by Markus E. Bouillon, David M. Malone, and Ben Rowswell, 23–39. Boulder, CO: Lynne Rienner.

Dziadosz, Alexander, and Raheem Salman. 2014. "After Years Off-Stage, Iraq's Sistani Takes Charge." Reuters, 29 June. http://www.reuters.com/article/2014/06/29/us-iraq-security-clerics-insight-idUSKBN0F30KX20140629#AyluHpVTEZulzUzM.99.

Easterly, William, and Ross Levine. 1997. "Africa's Growth Tragedy: Politics and Ethnic Divisions." *Quarterly Journal of Economics* 112, no. 4: 1203–1250.

Eberly, Don. 2009. *Liberate and Leave: Fatal Flaws in the Early Strategy for Postwar Iraq*. Minneapolis, MN: Zenith Press.

Ellickson, Robert C. 1991. *Order without Law: How Neighbors Settle Disputes*. Cambridge, MA: Harvard University Press.

Ende, Werner. 1978. "The Flagellations of Muharram and the Shi'ite 'Ulama.'" *Der Islam* 55, no. 1: 19–36.

Etherington, Mark. 2005. *Revolt on the Tigris: The Al-Sadr Uprising and the Governing of Iraq*. Ithaca, NY: Cornell University Press.

Fairweather, Jack. 2003a. "Britain's Chosen Sheikh Found to Have Ba'ath Link." *Daily Telegraph*, 11 April 2003.

———. 2003b. "British Anger Basrans by Bringing Back Ba'athists." *Daily Telegraph*, 18 April.

Fallows, James. 2004. "Blind into Baghdad." *Atlantic Monthly*, January/February.

Al-Fardan, Bandar Salim. 2013. *Salat al-jama'ah: Adwa' fiqhiyah wa-ahkam 'amaliyah li-salat al-jama'ah 'ala ra'y samahat Ayat Allah al-'uzma al-sayyid Ali al-Sistani dama zilluhu al-sharif*. Beirut: Dar al-Mahajjah al-Bayda' lil-Tiba'ah wa-al-Nashr wa-al-Tawzi.

Fathi, Asghar. 1980. "Preachers as Substitutes for Mass Media: The Case of Iran, 1905–1909." In *Towards a Modern Iran*, edited by Elie Kedourie and Sylvia G. Haim, 169–184. London: Frank Cass.

———. 1981. "The Islamic Pulpit as a Medium of Political Communication." *Journal for the Scientific Study of Religion* 20, no. 2: 163–172.

Faust, Aaron M. 2015. *The Ba'thification of Iraq: Saddam Hussein's Totalitarianism*. Austin: University of Texas Press.

Fernea, Elizabeth Warnock. 1969. *Guests of the Sheik: An Ethnography of an Iraqi Village*. New York: Anchor.

Fischer, Hannah. 2008. "Iraqi Civilian Casualty Estimates." CRS Report RS22547, Library of Congress, Congressional Research Service, Washington, DC.

Frances, Andrea Gastaldo. 2010. *War from a Broad: The Siege of Basrah*. Wellington, New Zealand: Travelling Broad Publications.

Gaffney, Patrick D. 1994. *The Prophet's Pulpit*. Berkeley: University of California Press.

Gordon, Joy. 2010. *Invisible War: The United States and the Iraq Sanctions*. Cambridge, MA: Harvard University Press.

Gordon, Michael R., and Bernard E. Trainor. 2006. *Cobra II: The Inside Story of the Invasion and Occupation of Iraq*. New York: Pantheon Books.

Granovetter, Mark S. 1978. "Threshold Models of Collective Behavior." *American Journal of Sociology* 83, no. 6: 1420–1442.

Greif, Avner. 2006. *Institutions and the Path to the Modern Economy: Lessons from Medieval Trade*. Cambridge: Cambridge University Press.

Gunter, Frank R. 2013. *The Political Economy of Iraq: Restoring Balance in a Post-Conflict Society*. Northampton, MA: Edward Elgar.

Habib, Mustafa. 2015. "Better Pay, Better Weapons: Are Shiite Militias Growing More Powerful Than Iraqi Army?" *Niqash*, 29 January. http://www.niqash.org/en/articles/security/3614/.

Haddad, Fanar. 2011. *Sectarianism in Iraq: Antagonistic Visions of Unity*. New York: Columbia University Press.

———. 2014. "A Sectarian Awakening: Reinventing Sunni Identity in Iraq after 2003." *Current Trends in Islamist Ideology* 17:145–176. https://www.hudson.org/research/10544-a-sectarian-awakening-reinventing-sunni-identity-in-iraq-after-2003.

Hadid, Foulath. 2014. *Iraq's Democratic Moment*. London: Hurst.

Halliday, Denis. 1999. "The Impact of the UN Sanctions on the People of Iraq." *Journal of Palestine Studies* 28, no. 2: 29–37.

Hardin, Russell. 1982. *Collective Action*. Baltimore: Johns Hopkins University Press.

———. 1991. "Acting Together, Contributing Together." *Rationality and Society* 3, no. 3: 365–380.

———. 2007. *David Hume: Moral and Political Theorist*. New York: Oxford University Press.

———. 2013. "The Priority of Social Order." *Rationality and Society* 25, no. 4: 407–421.

Harling, Peter, and Hamid Yassin Nasser. 2010. "The Sadrist Trend: Class Struggle, Millenarianism and Fitna." In *The Shi'a Worlds and Iran*, edited by Sabrina Mervin, translated by Bart Peeters, 281–302. London: Saqi Books.

Hechter, Michael. 1990. "The Emergence of Cooperative Social Institutions." In *Social Institutions: Their Emergence, Maintenance, and Effects*, edited by Karl-Dieter Opp, Michael Hechter, and Reinhold Wippler, 13–29. New York: Walter de Gruyter.

Hechter, Michael, and Christine Horne, eds. 2009. *Theories of Social Order: A Reader*. 2nd ed. Stanford, CA: Stanford University Press.

Helfont, Samuel. 2018. *Compulsion in Religion: Saddam Hussein, Islam, and the Roots of Insurgencies in Iraq*. New York: Oxford University Press.

Human Rights Watch. 2003. "Basra: Crime and Insecurity under British Occupation." *Human Rights Watch* 16, no. 6(E). https://www.hrw.org/report/2003/06/02/basra/crime-and-insecurity-under-british-occupation.

Ibn Battuta. 1962. *The Travels of Ibn Battuta, A.D. 1325–1354*. Vol. 2. Edited by H. A. R. Gibb. London: Hakluyt Society.

Ibn Khaldun. 1958. *The Muqaddimah: An Introduction to History*. Vol. 2. Translated by Franz Rosenthal. London: Routledge & Kegan Paul.

Ibrahim, Arwa. 2020. "'Hopeful Again': Iraqi Protesters Hail Ayatollah Sistani's Speech." Al-Jazeera, 7 February. https://www.aljazeera.com/news/2020/2/7/hopeful-again-iraqi-protesters-hail-ayatollah-sistanis-speech.

International Crisis Group. 2003. "Iraq's Shiites under Occupation." Briefing no. 8, International Crisis Group, 9 September. https://www.crisisgroup.org/middle-east-north-africa/gulf-and-arabian-peninsula/iraq/iraqs-shiites-under-occupation.

Jabar, Faleh A. 2003a. *The Shi'ite Movement in Iraq*. London: Saqi Books.

———. 2003b. "Sheikhs and Ideologues: Deconstruction and Reconstruction of Tribes under Patrimonial Totalitarianism in Iraq, 1968–1998." In *Tribes and Power: Nationalism and Ethnicity in the Middle East*, edited by Faleh A. Jabar and Hosham Dawod, 69–101. London: Saqi Books.

Al-Jazeera. 2020. "Iraq Protestors Look to al-Sistani Ahead of Friday Sermon." 7 February. https://www.aljazeera.com/news/2020/2/7/iraq-protesters-look-to-al-sistani-ahead-of-friday-sermon.

Kadhem, Fouad Jabir. 2012. "The Sacred and the Secular: The *'Ulama* of Najaf in Iraqi Politics between 1950 and 1980." PhD diss., University of Exeter.

Kadhim, Abbas. 2011. "Forging a Third Way: Sistani's *Marja'iyya* between Quietism and *Wilāyat al-faqīh*." In *Iraq, Democracy, and the Future of the Muslim World*, edited by Ali Paya and John L. Esposito, 66–79. New York: Routledge.

———. 2013. "The al-Shahristani under Siege: A Study in the Baʿth Party Archive." IIS BU Occasional Paper no. 1, Institute for Iraqi Studies, Boston University.

Kadhim, Abbas, and Luay al-Khatteeb. 2014. What Do You Know about Sistani's Fatwa?" *Huffington Post*, 10 July. http://www.huffingtonpost.com/luay-al-khatteeb/what-do-you-know-about-si_b_5576244.html.

Katz, Marion Holmes. 2013. *Prayer in Islamic Thought and Practice*. New York: Cambridge University Press.

Katzman, Kenneth. 2005. "Iraq: Elections and New Government." CRS Report for Congress RS21968, Library of Congress, Congressional Research Service, Washington, DC.

Katznelson, Ira, and Barry R. Weingast. 2005. "Intersections between Historical and Rational Choice Institutionalism." In *Preferences and Situations: Points of Intersection between Historical and Rational Choice Institutionalism*, edited by Ira Katznelson and Barry R. Weingast, 1–24. New York: Russell Sage Foundation.

Al-Khaffaf, Hamid. 2007. *Al-Nusus al-sadirah 'an samahat al-Sayyid al-Sistani fi al-mas'alah al-'Iraqiyah*. Beirut: Dar al-Mu'arrikh al-'Arabi.

Khalaji, Mehdi. 2006. "The Last Marja: Sistani and the End of Traditional Religious Authority in Shiism." Policy Focus no. 59. Washington, DC: Washington Institute for Near East Policy.

Khaleel, Ahmed. 2019. "The Future of the Iraqi Sunni Arabs." In *Iraq after ISIS: The Challenges of Post-War Recovery*, edited by Jacob Eriksson and Ahmed Khaleel, 39–55. Cham, Switzerland: Palgrave Macmillan.

Al-Khattab, Adill Abdullah. 1972. "Basra City: A Study in Urban Geography." PhD diss., University of London, School of Oriental and African Studies.

Al-Khayyun, Rashid. 2011a. *100 'am min al-Islam al-Siyasi bi-l-'Iraq*. Vol. 1, *Al-Shi'a*. Dubai: Al Mesbar Studies and Research Centre.

———. 2011b. *100 'am min al-Islam al-Siyasi bi-l-'Iraq*. Vol. 2, *Al-Sunna*. Dubai: Al Mesbar Studies and Research Centre.

Khoury, Dina Rizk. 2013. *Iraq in Wartime: Soldiering, Martyrdom, and Remembrance*. New York: Cambridge University Press.

———. 2016. "Making and Unmaking Spaces of Security: Basra as Battlefront, Basra Insurgent, 1980–1991." In *Violence and the City in the Modern Middle East*, edited by Nelida Fuccaro, 127–148. Stanford, CA: Stanford University Press.

Kubba, Laith. 2001. "Lessons from Iraq." In *Iraq, Democracy and the Future of the Muslim World*, edited by Ali Paya and John L. Esposito, 36–49. New York: Routledge.

Kuran, Timur. 1997. *Private Truths, Public Lies: The Social Consequences of Preferences Falsification*. Cambridge, MA: Harvard University Press.

Kurzman, Charles. 2004. *The Unthinkable Revolution in Iran*. Cambridge, MA: Harvard University Press.

Laakso, Marku, and Rein Taagepera. 1979. "'Effective' Number of Parties: A Measure with Application to West Europe." *Comparative Political Studies* 12, no. 1: 3–27.

Lafourcade, Fanny. 2012. "How to 'Turn the Page.'" In *Writing the Modern History of Iraq: Historiographical and Political Challenges*, edited by Jordi Tejel, Peter Sluglett, Riccardo Bocco, and Hamit Bozarslan, 181–201. London: World Scientific.

Laitin, David D. 1998. *Identity in Formation: The Russian-Speaking Populations in the Near Abroad*. Ithaca, NY: Cornell University Press.

Lake, David A. 2002. "Rational Extremism: Understanding Terrorism in the Twenty-First Century." *Dialog-IO* 1, no. 1: 15–28.

Lefebvre, Henri. (1974) 1991. *The Production of Space*. Translated by Donald Nicholson-Smith. Cambridge, MA: Blackwell.

Levi, Margaret. 2004. "An Analytic Narrative Approach to Puzzles and Problems." In *Problems and Methods in the Study of Politics*, edited by Ian Shapiro, Rogers Smith, and Tarek Masoud, 201–226. New York: Cambridge University Press.

Lewis, David K. 1969. *Convention: A Philosophical Study*. Cambridge, MA: Harvard University Press.

Liaison Office of Grand Ayatullah Seestani—London. 2003. "The Communiqué Issued by the Supreme Religious Authority of the Shia World, His Eminence Ayatullah al-Udhma as-Sayyid as-Seestani (Dama Dhiluh), on the Current Situation in Iraq." 15 Safar 1424 (18 April 2003). http://najaf.org/?lang=arabic&tab=article&cat=statement&id=18042003 (in Arabic); http://najaf.org/?lang=english&tab=article&cat=statement&id=18042003 (in English).

Litvak, Meir. 1998. *Shi'i Scholars of Nineteenth-Century Iraq*. New York: Cambridge University Press.

Louër, Laurence. 2008. *Transnational Shia Politics: Religious and Political Networks in the Gulf*. New York: Columbia University Press.

Lynch, Kevin. 1960. *The Image of the City*. Cambridge, MA: MIT Press.

Machlis, Elisheva. 2014. *Shi'i Sectarianism in the Middle East: Modernisation and the Quest for Islamic Universalism*. London: I. B. Tauris.

Mahdi, Qasim R. 1985. "The Spoken Arabic of Basra, Iraq: A Descriptive Study of Phonology, Morphology and Syntax." PhD diss., University of Exeter.

Makiya, Kanan [Samir al-Khalil]. 1989. *Republic of Fear: The Politics of Modern Iraq*. Berkeley: University of California Press.

——. 1993. *Cruelty and Silence: War, Tyranny, Uprising and the Arab World*. New York: W. W. Norton.

Al-Marashi, Ibrahim. 2002. "Iraq's Security and Intelligence Network: A Guide and Analysis." *Middle East Review of International Affairs* 6, no. 3: 1–13.

Matthiesen, Toby. 2014. "Mysticism, Migration and Clerical Networks: Ahmad al-Ahsa'i and the Shaykhis of al-Ahsa, Kuwait and Basra." *Journal of Muslim Minority Affairs* 34, no. 4: 386–409.

Mauriello, Raffaele. 2011. *Descendants of the Family of the Prophet in Contemporary History: A Case Study, the Shi'i Religious Establishment in al-Najaf*. Rome: Fabrizio Serra.

Mazaheri, Nimah. 2010. "Iraq and the Domestic Political Effects of Economic Sanctions." *Middle East Journal* 64, no. 2: 253–268.

McCants, William. 2015. *The ISIS Apocalypse: The History, Strategy, and Doomsday Vision of the Islamic State*. New York: Picador.

McCarthy, Rory. 2003. "Lead Cleric Threatened by Radicals." *Guardian*, 14 April 2003. https://www.theguardian.com/world/2003/apr/14/iraq.rorymccarthy.

Meijer, Roel. 2005. "The Association of Muslim Scholars in Iraq." *Middle East Report* 237 (Winter): 12–19.

Mellor, Noha. 2009. "Smile... You're on Iraqi TV." *New York Times*, 23 September. https://www.nytimes.com/2009/09/24/opinion/24iht-edmellor.html.
Michael, Maggie. 2016. "Egypt Standardizes Sermons, Tightening Grip on Mosques." Associated Press, 15 July. https://www.seattletimes.com/nation-world/egypt-standardize-muslim-sermons-tightening-grip-on-mosques/.
Middle East Eye. 2016. "Unified Friday Sermon Rings Out across Egypt for the First Time." 15 July. http://www.middleeasteye.net/news/unified-friday-sermon-rings-out-across-egypt-first-time-132910045.
Miguel, Edward, and Mary Kay Gugerty. 2005. "Ethnic Diversity, Social Sanctions, and Public Goods in Kenya." *Journal of Public Economics* 89, no. 11–12: 2325–2368.
Al-Mohammad, Hayder. 2012. "A Kidnapping in Basra: The Struggles and Precariousness of Life in Postinvasion Iraq." *Cultural Anthropology* 27, no. 4: 597–614.
Nakash, Yitzhak. 1994. *The Shi'is of Iraq*. Princeton, NJ: Princeton University Press.
North, Richard. 2009. *Ministry of Defeat: The British War in Iraq 2003–2009*. New York: Continuum.
Okabe, Atsuyuki, Barry Boots, Kokichi Sugihara, and Sung Nok Chiu. 2000. *Spatial Tessellations: Concepts and Applications of Voronoi Diagrams*. 2nd ed. New York: John Wiley & Sons.
Olsen, Ole Wøhlers, and Lally Hoffmann. 2004. *Beduin I laksko: Samtaler med Ole Wøhlers Olsen*. Copenhagen: Lindhardt og Ringhof.
Olson, Mancur. 1965. *The Logic of Collective Action: Public Goods and the Theory of Groups*. Cambridge, MA: Harvard University Press.
Oppel, Richard A., Jr. 2005. "In Basra, Militia in Control after Infiltration of Police." *New York Times*, 9 October 2005. http://www.nytimes.com/2005/10/09/international/middleeast/09basra.html.
Osman, Khalil F. 2015. *Sectarianism in Iraq: The Making of State and Nation since 1920*. New York: Routledge.
Oxford Research International. 2003. "First National Survey of Iraq—Selected Initial Findings. November 2003."
Packer, George. 2005. *The Assassins' Gate: America in Iraq*. New York: Farrar, Straus and Giroux.
Padgett, John F., and Christopher K. Ansell. 1993. "Robust Action and the Rise of the Medici, 1400–1434." *American Journal of Sociology* 98, no. 6: 1259–1319.
Panjwani, Imranali, ed. 2012. *Shi'a of Samarra: The Heritage and Politics of a Community in Iraq*. London: I. B. Tauris.
Parker, Ned. 2015. "Power Failure in Iraq as Militias Outgun State." Reuters, 21 October.
Patel, David Siddhartha. 2008. "The Last Gasp of the Iraqi Opposition: The Sadriyyun, the 1999 Uprisings, and the Roots of Intra-Shiite Divisions." Unpublished manuscript.
———. 2012. "Concealing to Reveal: The Informational Role of Islamic Dress." *Rationality and Society* 24, no. 3: 295–323.
Pellat, Ch., and S. H. Longrigg. 2007. "Basra (al-Basra)." In *Historic Cities of the Islamic World*, edited by Clifford Edmund Bosworth, 49–52. Leiden, Netherlands: Brill.
Pellat, Ch., and S. H. Longrigg. 2012. "Al-Baṣra." In *Encyclopaedia of Islam*, 2nd ed., edited by P. Bearman, Th. Bianquis, C. E. Bosworth, E. van Donzel, and W. P. Heinrichs. Brill online ed., 2012. http://dx.doi.org/10.1163/1573-3912_islam_COM_0103. First published online: 2012.
Phillips, David L. 2005. *Losing Iraq: Inside the Postwar Reconstruction Fiasco*. Boulder, CO: Westview Press.
Posner, Daniel N. 2004. "Civil Society and the Reconstruction of Failed States." In *When States Fail: Causes and Consequences*, edited by Robert I. Rotberg, 237–255. Princeton, NJ: Princeton University Press.

———. 2005. *Institutions and Ethnic Politics in Africa*. New York: Cambridge University Press.
Putnam, Robert D., and David E. Campbell. 2010. *American Grace: How Religion Divides and Unites Us*. New York: Simon & Schuster.
Al-Qarawee, Harith. 2019. "The 'Formal' Marjaʿ: Shiʿi Clerical Authority and the State in Post-2003 Iraq." *British Journal of Middle Eastern Studies* 46, no. 3: 481–497.
Qutbuddin, Tahera. 2019. *Arabic Oration: Art and Function*. Leiden, Netherlands: Brill.
Rabkin, Nathaniel. 2018. "The Sunni Religious Leadership in Iraq." *Current Trends in Islamist Ideology*, 2 June. https://www.hudson.org/research/14304-the-sunni-religious-leadership-in-iraq.
Rahimi, Babak. 2007. "Ayatollah Sistani and the Democratization of Post-Baʿathist Iraq." Special Report 187, United States Institute of Peace, Washington, DC, June 2007. https://www.usip.org/sites/default/files/sr187.pdf.
Ram, Chagay. 1991. "Islamic Symbolism: The Ideology of the Islamic Revolution in Iran as Reflected in Friday Communal Sermons, 1979–1989." PhD diss., New York University.
Raʾuf, Adil. 1999. *Muhammad Muhammad-Sadiq al-Sadr: Marjaʿiyyat al-Maydan. Mashruʾhu al-Taghyiri was Waqaʾi al-Ightiyal*. Damascus: Al-Markaz al-Iraqi li al-Alam wa al-Dirasat.
———. 2000. *Al-ʿAmal al-Islami fi al-Iraq bayna al-Marjaʿiyya wa al-Hizbiya: Qiraʾa Naqdiya li-Masira Nisf Qarn 1950–2000*. Damascus: Al-Markaz al-Iraqi li al-Alam wa al-Dirasat.
———. 2002. *Iraq bi-la Qiyada: Qiraʾa fi Azma al-Qiyada al-islamiya al-Shiʿa fi al-Iraq al-Hadith*. Damascus: Al-Markaz al-Iraqi li al-Alam wa al-Dirasat.
Rawls, John. 2001 *Justice as Fairness: A Restatement*. Cambridge, MA: Harvard University Press.
Rayburn, Joel. 2014. *Iraq after America: Strongmen, Sectarians, Resistance*. Stanford, CA: Hoover Institution Press.
Reuters. 1995. "No Surprise in Iraqi Vote." October 17. https://www.nytimes.com/1995/10/17/world/no-surprise-in-iraqi-vote.html.
Ricks, Thomas. 2006. *Fiasco: The American Military Adventure in Iraq, 2003 to 2005*. New York: Penguin.
Riggs, Robert J. 2012. "Partisan and Global Identity in the Historiography of Iraqi Religious Institutions." In *Writing the Modern History of Iraq: Historiographical and Political Challenges*, edited by Jordi Tejel, Peter Sluglett, Riccardo Bocco, and Hamit Bozarslan, 303–320. London: World Scientific.
Ripley, Tim. 2014. *Operation TELIC: The British Campaign in Iraq 2003–2009*. Lancaster, UK: Telic-Herrick. Kindle.
Rizvi, Sajjad. 2010. "Political Mobilization and the Shiʿi Establishment." *International Affairs* 86, no. 6: 1299–1313.
———. 2018. "The Making of a *Marjaʿ*: Sistani and Shiʿi Religious Authority in the Contemporary Age." *Sociology of Islam* 6, no. 2:165–189.
Rohde, Achim. 2010. *State-Society Relations in Baʿthist Iraq: Facing Dictatorship*. New York: Routledge.
Rosen, Nir. 2006. *In the Belly of the Green Bird: The Triumph of the Martyrs in Iraqi*. New York: Simon & Schuster.
Rossiter, Mike. 2009. *Target Basra*. London: Corgi.
Rotberg, Robert I., ed. 2004. *When States Fail: Causes and Consequences*. Princeton, NJ: Princeton University Press.
Rudd, Gordon W. 2011. *Reconstructing Iraq: Regime Change, Jay Garner, and the ORHA Story*. Lawrence: University Press of Kansas.

Sabl, Andrew. 2012. *Hume's Politics: Coordination and Crisis in the History of England*. Princeton, NJ: Princeton University Press.
Sachedina, Abdulaziz Abdulhussein. 1988. *The Just Ruler (al-sultan al-ʿadil) in Shiʿite Islam: The Comprehensive Authority of the Jurist in Imamite Jurisprudence*. New York: Oxford University Press.
Al-Sadr, Mohammad. 2002. *Fiqh al-ʿAshaʾir*. Beirut: Dar al-Adwaʾ.
Al-Sadr, Mohammad Mohammad Sadiq. n.d. *Minbar al-Sadr: Khutab al-Jumuʾah allati kana yulqiha al-Imam al-shahid al-Sayyid Muhammad al-Sadr fi Masjid al-Kufah al-Atheem*. Edited by Muhsin al-Nuri al-Musawi. Beirut: Dar al-Mutaqeen.
Al-Salihi, Najib. 1998. *Al-Zilzal (The Earthquake)*. London: Al-Rafid.
Al-Samaraʾi, Yunus Ibrahim. 2006. *Tarikh masajid al-Basrah, al-Zubayr, Abu Khasib, al-Faw*. Beirut: Al-Dar al-Arabiyah lil-Muwasuʿat.
Samuelson, Larry. 1998. *Evolutionary Games and Equilibrium Selection*. Cambridge, MA: MIT Press.
Sanders, Paula. 1994. *Ritual, Politics, and the City in Fatimid Cairo*. Albany: State University of New York Press.
Sassoon, Joseph. 2012. *Saddam Hussein's Baʿth Party: Inside an Authoritarian Regime*. New York: Cambridge University Press.
Sayej, Caroleen Marji. 2018. *Patriotic Ayatollahs: Nationalism in Post-Saddam Iraq*. Ithaca, NY: Cornell University Press.
Schelling, Thomas. (1960) 1980. *The Strategy of Conflict*. Cambridge, MA: Harvard University Press.
———. 1978. *Micromotives and Macrobehavior*. New York: Norton.
Shadid, Anthony. 2005. *Night Draws Near: Iraq's People in the Shadow of America's War*. New York: Henry Holt.
Al-Shahristani, Hussein. 1994. "Suppression and Survival of Iraqi Shiʿis." In *Iraq since the Gulf War*, edited by Fran Hazelton, 134–140. London: Zed Books.
Shapiro, Jacob N., and Nils B. Weidmann. 2015. "Is the Phone Mightier Than the Sword? Cellphones and Insurgent Violence in Iraq." *International Organization* 69, no. 2: 247–274.
Simons, Geoff. 1996. *The Scourging of Iraq: Sanctions, Law and Natural Justice*. New York: St. Martin's Press.
Sluglett, Peter. 2003. "The Marsh Dwellers in the History of Modern Iraq." In *The Iraqi Marshlands: A Human and Environmental Study*, 2nd ed., edited by Emma Nicholson and Peter Clark, 223–239. London: AMAR International Charitable Foundation.
———. 2006. "Blunder Books: Iraq since Saddam." *Middle East Journal* 60, no. 2: 361–368.
Smyth, Phillip. 2014. "Iranian Proxies Step Up Their Role in Iraq." PolicyWatch 2268, Washington Institute for Near East Policy, Washington, DC, 13 June 2014. https://www.washingtoninstitute.org/policy-analysis/view/iranian-proxies-step-up-their-role-in-iraq.
Snow, John. 1855. *Report on the Cholera Outbreak in the Parish of St. James, Westminster, during the Autumn of 1854*. London: Churchill.
Special Inspector General for Iraq Reconstruction. 2009. *Hard Lessons: The Iraq Reconstruction Experience*. Washington, DC: Office of the Special Inspector General for Iraq Reconstruction.
Starrett, Gregory. 1997. "The Anthropology of Islam." In *Anthropology of Religion: A Handbook*, edited by Steven Gazier, 279–303. Westport, CT: Greenwood Press.
Synnott, Hilary. 2008. *Bad Days in Basra: My Turbulent Time as Britain's Man in Southern Iraq*. New York: I. B. Taurus.

Ucko, David H. 2013. *Counterinsurgency in Crisis: Britain and the Challenges of Modern Warfare*. New York: Columbia University Press.

Ullmann-Margalit, Edna. 1977. *The Emergence of Norms*. Oxford: Oxford University Press.

Underhill, Paco. 1999. *Why We Buy: The Science of Shopping*. New York: Simon & Schuster.

United Nations Development Programme (UNDP) and Iraqi Ministry of Planning and Development Cooperation. 2005. *Iraq Living Conditions Survey 2004*. Vol. 1, *Tabulation Report*. Baghdad: Central Organization for Statistics and Information Technology.

United States Department of State, Office of Research. 2003. "Iraqi Public Has Wide Ranging Preferences for a Future Political System." Opinion Analysis M-151-03, 21 October 2003. https://govinfo.library.unt.edu/cpa-iraq/government/political_poll.pdf.

Vincent, Steven. 2005. "Switched Off in Basra." *New York Times*, 31 July. http://www.nytimes.com/2005/07/31/opinion/31vincent.html.

Visser, Reidar. 2005. *Basra, the Failed Gulf State: Separatism and Nationalism in Southern Iraq*. Münster, Germany: Lit Verlag.

Visser, Reidar. 2006. "Sistani, the United States and Politics in Iraq: From Quietism to Machiavellianism?" Paper no. 700, Norwegian Institute of International Affairs, Oslo, 1 July 2006. https://www.nupi.no/en/Publications/CRIStin-Pub/Sistani-the-United-States-and-Politics-in-Iraq-From-Quietism-to-Machiavellianism.

———. 2012. "The Sectarian Master Narrative in Iraqi Historiography." In *Writing the Modern History of Iraq: Historiographical and Political Challenges*, edited by Jordi Tejel, Peter Sluglett, Riccardo Bocco, and Hamit Bozarslan, 47–60. London: World Scientific.

Walbridge, Linda S. 2001. *The Most Learned of the Shiʻa: The Institution of the Marjaʻ Taqlid*. New York: Oxford University Press.

———. 2014. *The Thread of Muʻawiya: The Making of a Marjaʻ Taqlid*. Bloomington, IN: Ramsay Press.

Al-Wardi, Ali. 1969. *Lamahat ijtimaʻiyah min tarikh al-Iraq al-hadith*. Vol. 6.1. Baghdad: Matbaʻat al-Irshad.

Weber, Max. 1978. *Economy and Society*. Edited by Guenther Roth and Claus Wittich. Berkeley: University of California Press.

Weidmann, Nils B., and Idean Salehyan. 2013. "Violence and Ethnic Segregation: A Computational Model Applied to Baghdad." *International Studies Quarterly* 57, no. 1: 52–64.

Weingast, Barry. 2002. "Rational Choice Institutionalism." In *Political Science: The State of the Discipline*, edited by Ira Katznelson and Helen Milner, 660–692. New York: W. W. Norton.

Wensinck, A. J. 1986. "Khuṭba." In *Encyclopaedia of Islam*, 2nd ed., edited by P. Bearman, Th. Bianquis, C. E. Bosworth, E. van Donzel, and W. P. Heinrichs, 5:74–75. Leiden, Netherlands: Brill.

Wiley, Joyce N. 1992. *The Islamic Movement of Iraqi Shiʻas*. Boulder, CO: Lynne Rienner.

Wilson, James Q., and George L. Kelling. 1982. "Broken Windows: The Police and Neighborhood Safety." *Atlantic*, March. https://www.theatlantic.com/magazine/archive/1982/03/broken-windows/304465/.

Woertz, Eckart. 2019. "Iraq under UN Embargo, 1990–2003: Food Security, Agriculture, and Regime Survival." *Middle East Journal* 73, no. 1: 93–112.

Wolfe, Alan. 2003. *The Transformation of American Religion: How We Actually Live Our Faith*. New York: Free Press.

Wong, Edward. 2005a. "U.S. Journalist Who Wrote about Police Corruption Is Abducted and Killed in Basra." *New York Times*, 4 August 2005. http://www.nytimes.com/2005/08/04/international/middleeast/04journalist.html.

———. 2005b. "Sunni Candidates in Iraq Find Enemies on All Sides." *New York Times*, 5 December 2005. http://www.nytimes.com/2005/12/05/world/middleeast/sunni-candidates-in-iraq-find-enemies-on-all-sides.html.

Woods, Kevin M., Michael R. Pease, Mark E. Stout, Williamson Murray, and James G. Lacey. 2006. *Iraqi Perspectives Project: A View of Operation Iraqi Freedom from Saddam's Senior Leadership*. Norfolk, VA: United States Joint Forces Command. https://permanent.access.gpo.gov/lps68139/IraqiPerspectivesProject.pdf.

Worth, Robert F. 2005. "Reporter Working for *Times* Abducted and Slain in Iraq." *New York Times*, 20 September 2005. http://www.nytimes.com/2005/09/20/international/middleeast/20basra.html.

Wrong, Dennis H. 1994. *The Problem of Order*. Cambridge, MA: Harvard University Press.

Zeidel, Ronen. 2009. "The Association of Muslim Scholars: The Rise and (Temporary) Fall of a Sunni Arab Political Organization in Iraq." *Journal of South Asian and Middle Eastern Studies* 33, no. 1: 20–35.

Index

Note: Page numbers in italics indicate figures and tables. Names starting with "al-" are alphabetized by the subsequent part of the name.

Abdullah, Thabit, 58, 110, 177
Accord Front. *See* Iraqi Accord Front
al-Ahsa'i, Ahmad, 95
Akhbaris, 28, 62–64, 182n48; neo-Akhbari movements in postinvasion Iraq, 155, 158
Allawi, Ali, 134–35, 196–197n43
Allawi, Ayad, 138, 154, 170
AMS. *See* Association of Muslim Scholars
anarchy, 55–56, 66, 79, 176
Anderson, Benedict, 175
Anglo-Iraqi Treaty (1922), 31
Ansari, Murtadha, 28, 63
Araki, Muhammad Ali, 34, 183n80
al-'Askari Shrine (Samarra) bombing (2006), 141, 143, 170, 198n63
assassinations, targeted executions, and revenge killings: al-'Askari Shrine (Samarra) bombing (2006) as pretext for, 141, 143; in Basra, 26, 143; Ba'thists as targets, ix, x, 26, 43, 82, 126; grand ayatollahs assassinated in 1990s, 35, 65, 158, 188n49; Mohammad Baqir al-Hakim's assassination (2003), 93; al-Hasan, Yosuf's assassination (2006), 166; Islamist militant groups' operations, 104; journalists as targets, viii–ix, 179n10, 179nn1–2; lack of security and, 50; Movement of the Fifteenth of Sha'ban (1996) and, 179n10; mukhtars targeted by Basrawis, 80; prevalence in 2006, 143; al-Sadr, Grand Ayatollah Mohammad Mohammad Sadiq's assassination (1999), 35, 65, 158, 188n49
Association of Muslim Scholars (AMS), 11, 18–19, 162–163, 165–170
authoritarianism, 27, 37, 44

Baghdad: expansion eclipsing Basra, 109; Friday prayers and sermons in, 64; Green Zone, 17; Mother of All Villages Mosque (formerly Mother of All Battles Mosque), 166, 170; al-Muhsin Mosque, 67; Prophet Mohammed Mosque, 94–95; al-Rahman Mosque, 71; Sadr City, ix, 67; voting trends in January 2005 elections, 136
al-Bahadali, Abdul Satar, ix, 159, 183n75
Bahr al-Uloom, Mohammad Bahr, 70, 154, 199n103
Barakat, Sultan, 21, 111
Baram, Amatzia, 24, 25, 36–38, 168
Basra: al-Abila's grand mosque, 129–130; Arabic dialect of, 13, 180n14; 'Ashair area, 110; al-'Ashira al-Mubashara Mosque, 142–143; al-Asma'i neighborhood, 90–93, *92*, 111; author's field research in (September 2003 to April 2004), vii–viii, 12–13, 17; Ba'th regime's support in, 26, 42; British military and administration (CPA South), x, 1, 9, 17, 40–41, 85, 179n7; cell phone usage in, 78–79; Christians in, 78; correlation of Friday mosques and number of murders in, 105–108, *106–107*, 193n34; crime and security issues in, viii–ix, 49, 50–51, 94, 96–97; demonstration against constitutional drafting process (January 2004), 129–130; district advisory councils (DACs), 115; failure of occupation to reestablish order in, 48–50; Friday mosques and prayers in, 16, 64, 69, 71–72, *71*, 100–102, 105, 112–113, 115–118, *116–117*, 200n14; generalizable lessons learned from, 176–177; Grand Mosque of Ali, 109, 194n40; al-Hakimiyya Mosque, 134; Hayyaniah, 82–83, 91–93, 111; history of, 16, 108–112, 177, 193n38; al-Hooda Mosque in, 75, 93; Human Rights Watch report on, 49; hussainiyas in, 16, 113; invasion of, 40–41, 48–50; Iran-Iraq War's effect on, 82–83; Islamist militias and gangs in, ix, 179n2, 179n7; al-Jumhuriyya neighborhood, 82, 111; Kermani school of Shaykhiyya Islam, 96; Khamsa Meel, 82, 111, 194n50; local councils (postinvasion) in, 115, *117*; looting in, 1, 17, 41–44; *al-Manarah* newspaper, 86; Maqam Ali, 112; al-Maqil area, 110;

215

Basra (*continued*)
  migration to, 82–83, 105, 109–111; mosques in, 112–113; mukhtars' role, 79–80; murder events as indicator of social order in, 103–108; al-Musawi Grand Mosque (known as al-Hasawiyya Mosque), 95, 100, 192n14; name of, 193n38; neighborhood advisory councils (NACs), 115–118; Old Basra area, 74, 82, 110; postinvasion coordination problems in, 57–59; preinvasion neighborhood identity in, 80; public health issues in, 58; radio stations, 86; Rifaʿis in, 168–169; rooftop sleeping in, 97, 192n19; Sahlani Mosque in al-Asmaʿi al-Jadid, 90, 93; al-Saymar (al-Fursi) neighborhood, 95–96; sectarianism in, 26; Shaykhiyyas' provision of security in, 96–97; Shiʿi violence against Sunnis in, 142; social structure in, 79; Sunni mosques in, 63–64; teahouses and social clubs not operating in, 46; utilities committee established, 49; waste disposal and uncollected trash in, 1, 3, 58; water delivery in, 59–60
al-Basri, Muhammad, 134
Battle of the Camel (first Muslim civil war, 656), 109, 177
Baʿth regime: AMS roots in, 166; atomization of society and, 8, 10, 44, 47, 157; Basra's size and development under, 111–113; civil society in, 15, 44–45; collapse of, vii, 1–2, 15, 23, 40–48, 66; despotism of, 15, 22, 37, 44; discrimination against Shiʿa, 20, 25–27; dismissal of grand mufti of Iraq by, 38; distrust during, 44, 45–48; economy of, 22, 81; General Security Directorate, 36, 45, 79; Ministry of Endowments and Religious Affairs, 36, 113, 114, 164, 167; mosque sermons and, 65, 174; mukhtars' role, 79–80; paramilitaries in, 45; patronage of, 15, 21–23, 44, 82, 83; postinvasion exhortation of civil war, 140; preinvasion governance of, 21, 44; religiosity in society and, 24–25, 36–37, 76; reprisals against former members and sympathizers of, ix, x, 26, 43, 82, 126; school books on Iraqi history, 48; security agencies of Baʿth Party, 45; social networks connected to, 81–82; state-controlled radio station, 86; Sunni clerics' role under, 36–38, 163–165; tribal leaders and, 20, 22–23, 181n17
Berg, Nicholas, 179n1
bin Ghazwan, Utbah, 108
Binns, Graham, 42, 184n5

Brahimi, Lakhdar, 196n30
Bremer, L. Paul "Jerry," 125, 128, 149, 153, 184n10, 196n29
Brims, Robin, 184n5, 186n50
British role in 20th century: Anglo-Iraqi Treaty (1922), 31; Basra's occupation by British (1914), 109; fashioning of Iraq under British mandate, 8, 16; Iraqi revolt (1920) against, 31, 47, 80, 156, 167
British role in CPA South: 2005 operations against Sadrists, 179n7; in Basra, x, 1, 9, 17, 40–41, 85, 179n7; drawdown of troops, 9, 48–49, 185n48; plan for postconflict operations by, 48–50, 85, 184n7, 184–185n18
broken windows theory of policing, 103
Bulliet, Richard, 174
Burujirdi, Ali Muhammad, 35

Campbell, David, 61
celebratory and unauthorized gunfire, neighborhood variations in dealing with, 50, 97–99, 192n18
cell phone usage, 78–79, 154
Chalabi, Ahmad, 129, 138, 154, 199n103
Christians, 78, 128–129, 132, 160
Chwe, Michael, 9, 56, 186n9
civil society, 15, 44–45, 199n98
civil war in Iraq. *See* violence
clerics: Baʿth regime training and membership of, 24, 37–38; doctrine of emulation among Shiʿa, 27–28; filling void in absence of state authority, 20, 53, 75; iconography of martyred clerics, 6; marjaʿ taqlid's role among Shiʿa, 27–28, 30; mujtahid's role among Shiʿa, 27–28, 181–182n44; political activism and, 11, 30–33, 70, 121, 126, 134; preinvasion authority of, 20, 27–33, 75, 79; quietism tradition, 30–33, 35–36, 70, 121, 124, 126, 196n29; role of, 2, 8–10, 17, 30, 120; Shiraziyyin clerics, 123. *See also* Friday prayers and sermons; grand ayatollahs
Coalition Provisional Authority (CPA): "blunder books" about, 48; clashing with Sadrist militia, viii; communications' failure to create common knowledge, 10, 84; currency and, 85–86; de-Baʿthification policy of and disbanding of Iraqi Army by, 43; failure to plan for postinvasion Iraq, 48–50, 85; humanitarian assistance plan, 48; Office of Reconstruction and Humanitarian Assistance (ORHA) as predecessor of, 43, 48, 85; al-Sadr (Moqtada) advocating resistance to, 120; Sistani and, 4, 67,

149–150; state-run radio al-Iraqiya as mouthpiece of, 153; on Transitional Administrative Law (Iraq's interim constitution), 131–32. *See also* November Fifteenth Agreement

Coalition Provisional Authority South: in Basra, x, 1, 9, 17, 40–41, 85; inadequacies of, 9, 44, 48–50, 85; Shaykhiyyas' provision of security and local organization endorsed by, 96–97; town hall meeting on constitutional drafting process, 128

Cockburn, Patrick, 64, 67, 75

Cole, Juan, 143, 144

collective action problems, 54–57, 186n1

common knowledge: Ba'th regime's destruction of ways to generate, 44, 47–48, 159; defined, 56, 84, 186n9; exclusion from Shi'i mosques, effect on, 5–6, 77–78, 160, 175; generalizable lessons learned about, 177; gossip and, 46, 57, 87, 99, 114; hussainiyas (prayer halls) not conduits for, 114; individual efforts to create in neighborhoods, 80–81; individual Iraqis lacking knowledge of what other Iraqis know, 154; insufficient alone for group to coordinate together, 3, 56–57, 66, 99, 152; linked to community coordination, 10, 17, 18, 52, 119–120, 159; media's limited ability to create, 152–153; mosque sermons creating, 2, 3, 10–11, 18, 53, 60–66, 73–76, 78, 89, 119, 121, 150, 159; other potential sources of, 152–154, 160; political parties' failure to create, 154; Shiraziyyin's failure to create, 157; Sunnis' limited ability to generate, 163–165, 168, 171–172

communication. *See* common knowledge; Friday prayers and sermons; information and communication

community coordination: across Sunnis and Shi'a, 114, 176; based on clerics' sermons, 3, 11, 53, 73–76, 164, 175; Basra's postinvasion coordination problems, 57–59; coercion or reward to achieve, 52, 54–55, 66, 94–95; common knowledge linked to, 10, 17, 18, 52, 119–120, 159; coordination dilemmas and, 10, 53–54; costs of, 53–55, 66, 76, 91, 120, 122–124, 133; demonstration against constitutional drafting process (January 2004), 129–130; on directly elected council to draft Iraqi constitution, 128–131; exclusion of those not hearing sermons, 5–6, 77–78, 160, 175; Friday sermons creating, 11, 14, 17, 73–76, 79, 160; generalizable lessons learned about, 177; importance of, 7, 9–10; participation of neighbors in, 52; preinvasion lack of, 44–45; Save the Children's community action program, 66–67; self-enforcing aspects of, 55, 57, 75, 115, 118, 144, 159, 176, 178; Sistani's ability to coordinate behavior, 11, 18, 34–36, 67, 119–120, 125–127, 130, 138, 163, 168, 170, 172, 175, 195n6; Sunni clerics' sermons preinvasion not used for, 36, 164; taking for granted, 55–56; tipping quality of incentives to participate, 57; on Transitional Administrative Law (Iraq's interim constitution), 131–132; types of problems requiring, 53–57; on voting in December 2005 elections, 138–140, *139*; on voting in January 2005 elections, 132–138, *136–137*. *See also* free-rider problem; geographical limit on mosque sermons' effectiveness

constitution: CPA call for drafting of, 4; national referendum on proposed permanent constitution (October 2005), 169; Sistani's position on drafting of (November Fifteenth Agreement), 126–131, 196n30; Transitional Administrative Law (TAL, Iraq's interim constitution), 120, 127, 131–132, 196n32

Corboz, Elvire, 32, 34

corruption, 15, 76, 145, 149, 174

crime and security issues: in Basra, viii–ix, 49, 50–51, 90–91, 94, 96–97; community coordination to deal with, 9, 66, 94; costly contributions to maintain security, 93–94; failure to recreate Shaykhiyyas' local organization elsewhere, 97; gun availability and, 50, 186n59; kidnapping, prevalence of, 94; mosques addressing, 69, 93–97; in preinvasion era, 81–82, 185n29; social disorder and, 53–54; stray gunfire, neighborhood variations in dealing with, 50, 97–99, 192n18; tribal sheikhs providing protection, 81–83. *See also* assassinations, targeted executions, and revenge killings; traffic enforcement

currency, 85–86, 174

Da'wa movement and party, 26, 131, 138, 145, 153, 154

de-Ba'thification, 8, 43, 184n17

al-Dhari, Harith, 165, 167–168, 170

Diamond, Larry, 125, 130, 132, 196n23, 196n29

district advisory councils (DACs), 115

al-Dulaimi, Adnan, 167, 170

Eberly, Don, 43–44
Empirical Studies of Conflict Project (ESOC), 103
Egypt: Fatimid rule of, 174, 201n3; mosque sermons in, 19, 62, 174; standardization of Friday sermons in, 174–175
elections: October 2002, 42; January 2005, viii, 120, 132–138, *136–137*, 169–170, 197n45, 197n50; October 2005 national referendum, 169; December 2005, 120, 138–140, *139*, 163, 167, 169–170, 197n53; January 2009, 145; 2010, 145; 2014, 145; 2018, 148; Anglo-Iraqi Treaty ratification (1922), Khalisi's opposition to, 31; clerics running for office, 11, 30–33, 70, 121, 126, 134, 164; governate council ballot (January 2005), 135–136, *136*; Sistani's demand for directly elected council to draft Iraqi constitution, 126–131, 196n30; United Iraqi Alliance (UIA) and, 134–136, 138–139; voting strategies, 18, 120, 126–140, 170
ethics, 46, 73, 77
ethnography and ethnographic evidence, vii, 12, 17, 79, 90–93
exiles, 26–27, 50, 91

Fadlallah, Grand Ayatollah Mohammed Hussein, 34, 155
failed states: generalizable lessons learned applicable to, 177; Iraq distinguished from, 15, 21, 23, 181n19
Faith Campaign (1993), 17, 20, 24–25, 64, 113, 164
Fatah Alliance, 148
fatwas: in 1991 uprising, 33, 123; in 2005 (December) elections, 138; anti-communism, 31–32, 123; anti-Israel, 35; anti-looting, 70–71, 74–75, 126; anti-violence, 126; Ba'th Party support from, 35, 67, 126, 195n3; condoning something that would happen regardless, 75; constitution writing, opposing process for, 126; differentiated from other edicts, 122; Friday prayers, 69; political restraint of clerics, 32, 70; power of, 122, 124; religious dues collected and spent locally, 126, 195n18; Sistani's jihad fatwa (June 2014), 146–149; Sunnis issuing, 170; tobacco prohibition, 63, 123–124; wording to avoid forcing followers from taking costly actions, 123
Fayyad, Grand Ayatollah Muhammad, 125
Feda'yeen Saddam (paramilitary), 40, 45
federalism, 18, 159

field research in Iraq, vii–viii, 12–13, 17
Fifteenth Sha'ban (Islamist militia group), ix, 179n10
free-rider problem, 2–3, 5, 7, 52, 54–56, 97, 122, 124, 152
Friday prayers and sermons, 60–78; author attending, 13–14, 72, 75–77, 87, 93, 160, 200n108; common knowledge and, 2, 3, 10–11, 18, 53, 60–66, 73–76, 78, 89, 119, 121, 150, 159; community coordination based on religious authority, 11, 14, 17, 73–76, 79, 160; compared to Christian church congregations, 192n22; congregations and, 61–62, 191n7; on constitutional drafting, 126–131; cost of compliance as factor, 3–5, 10–11, 18, 53–55, 66, 76, 91, 122–124, 133, 145, 149; in Egypt, 19, 62, 174–175; making communities imaginable, 175; as new institution in Shi'a areas, 2–3, 24, 63, 67, 72, 176; postinvasion role of, 2–6, 10, 17, 53, 66–72, 126; previous research on, 62; as protests and demonstrations, 170; reliable and routine delivery of messages via, 10, 18, 79, 119, 155–156, 159, 176, 200n14; ritual associated with, 53, 60–61, 72–73; ruler's name omitted from, as act of rebellion, 65, 173; al-Sadr reinstituting (1995–1999), 11, 24, 26, 64–65, 71; self-enforcing aspects of orders from, 55, 57, 75, 115, 118, 144, 159, 176, 178; sermon content and messages, 2–3, 10–11, 18, 53, 66, 72–73, 76–77, 89, 91, 121–122, 150, 155, 173; Shiraziyyin lacking Friday mosques, 157; Sistani's influence through, 65, 67–70, 76, 100, 124, 126–127, 130, 159–160, 174; Sunnis and, 36, 60, 64, 67, 78, 112–113, 163–165; on Transitional Administrative Law (Iraq's interim constitution), 131–132; on voting in 2005 elections, 132–140. *See also* geographical limit on mosque sermons' effectiveness; limits of sermon-based social orders

Garamshi tribe, 50, 83, 96
Garner, Jay, 43, 125
gender norms. *See* women
geographical limit on mosque sermons' effectiveness, 89–118; catchment area of mosques' attendees, 89, 100–102, *101*, 105, 115, 118, 165, 192n25, 193n35; limitations on sermon-generated orders, 93–97; multiple-mosque areas, 89, 93, 102, 174; murder events as indicator of social order correlated with mosque catchment areas,

103–108, *106–108*, 193n34; single-mosque areas, 89, 90, 102; stray gunfire, neighborhood variations in dealing with, 97–99
geographic information system (GIS). *See* spatial analysis techniques
Gharawi, Mirza Ali, 35
al-Ghita, Muhammad Hussain Kashif, 31–33
Golpaygani, Mohammad Reza, 34, 183n80
Gordon, Joy, 22
gossip. *See* information and communication
Governing Council (GC), 128–131, 134, 137, 159, 164, 195n23, 199n103
grand ayatollahs: assassinations of (1990s), 35, 65, 158, 188n49; avoidance of controversial rulings, 123; *bayan*, issuance of, 122, 124, 127; competition among, 5, 122–123; fear of losing followers, 122–123, 144; *hokm*, issuance of, 122; influence of, factors limiting, 12, 29, 121–122, 125, 144; marja'iyya hierarchical networks of, 18, 28–29, 35–36, 114, 119, 121, 122, 157, 158, 182nn52–53; role among Shi'a, 27–30; self-harming rituals not condemned by, 123; sources of authority, 11, 120–122; Sunnis and, 163; types of edicts issued by, 122. *See also* fatwas; Friday prayers and sermons; *specific grand ayatollahs by name*
Greif, Avner, 9, 12, 56–57

Haddad, Fanar, 20, 23–24, 25, 33, 38, 73, 171–172, 176, 197n57
al-Haeri, Kazem, 67, 75, 100, 155, 158, 192n23
al-Hakim, Abdul Aziz, 70, 129, 154, 199n103
al-Hakim, Mohsin, 28, 32, 63, 69, 123, 191n5
al-Hakim, Muhammad Saeed, 34, 125
Hardin, Russell, 9, 55
Harling, Peter, 20, 180n1
al-Hasan, Yosuf, 166
al-Hashd al-Sha'bi. *See* Popular Mobilization Forces
al-Hassan, Ahmad, 155
Helfont, Samuel, 24, 37–38, 166, 200n3
Hobbes, Thomas, 55, 191n7
Hume, David, 55, 191n7
hussainiyas (prayer halls), 8, 16, 63, 87, 100, 104, 113–114, 155
Hussein, Saddam: 1991 uprising against, 8, 20, 23, 33, 46, 47, 123; 1995 election of, 133; capture of, 153, 199n100; despotism of, 44; institutional control by, 80; mukhtars and, 80; patronage system of, 22–23; prison amnesty issued by (October 2002), 9, 42, 50; Sunni clerics and, 36–37; Supreme Committee for the Reconstruction of Basrah and Fao headed by, 112. *See also* Ba'th regime; Faith Campaign
Hussein, Uday, 65, 153, 179n10

Ibn Battuta, 109, 194n40
Ibn Khaldun, 173
Ibn Lanak, 58
ICP (Iraqi Communist Party), 32, 154
identity: common knowledge as part of shared identity, 119–120, 175, 177; ethnic identity from previous generations, 194n62; identity politics, rise of, 20, 26–27, 140; Iraq's failure to achieve national identity, 8; political salience of, vii, 6–7, 9, 19; pre-2003 factors and, 20, 171; sect-based identity, rise of, vii, 78, 95, 160–161; Sunni lack of identity-assertion, 171; we-ness, 5, 165, 171–172, 176
Imam Ali, 62, 64, 72, 112
Imam Husayn, 63, 73, 87, 155
IMN (Iraqi Media Network), 86, 153
information and communication: CPA messages, failure of, 85; exclusion of those not hearing sermons, 5–6, 77–78, 160, 175; gossip and, 46, 57, 87, 99, 114; individual efforts in neighborhoods, 80–81; Internet and cell phone use to obtain, 78–79, 154, 157; newspapers and, 86, 152, 199n98; radio stations and, 86, 152–154, 157, 199n99; role in producing social order, 19, 52, 119; signs, effectiveness of, 87–88, 98–99; tribes and tribal leaders, 81–84; word of mouth as way to convey, 78, 84. *See also* common knowledge; Friday prayers and sermons
Institute for the Preparation of Imams and Sermon-Givers, 37, 166
institutional genesis, problem of, 56
international networks of Shi'i factions, 126, 156
Internet and cell phone messaging, 78–79, 154, 157
Iran: clergy as civil servants in, 63, 181n42; Constitutional Revolution (1905) in, 31; Friday sermons in, 62, 63, 174; Iraqi militias with ties to, 147; Islamic Revolutionary Guard Corps, ix, 147; Seljuk Turks' occupation of northeast area (1037 or 1038), 174; Shaykhiyya Islam from, 96; al-Shirazi moving to post-revolution, 156; tobacco monopoly in, 31, 156; tobacco use prohibited in, 63; Tudeh Party, 32
Iran-Iraq War, 33–34, 37, 42, 46, 82–83, 111, 112

INDEX

Iraqi Accord Front, 139, 170
Iraqi Body Count project (IBC), 104
Iraqi Communist Party (ICP), 32, 154
Iraqi Islamic Party (IIP), 142, 153, 162, 167–170
Iraqi Media Network (IMN), 86, 153
al-Iraqiya (state-run television station), 153
Islam: congregations and, 61–62; ecclesiastical hierarchy lacking in, 29, 30; increased religiosity in Iraq in 1990s, 3, 11, 23–25, 36–37, 53; interfaith solidarity, 77, 141; primordial attachments in, 7–8; role after collapse of state government, 1–2, 76–77; Safavids and, 63; Shaykhiyya branch, 95–97. *See also* clerics; Faith Campaign; Friday prayers and sermons; Shi'i Muslims; Sunni Muslims
Islamic Action Organization (Amal), 153, 156
Islamic State in Iraq and Syria (ISIS), 6, 127, 145, 146, 172, 175, 177
Islamist militias: in Basra, ix–x; enforcement by, 6, 11; kidnapping and execution of journalists and foreigners by, viii–ix, 179nn1–2, 179n10; operating with impunity, ix; Sunni clerics' role in, 25. *See also* assassinations, targeted executions, and revenge killings; violence

Jaafari, Ibrahim, 131, 145, 154
Jabar, Faleh, 24, 82, 125, 155, 200n7
jihadists, 140, 170, 177

Kadhem, Fouad, 31–32
Kadhim, Abbas, 147–148
Karbala, 63, 82, 146, 156–157; pilgrimages to, 24, 27, 36, 67
al-Karbalai, Abdul Mehdi, 146
Kernaghan, Paul, 49–50
al-Khaffaf, Hamid, 195n3
Khaleel, Ahmad, 168–69, 171
al-Khalisi, Muhammad Mahdi, 31, 63
al-Khatteeb, Luay, 147–148
Khoei, Grand Ayatollah Abu al-Qasim, 28, 30, 32–36, 123, 125, 183n69, 183n76, 191n5
al-Khoei Foundation, 34–35, 183n80, 191n5
Khomenei, Grand Ayatollah Ruhollah, 123, 156
Khoury, Dina, 79–80
Khurasani, Wahid, 34
kidnapping: of foreigners and journalists, viii–ix, 179nn1–2; increase (2004–2008), 47; by known acquaintances, 47
al-Kubaisi, Abdul Salam, 165
Kubba, Laith, 44
Kurds, 131–132, 134–136, *137*, 139, *139*, 197n48, 197n51, 197n54

Lewis, David K., 186n9
limits of sermon-based social orders, 3, 17, 53, 76, 91, 93–97, 114–118, *116–117*, 175; informality of, 118; militias supplanting sermon-generated coordination, 118; reasons for failure to scale up, 115–118. *See also* geographical limit on mosque sermons' effectiveness
Litvak, Meir, 29
local social order: beliefs based on history of issuing information that is obeyed, 56; CPA and, 84–86; currency and, 85–86; district advisory councils (DACs) and, 115; emergence of, 52; exclusion of those not hearing sermons, 77–78; local alternatives to mosque orders, 78–88; local councils' (postinvasion) role, 115–118, *117*; mosques' role in, 65–88; mukhtars' role, 79–80; neighborhood advisory councils (NACs) and, 115–118; newspapers and, 86; notable intellectuals and professionals and, 80; preinvasion neighborhood identity in, 80; preinvasion social networks and, 81, 96–97; radio stations and, 86; Sadah or sayyid families and, 80, 109; tribal groups and, 81–82; variations of social norms by localities, 77. *See also* limits of sermon-based social orders
looting: in Basra, 1, 17, 41–44, 50, 74; clerics' condemnation of, 2–3, 53, 68, 70, 74, 95; cost of, 44; governmental collapse and, 9, 43–44, 52; Sadrists condoning under certain circumstances, 75; shunning looters, 2, 74
Lynch, Kevin, 118

al-Mahdi, Adel Abd, 134
al-Mahdi, (Imam) Muhammad, 2, 28, 62, 141, 151, 179n10
Mahdi Army, ix, 95, 147, 159
Makiya, Kanan, 21, 185n29
al-Maliki, Nuri, 144, 145, 147, 179n11, 201n24
marja'iyya: defined, 29; origins of, 27–30. *See also* grand ayatollahs
Massignon, Louis, 109
Matthiesen, Toby, 95
McCants, William, 177
Medici social network structure, 182n53, 198n87
militias: anti-militia stance of Sistani, 126, 141–142, 146, 148–149; enforcement by, 87, 93–95, 120; with Iran ties, 147; in neighborhood advisory councils (NACs),

118; popular mobilization and, 147; rise of, 148–149; Sunni mosque desecration by, 142–143; supplanting sermon-generated coordination, 118. *See also* Islamist militias
minorities: exclusion from common knowledge, 175; religious oversight postinvasion, 164; rights in Transitional Administrative Law (Iraq's interim constitution), 131–132. *See also* Christians; Kurds
al-Modarresi, Mohammed Taqi, 156–157
Mohammad (Prophet), 60, 64
al-Mohammad, Hayder, viii, 94
al-Mosawi, Ali Hakim, 74
al-Mosawi, Yusuf, x, 179n11
mosque sermons. *See* Friday prayers and sermons
Mosul, 127, 146–147, 175
mukhtars' (local leaders) role, 79–80
murder events: as indicator of social order, 18, 103–108. *See also* assassinations, targeted executions, and revenge killings
al-Musawi, Ali, 96–97
Muslim Brothers, 153, 167, 199n102
Mustanbit, Nasrullah, 183n76
al-Mutlaq, Saleh, 170

Najaf: burial plots in, 27, 82; pilgrimages to, 27; public services in, 33; Sistani in, 4, 35
al-Najafi, Bashir, 123
al-Najafi, Muhammad Hasan, 28
Naji, Abu Bakr: *The Management of Savagery: The Most Critical Stage through which the Islamic Nation Will Pass*, 177
Nakash, Yitzhak, 31
Naqshbandiyya sect (Sufi), 25, 168
Nasser, Gamal Abdul, 32
National Dialogue Front, 139, 170
national unity advocated by Sistani, 140–141, 150, 175–176
neighborhood advisory councils (NACs), 115–118
newspapers, 86, 152, 199n98
NGOs, 59, 84, 90, 94
November Fifteenth Agreement (Agreement on Political Process), 120, 126–131, 195–96n23, 196n30

October Revolution (2019), 149
Office of Reconstruction and Humanitarian Assistance (ORHA, predecessor of CPA), 43, 48, 85
Oil-for-Food Programme (UN), 15, 21–22, 80, 81, 105, 180n6
Olsen, Ole Wøhlers, 49, 85
Operation Charge of the Knights (2008), ix, 104, 118, 179n11
Ottoman empire, 8, 27, 109, 174, 181n42

Pachachi, Adnan, 154, 162, 199n103
political influence: doctrine of absolute noninvolvement, 32; origins and limits of, vii, 6–7, 11, 176–177; quietism and clerical noninvolvement in politics, 31–36; religious leaders' increased role in, 7–9, 11–12, 23–25, 121; Sistani's political authority (postinvasion), 4–5, 9, 11, 18, 34–36, 67, 119–120, 125–127, 130, 132–138, 163, 168, 170, 172, 175, 195n6. *See also* Friday prayers and sermons; grand ayatollahs; limits of sermon-based social orders
political parties and organizations, 10, 17, 32, 81, 84, 86, 153–154, 163, 199n98. *See also specific parties*
Popular Mobilization Forces (PMF, al-Hashd al-Shaʿbi), 146–148
Posner, Daniel N., 197n55
primordialism, 7–8, 180n3
prisoner release by Saddam (October 2002), 9, 42, 50
protests and demonstrations: against constitutional drafting process (January 2004), 129–130, 196n29; Friday prayer services used for, 170; largest of post-Baʿth era (October 2019), 149; Sunni al-Anbar 2012–2014 protest movement, 170, 171
Putnam, Robert, 61

Qadiriyya sect (Sufi), 25, 168
al-Qaeda, 6, 140
quietism tradition (1923–2003), 30–33, 35–36, 70; coups during, 182n62; Sistani moving away from, 120–121, 126, 196n29

Rabkin, Nathaniel, 167, 170
radio and television stations, 86, 152–154, 157, 199n99
Ra'uf, Adil, 183n75
religion. *See* clerics; Friday prayers and sermons; Islam
Research Triangle Institute's (RTI International), 131; Local Governance Program, 115
Rida, Mohammad, 131
Rifaʿiyya sect (Sufi), 25, 168–169

rituals, 2–3, 13, 19, 26, 36, 87, 186n9. *See also* Friday prayers and sermons
Rizvi, Sajjad, 145
Rotberg, Robert, 23, 181n19
Rouhani, Mohammad Sadeq, 34, 183n76
al-Rubaie, Mowaffak, 129, 131

Sadah or sayyid families, 80, 109
Saddam Institute for Imams and Sermon-Givers, 37, 38
Saddam University for Islamic Studies, 37, 38, 166
al-Sade, Hassan, ix, 179n8
al-Sadr, Mohammad Baqir, 155, 157, 182n52
al-Sadr, Mohammad Mohammad Sadiq: assassination of (1999), 35, 65, 158, 188n49; Friday mosque network of (1995–1999), 11, 24, 26, 64–65, 71; Khoei's death creating competition for his successor and, 34; Najaf's dominant quietest tradition criticized by, 33; name of, 180n11; rival to Sistani, 123; splintering of followers after his death, 29–30, 100. *See also* Sadrists
al-Sadr, Moqtada: costliness of messages causing low motivation of followers, 158–159; fatwa allowing looting in certain circumstances, 75; Friday sermons network of, 124, 158, 159–160, 174; inheriting status and his father's network, 67, 71, 120, 157–158, 192n23; overreaching by, 120, 124, 158–159; political authority of, 18; resistance initiatives of, 119–120, 130, 158; rival to Sistani, 125, 155–158
Sadrists: coercion used to obtain compliance, 94–95, 120, 159; Friday sermons and prayers, 64, 67, 71, 124; government boycotts by, 120; Office of the Martyred Sadr II (OMS), 71, 158–159; political authority of, 11; in quietism era, 33; on Sistani vs. Sadr, 183n88; splintering of, 29–30, 67, 71, 100, 155, 158, 192n23; violence associated with, viii, 149, 179n10. *See also* Islamist militias
al-Safi, Ahmad, 133
al-Safi, Ali Abd al-Hakim al-Musawi, 129
al-Sahlani, Abu Dhar, 91
al-Sahlani, Fadil, 191n5
al-Sahlani, Muhammad Jawad, 91, 191n5
Salafism, 25, 26, 170
al-Salihi, Najib, 25
al-Samarrai, Ahmad Abd al-Ghafur, 167
sanctioning to enforce compliance, 55, 86–87, 94–95, 141, 192n21

sanctions era (1990–2003), 8, 21–27, 76, 81, 160
Sassoon, Joseph, 22, 36, 47
Save the Children, 59, 66, 98, *98*, 192n21
al-Sayyab, Badr Shakr, statue of, 184n15
al-Saʿadi, Farhan, 124
Schelling, Thomas, 9, 160, 186nn8–9
Science Applications International Corporation (SAIC), 153
sectarianism: antagonistic notions of nationalism and, 176; exiles and, 26–27; as legacy of Ottoman empire, 8; preinvasion, 25–27; rise of, 5, 26–27, 38–39, 120, 135–136, 140, 159–161, 180n3, 201n24; types of, 7–8; US imposition of ethnosectarian quota systems, 8; violence associated with, 124–125, 127, 140–143, 170
secularism, 24, 134, 138, 153–154, 161
self-enforcing aspects of community coordination, 55, 57, 75, 115, 118, 144, 159, 176, 178
self-harming rituals (flagellation or cutting), 123, 155, 157, 195n9
Shadhili Sufi order, 112
Shadid, Anthony, 94, 127
al-Shahristani, Husayn, 197n46
al-Shahristani, Jawad, 35, 126
Shawki, Ali, 94–95
Shaykhiyya families, 96–97, 100
sheikhs. *See* tribes and tribal leaders
al-Shirazi, Mohammad, 28, 33, 156–157
Shiraziyyin religious and political movement, 156–157
Shiʿi Muslims: Baʿth discrimination against, 20, 25–27; classical period (1000–1300s), 62; "Declaration of the Shiʿa of Iraq" (2002), 25; differences from Sunnis, vii, 5–6, 18, 38–39, 77–78, 119, 165; financing and religious endowments, 87; hierarchy of authority among, 27, 30; hussainiyas (prayer halls), 8, 16, 63, 87, 100, 104, 113–114, 155; lamentation responses of, 13, 63, 73, 87; pilgrimages and commemorations by, 24–25, 26, 27, 36, 67, 113; quietism, years of (1923–2003), 30–33; Sadah or sayyid families' status, 80, 109; separatist movement (1927), 33; Shaykhiyya branch, 95–97; Twelver Shiʿa, 27, 96, 120, 141, 192n24; Usuli-Akhbari debate, 62–63; Usuli jurisprudential school of, 27–28, 120, 122, 163; as voting bloc, 18, 120, 126–140, 170. *See also* clerics; Friday prayers and sermons; Islam
SIGACT dataset, 103–104, 193n33
Silawi, Adnan, 64, 158

INDEX

Sistani, Ali: alternative explanations for influence of, 150–152; annual income of, 195n18; anti-smoking rulings by, 123–124; charisma of, 151; choosing when to intervene, 145; on constitutional drafting, 4–5, 126–131; Friday prayers and sermons and, 65, 67–70, 76, 100, 124, 126–127, 130, 159–160, 174; on government accountability, 145; as indecipherable sphinx, 149–150, 198n87, 199n91; international network of, 126; jihad fatwa (June 2014), 146–149; al-Khoei Foundation and, 34–35, 191n5; limitations on authority of, 11, 18, 120, 140–145, 150; list of announcements of, 195n3; marja'iyya system and, 12, 33–36, 181n44; moving away from quietism tradition, 120–121, 125, 196n29; on national unity, 140–141, 150, 175–176; non-resistance statements after invasion, 126; October Revolution (2019) and, 149; political authority wielded by (postinvasion), 4–5, 9, 11, 18, 34–36, 67, 119–120, 125–127, 130, 132–138, 163, 168, 170, 172, 175, 195n6; postinvasion assessment of, 150, 195n6; post-invasion disengagement from politics by (2006–2008), 11, 120, 143–144; preinvasion assessment of, 125–126; as rival to Sadrists, 70, 123, 125, 155–156; seclusive lifestyle of, 151; on sectarian violence, 140–143; size of network of, 120, 122, 159–160, 174; on status of forces agreement (SOFA), 145; as successor of Khoei, 30, 33–34, 70; on Transitional Administrative Law (Iraq's interim constitution), 131–132; on voting in December 2005 elections, 138–140, 170; on voting in January 2005 elections, 132–138

Sluglett, Peter, 48
smoking, 46, 123–124, 151
smuggling, 22, 23, 45
social norms and conventions: community coordination relying on, 55; al-Sadr's sermons focusing on, 65; women and, 6, 14–15. *See also* trust issues
social order: in absence of a state, 1, 6–7, 9, 13, 50–52, 176, 178, 184–185n18; contribution problems and, 10–11; failure of mosques to control militias, ix; mosque sermons aimed at producing, 2–6, 14, 65–88; murder events as indicator of, 103–108; occupation authorities' inability to maintain, 9, 44, 48–50, 85; origins of, vii. *See also* community coordination

spatial analysis techniques, 14, 18, 90, 105–108, 118, 192n25
stateless society, 1, 6–7, 9, 13, 50–52, 176, 178, 184–185n18. *See also* anarchy
status of forces agreement (SOFA), 145
Sufi orders, 25, 112, 168–169
Sunni Muslims, 18, 162–172; Basra mosques, 112–113; challenge of inclusion of, 171–172; clerical hierarchy lacking in, 38, 163, 165; clerics' influence in postinvasion society, 25, 163–164, 168; clerics' role under the Ba'th, 36–38, 163–165; common knowledge, limited ability to generate, 163–165, 168, 171–172; on constitutional drafting process, 128–129; differences from Shi'i Muslims, vii, 5–6, 18, 38–39, 77–78, 119, 165; disunity of, 5–6, 11, 18–19, 25, 162, 165, 168–172, 200n14; exclusion from common knowledge, 5–6, 78, 160, 175; Friday prayers and sermons, 5, 36, 60, 64, 67, 78, 112–113, 163–164, 174–175; Iraqi Islamic Party supported by, 153, 162; mosque location and usage of, 63, 164–165, 174; opposition to foreign occupation of Iraq, 167; postinvasion governmental role of, 172; Shi'i conflict with, 140–141, 171; US and neighboring states' attempt to nurture leaders among, 172; US disenfranchisement of, 8; victimhood mentality and, 172; voter coordination and, 136, *137*, 139, *139*, 170. *See also* Association of Muslim Scholars; clerics; Islam
Supreme Council for Islamic Revolution in Iraq (SCIRI), 86, 131, 134, 138, 153, 154
Synnott, Hilary, 49, 85, 97
Syria, 147, 148, 156, 177

al-Tai, Qasim, 147
al-Tamimi, Muzahim Mustafa Kanan, 49
TharAllah (God's Revenge, Islamist militia group), ix, 104, 179n10, 180n11
Thiessen polygons, 115, *116*, *117*, 192n25
traffic enforcement, 80–81, 86–87, 91
Transitional Administrative Law (TAL, Iraq's interim constitution), 120, 127, 131–132, 196n32
tribes and tribal leaders, 10, 20, 22–23, 81–84, 109, 111, 181n17
trust issues, 45–47, 55, 79

uncertainty, feelings of, 50–51
Underhill, Paco, 88
United Iraqi Alliance (UIA), 4, 134–136, 138–139, 170, 197n46

United Nations (UN): desirability of involvement in Shi'i viewpoint, 120; Oil-for-Food Programme, 15, 21–22, 80, 81, 105, 180n6; sanctions, 8, 10, 15, 17; Sistani and, 125, 196n30

United Nations Development Programme (UNDP), 97–98, 192n18

United States. *See* Coalition Provisional Authority

Vincent, Steven, viii–ix, 179n11

violence: cleric's condemnation of, 70; extremists' use to provoke retaliation against their own group, 140–141, 143, 159, 198n58; murder events as indicator of social order, 18, 103–108; sectarian violence and civil war, 124–125, 127, 140–143, 170. *See also* assassinations, targeted executions, and revenge killings; Islamist militias; Sadrists

Visser, Reider, 126, 195n3, 197n46

Voronoi diagram, 115, 192n25

al-Wa'eli, Ahmad, 152, 155

Walbridge, Linda S., 125, 183n82, 195n18

waste disposal and uncollected trash: al-Asma'i neighborhood in Basra, 90–91; in Baghdad, 43; in Basra, 1, 3, 58; collapse of state government and, 9, 50, 52, 66; community coordination to deal with, 9, 52, 53, 58

water supply, 59–60

Weber, Max, 11, 30, 121, 151

women: ability to coordinate solutions or resolve problems, 89–90, 191n1; face covering by, 123; social norms and, 6, 14–15

al-Yaqoubi, Muhammad, 67, 71, 149, 155, 158, 195n6

Yazdi, Muhammad Kazim Tabataba'i, 182n49

Zaidan, Abdul Karim, 168

al-Zarqawi, Abu Musab, 140–141, 198n59

www.ingramcontent.com/pod-product-compliance
Lightning Source LLC
Chambersburg PA
CBHW030825230426
43667CB00008B/1375